Survey of Media

An accessible and exciting new textbook that provides students with an in-depth historical and conceptual understanding of the nature and function of media in society.

Stacey O. Irwin contextualizes media objects and experiences—including cinema, TV, phones, gaming, radio and podcasting, journalism, publishing, advertising, and more—into three descriptive sections: screens, sounds, and synergies. The text examines how technology is enfolded into the cultural process of contemporary media experience, exploring topics such as social media, augmented reality, and other trends from the metaverse. It also reflects on the impact of legacy media and highlights instrumental moments in media history along the way. By examining media history from the perspective of future decision-making, this textbook explores how media technologies have a positive and negative sociocultural impact. This provides students with a more accessible entry point to the topic, and readers are left with a well-rounded understanding of media and the interplay between media, culture, technology, and society. Each chapter concludes with things to consider and additional takeaways to enhance student learning.

This is an essential text for students taking classes such as Introduction to Mass Media, Survey of Media, Media History, Media and Society, and Media Culture.

Stacey O. Irwin is Professor of Media Arts Production, Department of Communication & Theatre, Millersville University of Pennsylvania, USA. She has taught courses in media production, writing, and theory for more than thirty years. Her documentary film *Raising Faith: Stories About Dyslexia* (2020) has won more than twenty-five national and international competitions in IMDb qualifying film festivals. Her book *Digital Media: Human-Technology Connection* (2016), won a Choice Book Award.

Survey of Media

Screens, Sounds, and Synergies

Stacey O. Irwin

Routledge
Taylor & Francis Group

NEW YORK AND LONDON

Designed cover image: godfather744431 / Getty Images

First published 2025
by Routledge
605 Third Avenue, New York, NY 10158

and by Routledge
4 Park Square, Milton Park, Abingdon, Oxon, OX14 4RN

Routledge is an imprint of the Taylor & Francis Group, an informa business

© 2025 Stacey O. Irwin

Library of Congress Cataloging-in-Publication Data
Names: Irwin, Stacey O., 1965– author.
Title: Survey of media : screens, sounds, and synergies / Stacey O. Irwin.
Description: New York : Routledge, 2025. | Includes bibliographical references and index.
Identifiers: LCCN 2024021347 (print) | LCCN 2024021348 (ebook) | ISBN 9781032502502 (paperback) | ISBN 9781032502502 (hardback) | ISBN 9781003397588 (ebook)
Subjects: LCSH: Mass media—Social aspects—United States. | Mass media—United States. | Popular culture—United States.
Classification: LCC HN90.M3 .I79 2024 (print) | LCC HN90.M3 (ebook) | DDC 302.23—dc23/eng/20240523
LC record available at https://lccn.loc.gov/2024021347
LC ebook record available at https://lccn.loc.gov/2024021348

ISBN: 978-1-032-50250-2 (hbk)
ISBN: 978-1-032-50249-6 (pbk)
ISBN: 978-1-003-39758-8 (ebk)

DOI: 10.4324/9781003397588

Typeset in Sabon
by Apex CoVantage, LLC

This book is dedicated to my parents, husband and three grown children, who have taught me so much about media literacy.

Contents

Preface   *ix*
Acknowledgements   *xi*

1 Introduction   1

PART ONE
Screens   13

2 Printed Text   15

3 Cinema   32

4 Television and Broadcasting   49

5 Video   66

6 Journalism   77

PART TWO
Sounds   93

7 Music Recording and Foley   95

8 Radio, Audio, and Podcasting   111

9 Phones   128

PART THREE
Synergies   145

10 Sports Media   147

11 Marketing, Advertising, and Public Relations   156

12 Social Media   171

13 Video Gaming and the Metaverse   181

14 Digital Synergies   194

Index   *207*

Preface: How to Use This Book

Survey of Media: Screens, Sounds, and Synergies delves into the historical story of media and its convergence to digital. This survey examines media technologies, including cinema, radio, television, gaming, and social media. It shows how current practice uses concepts and content. The sections in the text, Screens, Sounds, and Synergies, explore how legacy media technologies are still relevant today. The chapters in this book redefine media history by using technology to connect with readers on their contemporary media journey. Understanding media history helps us become better content creators, leaders, and consumers. The content focuses on important media technologies, their growth over time, and their impact on the current media landscape.

A survey study works well as an introduction that provides baseline knowledge. Using that foundation helps readers make educated guesses about future technologies and experiences. Each chapter explores a medium and its technological underpinnings. Chapters are concise and designed for reading and discussion, either in person or through online formats. A section at the end of each chapter focuses on Things to Consider and chapter Takeaways that learners can build on. Readers are encouraged to delve deeper and explore topics, concepts, and sociocultural changes related to these media technologies and subjects. Integrating the content into everyday experiences of mediated life requires reading, thinking, and conversation.

This historical take does not include all media-related technologies, events, and sociocultural moments, but provides tent poles for understanding overall concepts. "Painting with a broad stroke" can sometimes mean missing notable topics. Discussing "what is missing" from the book can provide many exciting and enriching in-class conversations. If all historical media technologies, the specific events they grew and fostered, and their sociocultural significances and events were shared, the book would be large, expensive, and still miss some things. This approach to media history is designed to be an accessible introduction for media studies students and those interested in general education. The content included in the text allows readers to become media-literate consumers without feeling overwhelmed by too much information.

The idea of what content goes into which chapter took some thought. Media overlap each other, sharing similar histories and periods. Convergence makes it challenging to identify overarching topic areas because subject lines are blurred. The book's premise proves itself. Screens and sounds provide increasingly synergistic experiences, and the converged environment is to thank for this. Occasionally, a concept in the Screens section might also be addressed in the Sounds or Synergies sections. Perhaps something from the Synergies section could be moved earlier. This is true. Organizing chapters concerned keeping each section reasonably even and focusing on technologies as the catalyst for each medium within the survey landscape. The disparate technologies have moved from their silos into synergies. The text converts dates into decades or windows of time that mark essential periods of technological shifts and advancements. Also, the aim was for minimal references for a thinner text, but sources are required for academic rigor. *Survey of Media: Screens, Sounds, and Synergies* offers a comprehensive perspective on media, drawing from the author's personal and professional experiences.

Acknowledgements

Thank you to everyone who has offered insights on this book topic, especially my students. In the Survey of Media class I've been teaching for numerous years, I ask students to share what media topics they are interested in studying. These ideas have guided the chapters of this book. I organized the book into sections based on class discussions about media history and its relevance to the current media landscape. These sections are called screens, sounds, and synergies. I found our in-class discussions about media literacy helpful for the end sections of each chapter called Things to Consider and Takeaways.

I would like to express my gratitude to my colleagues nationwide for their valuable input and support as I created the proposal for this book. They have openly shared their knowledge and experiences with me through conversation, conference presentations, articles, and book chapters. This exchange of ideas is essential for professional development, nurturing academic areas of study, and enhancing student learning.

I would like to thank my Millersville University Provost Gail Gasparich, my College of Arts, Humanities & Social Sciences Dean, Ieva Zake, my Department of Communication & Theatre Department Chair, Lowery Woodall III, and my respected department colleagues for their support and encouragement. You are all experts in your fields, and I am honored to work with you. I'd also like to acknowledge BEA: Educating for Tomorrow's Media for creating enriching conventions and faculty development opportunities so I can continue to grow my understanding of media, The Television Academy Foundation Faculty Seminar, my dear friends in the Postphenomenology Research Group, including Don Ihde, and my Society for Phenomenology and Media colleagues for sharing their research and conversation around media. Thank you to Danielle Agabedis, Melina O'Neal, and John Sievers for content advice and Keira O'Neal for photo help.

Also, a big thank you to the Taylor & Francis editorial team for guidance and patience including Sheni Kruger, Grace Kennedy, Jacqueline Lawless and Emma Harder-Collins.

To my husband Dukie, grown children Faith, Daniel, and David, parents Judith and Bradford, in-laws Linda and Duke, family, and friends, thank you for your love and encouragement.

1   Introduction

Writing an introduction highlighting the importance of a historical event or idea through technological advancements is challenging. However, outlining the scope and potential of that history is crucial. Like history, introductions have multiple starting points. Does the first dot on the timeline start when someone etched the first sign, perhaps a hieroglyph, into a wall to signify the first visual media? Or does it begin with the invention of electricity, the means that allowed people to plug in and connect? Where a book starts and ends holds significance. One way to think of media is to consider its role in society. Media can also be the channels and platforms we access. Another way is to consider media based on the tools and technologies they employ. Frankly, hundreds of things make up *the media,* and this book will get to many of them. While no specific entity in the world is labeled *the media*, this book requires a generic term. The assumption here is not biased or pejorative. It is an all-encompassing way to discuss this topic. This book's title has the word survey because the focus is on providing a structure or landscape for the topic. Surveys offer a glimpse into development, touching on key points. The text is not comprehensive. It touches on many areas, and might not be satisfying on many subjects. In this case, active reading and research become essential. Search and explore the missed and briefly mentioned topics on your own. This chapter shares some introductory ideas about defining media, media effects, and media saturation and briefly touches on content in each chapter at the end.

What precisely defines something as media? In this text, media is the plural form of medium. A medium is a form of communication that can be digital, written, oral, visual, or experienced, such as in extended reality platforms. The text shares the history of legacy media, those media that came first in the historical trajectory of media, then converged media, or the convergence of many media into one device in the contemporary digital landscape. The text is divided into three categories that reflect how media history sifts into major experiential fields over time. The spheres include

DOI: 10.4324/9781003397588-1

media focusing on visual media viewed on screens, sound in media, and media convergence into synergistic technologies and experiences. Readers grasp critical historical events by studying the evolution of the media technologies integrated into the media process. The aim is to contextualize how media of the past are reflected in the current media experience as we look toward the future.

Although this text is not interactive, it encourages thinking about technology as essential in media. For instance, much of the media story starts with telephone-linked technology. The telephone revolutionized communication by allowing people in different locations to have real-time conversations. Auditory information became more popular than written communication and the phone became the fastest way to communicate person-to-person. This invention laid the foundation for developing all future communication technologies. Many contemporary mobile phone users prefer typing and texting to talking, but the early phone brought people together as a global community of vocal communicators and has altered how humans communicate. Developing a historical context for technologies, like the telephone as an example, helps define future directions and acknowledge technology's place and influence in media history.

Context Matters

Historical context helps a society understand how a specific topic has shaped the economic, sociocultural, and political landscape through its existence. For media, as a collective of technologies, processes, and messages, the history started in tandem with tool use. Artifacts share origins of communication way back. Communication, through media tech, links back to paper's creation. Indeed, the printing press is early in the media technologies timeline. This invention is one of many mentioned in this textbook. Why? Mass production through inventions like the printing press pushed the rise of mass media. These technologies revolutionized communication by transmitting information over long distances. When a media consumer, a media professional, or a citizen of the digital world understands the cultural artifacts (content creator + content + technology + world), they make informed decisions about the past, the current, and the future. These insights can be motivating and perceptive. They help to avoid assumptions and provide a broader perspective on how we arrived here, to our contemporary mediated world. An accurate interpretation and analysis allow everyone to move forward together in an even historical context to understand a more complete and insightful interpretation of media and all it entails.

History, Popular Culture, or Both?

So much of the history of media technologies and content is part of the popular culture of a specific period. That popular sociocultural element travels with the media industry and experiences throughout its history. Media spread and preserve a particular period's practices, experiences, arts, languages, and objects. Media can change depending on political events, such as violence against a president or politicians using media to share their messages. In other cases, the coverage moves the public, and they embrace the images and sounds from a live broadcast. These events can be everything from a 1985 multi-venue benefit concert called Live Aid, to televised riots across time zones and countries, natural disasters, political elections, international sporting events, and innovative experiences, such as astronauts landing on the moon.

Countless markers fill time, each holding meaning. As you read the text, developing those markers will be your work. The history of our media environment reveals how technology and its content affect human experiences. Popular culture is current within a time but also embedded into history. Many media points we now see as historical facts were pop culture movements in a specific time window, surrounded by everyday life.

Consider how media technologies, media devices, and media representation impact behavior, sociocultural experience, and communication. Current technology integrates into society and affects how we consume media daily.

However, where to start? This book, this survey, and this story begin with media technology. Author and philosopher of technology Don Ihde (1990) has shared that technologies transform human experience. They are not just neutral pathways for our content but complex interactions between humans, technology, and the world, with positive and negative consequences. This premise guides this text and starts your work in various ways. Every media technology, along with its intertwined content, has the power to reshape human experience and impact the world and our lives, both positively and negatively. Knowing that particular media or devices exist changes the nature of the relationship, which can no longer remain neutral. So, the philosophy of technology encompasses media technologies and mediated experience. As each chapter mentions different media technologies, consider the entanglements, sociocultural influences, and embodied ways that create positive and negative effects, sometimes simultaneously. A book that notes all of these effects would be too long and rely on so many different positives and negatives, based on diverse points of the sociocultural scale, that it would require a series of books or a sizable tome. Starting a study on media history requires a different approach.

This textbook aims to provide a survey of media. Admittedly, an overview perspective only scratches the surface. Still, this focus allows readers to search, explore, and learn as they go. The term used to describe this activity is research. Your thoughtful experience and additional research can enable you to engage with media and mediated environments in a more literate and unique manner (Folkerts et al., 2009).

Hear Ye, Hear Ye

Through millennia, oral communication, the spoken word, was the primary way to exchange information. The town crier walked through town, sharing news, event ads, and government information. Oral communication was amplified to high communication status when the town crier made proclamations and shared important information, based on the day's news. Access to news through oral tradition was crucial for those who could not read. The town crier, usually an officer in a royal court, would ring a bell or drum to get people's attention. Then, they would give a clear message that everyone could hear. Government officers carried a printed version to read from and post on a designated door for literate individuals to access. Hurting a town crier was considered treason because town criers were protected citizens. While town criers are mostly ceremonial today, they are still used to disseminate information in some communities. In contrast, today's spoken word is streamed worldwide through the internet and various media.

Before the invention of the printing press, oral communication was the primary method of information exchange. The printing press allowed written works of all kinds to be mass-produced and available to the general public. The availability of written works led to increased literacy rates, as more individuals wanted to read this new information they had access to. Educational materials were also printed and distributed. This new one-to-many technology, called mass media, advanced mass literacy, transforming society.

Mass Communication Bound?

The history of language is ancient, extending at least as far back as to ancient Greece and Aristotle's rhetorical theory. Media history is part of this communication history as much as the history of mass communication because media disseminate ideas and information through language, to many at once, creating both diverse and homogenous groups. The diversity element often depends on the brand, channel, platform, and ideas of the communicated message. Media technology uniquely provide the communicative element that can simultaneously push information and messages to large groups of people over great geographic distances. One by-product is that the receiver of this one-way information or message, for many years, had yet to have the opportunity to provide immediate feedback. This has changed. Media consumers can rely on live social media feeds and message areas to respond instantly to content that everyone can see or read. Researchers often thoroughly study target audiences' demographics by analyzing census information, geographic data, household income projections, and algorithms from this instantly available participation.

Instant communication can help us share stories and ideas and understand events better. In addition, this participation serves to connect audiences. Through this communication, we can shape stories, meanings, and a collective comprehension of events and concepts. Media effects can promote growth and breakdown, eloquence and disruption. For instance, advertising affects a mass audience because of a specifically crafted message. This strategic process effects audience behavior, signifying sociocultural, ideological, and commercial impacts. It is worth examining the extent to which media affect us and the potential implications of this influence.

Who Makes Content?

Who makes media content has also shifted as innovations, technologies, and devices change. In the 20th century, a legacy news organization had many content professionals who read the news before it was printed, including the writer, several editors, typesetters, and printers. Although the editorial content was thoroughly edited, numerous people viewed it and could additionally suggest or make changes. The same occurred in legacy television, as several producers read and edited scripts before airing. Media companies editorially decided which stories to share, resulting in theories like agenda-setting and gatekeeping. News management also restricted access to stories or sets of information, that slowed or deleted specific news topics from the broadcast. Even in contemporary journalism, only some journalists receive press passes, and only some of the day's news fits into a 22-minute news broadcast or onto the front page of an online news site.

In contemporary news-making, there is a 24-hour news cycle. However, this was only sometimes true in the media's first century. Consumer-targeted products, like camcorders and in-camera editing, allowed consumers to make their own "edit style" content. In the digital age, when content quality matches that of the legacy media, citizen journalists readily share digital video footage of events. Bloggers publish stories instantaneously on web platforms, and the entire nature of content creation changes. Over a short period, three, then four flagship media content channels turned to one hundred choices between live and recorded content. In the era of participation, anyone can do a live shot and use a mobile phone to record images, load them to a video platform, and share them in seconds. The model is known as the one-to-many model. However, will consumers find the content? If so, it might go viral, bringing in more viewers than the local media outlet. These messages have no gatekeepers. They alone set the agenda. Moreover, perhaps the message in video, text, or audio format is anonymous, with a positive or negative message. Traditional media and newer platforms both create content, but users also contribute their content.

Before diving into specifics, it is crucial to contemplate a few more introductory concepts. The book explores media technologies from innovation in the 1800s and 1900s through current times. Every historical take has to start somewhere. The previous two hundred years encompass, to a large extent, the media environment you experience today. This insertion point also keeps this book on the shorter side. Media technologies were among the top technologies invented in these centuries, and almost all chapters jump off from these centuries. This is where the "one-to-one" communication model expanded to the "one-to-many" models of information transference.

Another essential idea is the fact that numerous prototypes failed before they succeeded. Media history rarely notes Ernest Lawrence's color tube, the Sony Betamax machine, or the Microsoft Zune. Each largely failed because of their competitor's marketing prowess. Many failures mean numerous innovations and inventions. Technologies, devices, and content are influenced by research, marketing, economics, world politics, and popular culture. The same goes for media programming. There are no guarantees.

Moreover, you may ask, exactly what makes something "media technology"? Technology allows the creation of media content. There is a lot to consider. The idea to help figure this out is to study whether a specific technological innovation helps to create media content. Perhaps the technology records media content. Still other technologies move the content to circulate it to the media consumers, the public, the residents, and humans to experience and use them. Technologies, those infrastructures and devices that compose, create, produce, deliver, and manage media, like audio, video, and digital content, through numerous devices, are the media technologies considered in this text. Media technologies have started and also transformed the timeline of media history. These transformations have positive and negative effects that bring about opportunity and challenge. Print, digital, new media, multimedia, and electronic media require technologies constantly developing in alternative forms and structures. What legacy experiences, ideas, and technological underpinnings remain in contemporary culture? At the survey level, it is essential to know that media technology aids in creating media (Turkle, 1995).

Key characteristics of the media in this text include those that expertly and creatively communicate information to people by leveraging various technologically mediated channels. Additionally, its replication and distribution reach large audiences. When recorded through analog or digital means, this media material transforms into a product for a specific audience. The scope of this introductory text focuses on American media, although some global history is shared. Media have increased in American society through an economic model of capitalism—efforts to make money for those who work in various business models, defined and developed American media. Media markets, or designated market areas (DMA), are named and labeled as small, medium, and large-sized markets, and each has its similarities and differences. The most significant city around it designates that market. There are over 200 American media markets.

This book focuses on text/visual and aural media, whether distributed through legacy or digital means. The term "digital" is obsolete now that all media are in digital format. When considering media, it is essential to acknowledge their role in communication. Media do this through broadcasting, circulating, spreading, publicizing, and publishing to many. Media do what they do and are what they are because of the people who create these messages and the technology they use to create and disseminate them, like content creators, broadcasters, filmmakers, journalists, communication and marketing specialists, public relations professionals, and advertisers (Malin, 2014).

Saturation Point

Saturation is a term that describes when a specific item has reached a particular fullness or completeness. Things combine or add to compare capacity or absorption. Sometimes, it takes work to gauge the fullness of something relative to its maximum capacity. It is the same with media saturation. What is the number of viewers for a specific program or stream? What amount of media are excessive for a consumer? How does media saturation affect things like mental and physical health? How many individuals saw this commercial? At what point does the influx of information, advertising, data, and messages overwhelm? Knowing the statistics of media saturation and access to media technologies worldwide is challenging. Some data suggests that approximately three-quarters of people in the US aged over ten own a cell phone. Three-quarters of youth aged 15–24 can access internet connectivity. Many who have access use it daily, weekly, or monthly, but one-third of the global population still needs internet service (Nielsen, n.d.). The Nielsen Corporation has measured media use for over one hundred years. Their research shows that over 95 percent of households worldwide have televisions connected to various sources like antenna, cable, DBS, Telco, or broadband internet. From an audio perspective, over 80 percent of people aged 12 and over listen to legacy radio, and over 40 percent listen to podcasts, which is up substantially in the last decade (Forman-Katz, 2023).

What about the saturation of social media platforms? "When Pew Research Center began tracking social media adoption in 2005, just 5% of American adults used at least one of these platforms. By 2011, that share had risen to half of all Americans", and in the 2020s, over 70 percent of the public used social media. Moreover, this statistic is growing (Pew Research Center, 2021). Studies on media use are primarily self-reported unless they are data-driven based on researched algorithm use. Different media use various methods to conduct usage research and collect data. In short, measuring and illustrating usage across media is tricky. However, advertisers, app developers, algorithms, and other data-driven measures shape media content. Devices deliver this content, while platforms and other technologies facilitate its delivery and use. Media consumers then see, hear, and experience it.

Effects Integration

Some media history textbooks have a chapter highlighting media effects. This book shares information on media effects at the end of most chapters to highlights a bit about this broad topic area and its importance to many different kinds of media. Understanding media effects is an act of media literacy, which is also a focus of this book. "Media refers to all electronic or digital means and print or artistic visuals used to transmit messages", and "Media literacy is the ability to encode and decode the symbols transmitted via media and synthesize, analyze, and produce mediated messages" (NAMLE, 2021). Media literacy, as defined by the National Association of Media Literacy Education, involves accessing, analyzing, evaluating, creating, acting, and using various forms of communication. Learning about media history helps people explore and evaluate media use as media consumers, content creators, and leaders.

Does media literacy work? Various research have shown that the capacity to analyze media content influences how it is perceived. One research study examined whether media literacy intervention efforts could change the perception of advertisements persuading media consumers about eating unhealthy foods. Parents and children attended a workshop to learn about critical thinking and how it relates to the advertisements they see. The research showed that those in the post-intervention focus group learned about media literacy and the impact of unhealthy food ads. "Researchers observed that the media literacy workshop functioned as a consciousness-raising intervention, teaching participants to be more critical of the advertisements they are exposed to. In addition, parents and children revealed positive changes regarding intentions and behaviors in eating healthy" (Powell, 2018, pp. 87–89).

Each chapter provides historical information about the medium's positive and negative effects. Media, like technology, are not neutral entities or conduits. Media effects are the sociocultural, behavioral, and psychological impacts that an individual's thoughts, attitudes, beliefs, and behaviors have when consuming media. The user can be influenced, either implicitly or explicitly, by the content.

Over time, media effects theories have changed. Media researchers and theorists started by looking at how media affect individual behavior and then focused on how people use and think about media messages. They use neuroscience and network control theory to study how media influences perception and thinking (Schmälzle & Huskey, 2023). The content may directly or indirectly impact the user in immediate or gradual ways. Studying media effects is essential to understanding the media and the technology linked to it. One psychological idea from a media literacy perspective involving media effects is media priming (Ewoldsen & Rhodes, 2019). The theory of media priming focuses on the idea that a media consumer relies on a prior frame of reference to interpret subsequent related content (Hoewe, 2020; Roskos-Ewoldsen et al., 2002).

Our media consumption can influence our thoughts and choices. For instance, a viewer of a specific genre of streamed media about crime may make future judgments in their physical world based on that mediated experience, whether the content consumed was fiction or nonfiction based. A primed media consumer is prepared to act in a particular situation based on prior knowledge. That prior knowledge may be achieved through media. The media they use can affect a media consumer's perspective and what they account for in their everyday life. In addition, the less prior knowledge a viewer of a mediated experience, for instance, has, the more the mediated associations have meaning and are integrated. Chronic accessibility is the term used to describe how readily our brain recalls past events about present ones. Psychologists also research the theoretical idea of priming, but more research is needed. Multiple studies have shown that the media have been proven to impact our judgments and behavior.

Quick Look Ahead

Chapters 2 to 6 discuss the various visual topics of print media, cinema, television, video, and journalism. Chapters 7 through 9 focus on sound-assembled media, like music recording and Foley, and audio-focused phones, radio, and podcasting. Chapters 10 to 13 discuss the combination of various technologies in sports media, marketing, advertising, and public relations, as well as video games and the metaverse. Chapter 14 explores the whole of these converged media and their synergistic nature. On the way, the book highlights media inventions, innovations, and effects from early media through the Industrial Revolutions, Y2K, and into the future.

Things to Consider

- Consider keeping a log of your media use for one week. Write the way you consume (platform), the times you consume, the kinds of media you use, and the content of what you consume. After a week, review your data. What did you learn from this exercise?
- Brainstorm some historical language and working knowledge that is still part of media use today.

Takeaways

- The book examines how historical media impact and shape present-day media through a structured survey method. It focuses on screens, sounds, and synergies as three critical areas of knowledge and experience. This systematic approach aims to offer people a framework for comprehending the evolution of media over time while recognizing that a single narrative cannot adequately explain the complex history of media.
- This book perspective focuses on understanding media history through technology and how it has changed our lives.
- Popular culture is deeply embedded and interwoven with the history of media. Comprehending how media weave into our everyday lives is crucial.
- Technology is not neutral but has both positive and negative effects.
- Media are part of mass communication. With the advancement of media technologies, our communication model shifted from one-to-one to one-to-many. This transformation has led to the development of target audiences and the chance to profit significantly from different media types.
- Name some of your chapter takeaways.

References

Ewoldsen, D.R., & Rhodes, N. (2019). Media priming and accessibility. In *Media effects*, pp. 83–99.

Folkerts, J., Teeter, D.L., & Caudill, E. (2009). *Voices of a nation: A history of mass media in the United States*. Pearson/Allyn and Bacon.

Forman-Katz, N. (2023, August 17). *For National Radio Day, Key Facts about Radio Listeners and the Radio Industry in the U.S.* Pew Research Center. https://www.pewresearch.org/short-reads/2023/08/17/for-national-radio-day-key-facts-about-radio-listeners-and-the-radio-industry-in-the-us/

Hoewe, J. (2020). Toward a theory of media priming. *Annals of the International Communication Association, 44*(4), 312–321.

Ihde, D. (1990). *Technology and the lifeworld: From garden to earth.* Indiana University Press.

Malin, B.J. (2014). *Feeling mediated: A history of media technology and emotion in America.* New York University Press.

NAMLE. (2021, February 10). *Media literacy defined . . .* https://namle.net/resources/media-literacy-defined/

Nielsen. (n.d.). *Nielsen estimates 121 million TV homes in the U.S. for the 2020–2021 T.V. season.* Nielsen Insights. https://www.nielsen.com/insights/2020/nielsen-estimates-121-million-tv-homes-in-the-u-s-for-the-2020-2021-tv-season/#:~:text=Additionally%2C%20the%20percentage%20of%20total

Pew Research Center. (2021, April 7). *Social Media Fact Sheet.* Pew Research Center: Internet, Science & Tech. https://www.pewresearch.org/internet/fact-sheet/social-media/

Powell, R.M., & Gross, T. (2018). Food for thought: A novel media literacy intervention on food advertising targeting young children and their parents. *Journal of Media Literacy Education, 10*(3), 80–94.

Roskos-Ewoldsen, D.R., Roskos-Ewoldsen, B., & Carpentier, F.R.D. (2002). Media priming: A synthesis. In *Media effects* (pp. 107–130). Routledge.

Schmälzle, R., & Huskey, R. (2023). Integrating media content analysis, reception analysis, and media effects studies. *Frontiers in Neuroscience, 17*, 1155750.

Turkle, S. (1995). *Life on the screen: Identity in the age of the internet.* Simon & Schuster.

Part One

Screens

2   Printed Text

Chapter 2 explores the origins and development of printed text and various forms of media, such as newspapers, magazines, books, and comics. In the past, technologies did not have screens, but now, we use screens to view printed and published materials. Initially, screens served as guards, but later, they became used for projections and computer monitors. Screens are part of creating any printed text today, but this media survey starts before their use.

The printing press changed the world by making it easier to share information, and influenced how we communicate today. Print media turns one-on-one or small-group communication into mass communication. Mass media, achieved through large-scale printing, revolutionized communication by reaching countless individuals. For the first time, people quickly shared large amounts of information, reaching vast numbers of people across different time zones, geographies, and societies. In this chapter, we delve into the history of publishing, focusing on the invention of printing and the display of printed materials. The technology called the press disseminated information rapidly and efficiently, making printed materials more widely accessible. The form of the information? Books, newspapers, pamphlets, magazines, and other print materials. Mass distribution to a broader audience was pivotal in the history of print media. The chapter discusses copyright, the rise of newspapers as a business, and the impact of digital technologies on publishing. The chapter ends with ideas about media effects from mass media consumption.

How Did We Get Here?

Before printing, everything was orally shared or written by hand. Each letter was recorded by hand by one individual and made into a single entity that one person could read or share with a group of people in the same vicinity who could hear the voice reading the lettered words or characters. Ancient texts scribed by monks and other religious officials

DOI: 10.4324/9781003397588-3

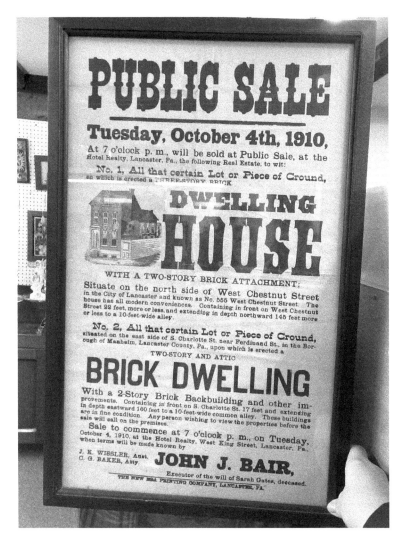

Figure 2.1 Public Sale poster from 1910.

Photograph by the author.

show a high margin of error in interpretation. The printing press minimized these errors to be, in many ways, more accurate. Yes, there were still typos, misspellings, and misinformation, aka fake news, because people run the presses, people change the type, people create the information, and people are fallible.

The use of technology shifted the socio-cultural experience. The printing press increased the standardization and affordability of information. Language also became more standard-specific, and vocabulary usage became more common in print. Somebody made choices about printing and sharing. Printed materials, like newspapers and books, were more affordable to mass audiences because of the lower costs of printing materials on a press. As access to printed materials increased across economic levels, standardized information about the world became available to more people. Literacy and education grew from this availability and access to printed materials helped spread scholarly ideas and encouraged more discussion and the development of new ideas. Education, literacy, and the evolution of ideas and culture were also impacted and advanced by printed materials, which became the first mass media. The printing press transformed communication, media, and knowledge access, and its influence continues today.

Turning The Page

Publishing and written materials have been around for a long time, starting with cave drawings and clay tablets and then evolving to include coins, pottery, papyrus, and parchment. Wood blocks, too, were used to print books. Textiles and printing on fabric have also been part of the history of visual communication. People have used textile printing as a form of political resistance and to express and distribute political views and criticisms of social issues. Stitching on fabric has also been used to pass messages between groups to spread political ideas. Quilting became popular in the 1800s and 1900s because of advancements in textile production, allowing women of the time a way to share their opinions. Textile art is an early form of communication that shares cultural, storytelling, and political ideas. In cultures around the globe, numerous countries share information and cultural signifiers through color and prints in fabric in the face of oppression.

Like contemporary media, these earlier forms of text use have helped communities express views, resist oppressive systems, and commemorate important people and places. Along with these early uses of text and visual communication, the invention of the printing press, the growth of the publishing industry, and the convergence of numerous kinds of media are crucial elements to understanding the contemporary media landscape. The idea of literacy acquired focus as this "new" print media, facilitated by new technology, became accessible to more and more people. The working definition used for literacy in the basic sense of the time is the ability to read and write. This fundamental shift in printing technologies moved communication out of the oral tradition and into the written one. Literacy now encompasses digital skills, such as accessing, organizing, evaluating, and creating information. Technological developments have enhanced literacy, especially in early education. However, there are still individuals in society who face challenges in reading and writing because of factors such as poverty, dyslexia, dysgraphia, dyscalculia, and other learning differences. Media technologies have not ended illiteracy but have allowed people to experience the world in new ways. Although not unfiltered, the mediated view has provided a broader understanding for people worldwide through various media platforms. Encoding and decoding information, how we hear something and then make sense of it, are different for each of us.

The Gutenberg printing press, invented in the mid-15th century, revolutionized book production and marked the start of printing in Europe. Letterpress technology expanded access to literature, knowledge, and information for more people who could read or distribute printed text. The early publishing companies' printing houses facilitated the spread of various published works. Printing technology advancements improved book production and distribution for publishing houses. The Renaissance heralded an era of cultural, economic, political, and artistic revival from the 14th to 16th centuries. The printing press helped spread science, philosophy, and literature to more people.

Ancient books were printed by Monastic scribes, who wrote books in scripted handwriting, and illuminators, who illustrated the books. Monastic monks from many religious cultures often wrote manuscripts on parchment. The Book of Kells and selected manuscripts from the Monasteries of Mount Athos are two examples of hand-scripted books still available today. While Gutenberg is credited with the movable type printing press, printing was already occurring in China and Korea. The writing process shifted from handwriting to using movable type and printing. Print artists in China chiseled pages of text into wooden blocks similar to a lithograph. China's Bi Sheng developed a movable type using porcelain. Korea's Choe Yun-ui cast three-dimensional characters in metal to press on sheets of paper to create documents (Doo-Jong, 1963). From the 1440s onward, people maintained the mechanics of the movable type printing press until they replaced the wooden parts with iron and integrated levers into the machine. From that time forward, countless printing press inventions and innovations tweaked the technology until the early 1980s and the birth of the digital revolution.

In the 1900s, newspapers focused more on making money and less on special interest funding. Profits increased for newspaper owners, and their companies became lucrative. Major cities used news collection to their advantage, publishing morning and evening and special weekend or themed editions. With urban areas' growth and city-focused newspapers' rise, the press has become an influential part of today's media conglomerates.

Political party alignment shifted to independent media driven by profit, moving from partisan sponsorship to commercial profitability. Sometimes, commercial profit and partisanship still align. The chapter on journalism shares more ideas about the newspaper industry. The American government also continued to use printing as a tool, especially in the military. They used printing during World War I and World War II by developing portable field army presses to print various documents as military companies moved from one geographic location to another. During World War II, aircraft distributed propaganda leaflets and newspapers behind enemy lines across the globe to shape opinion. Posters and other literature were also used to recruit Americans into military service. That changed in the mid-1900s, when analog computers and digital technologies became central to printing. All publishing and print work, and their associated publications, now use screened technologies as part of the process. In numerous cases in contemporary publications, the type is cast on the screen and never printed. However, this only happened with the advent of the World Wide Web and the internet.

Magazines Develop

Magazines trace their history back to the 1600s. However, in the early 1900s, they flourished and became an industry. Magazines grew from catalog inserts in newspapers to a new genre. As photography developed as a technology, magazines used it in a new stylistic way, focusing on longer-form photojournalism that highlighted photos in a vivid and often stylized way. Staged visuals, called "photoshoots", developed in the early 1900s and became a staple in fashion. Magazine photos provided an enhanced visual impact of stories. They changed the reporting style from hard news to feature and lifestyle news, developing a new content genre. The magazine format was larger and often targeted different demographics for its content. Halftone printing and photogravure perfected the printing process by accurately reproducing shadows in photographs and enhancing visual images. Some magazines had a reputation for providing in-depth coverage of current events.

In contrast, others shared information about the world, focusing on landscape and geographic photography and travel journalism. Magazines fostered content for many demographics. Teens loved magazines focused on popular culture. Women's magazines covered fashion, beauty, relationships, recipes, and household tips. Magazines targeting men concentrated on sports, health, hunting, and cars. Other magazines focused more on in-depth coverage of business and financial news, or in-depth reports on the general news of the day. Magazines like *National Geographic*, *Time*, and *Life* covered various topics like geography, science, history, world

Figure 2.2 Print advertisement from the 1960s.
Photograph by the author.

culture, and fascinating people. Hobby magazines focused on cars, dolls, and stuffed animals were also popular printed entertainment (Brooker & Thacker, 2015; Sumner, 2010), and children's magazines, like *Highlights for Children*, started in the mid-1900s. Urban lifestyle magazines gained popularity by targeting specific audiences and tailoring ads to their interests, making a name for themselves in local markets.

Continued Advancements and New Industries

The improvements in printing technology, mass paper production, and transportation upgrades made producing and distributing books easier. Bookstores became an economic force in the late 1800s and early 1900s. Both cities and small towns invested in local bookstores. The American Booksellers Association (ABA) was formed in 1900 and fostered the independent bookstore industry. American cities created big book districts, and independent bookstores opened to meet the book demand. Book Expo conferences and publishing conventions also grew the publishing industry. Popular regional department stores opened in-store book departments in the early 1900s, and National Book Week started in 1919. After World War II, publishing expanded through increased bookstore ownership and a growing academic market for higher education (Hyland, 2016).

Furthermore, education reform, the literacy movement, and the availability of more mass transit options fueled the growth of public libraries. While libraries were being built throughout Europe as early as the 7th century, citizens of Boston, Maryland, Philadelphia, and South Carolina established libraries in the first half of the 1800s. They donated book collections to create repositories of books that citizens could check out (Bell, 2021; Harris, 1995; Johnson, 1960).

Children's Literature

Children's literature and comics also became an essential part of the legacy of print and publishing history. Children's picture books have been handmade since the 1600s. Still, independent literature, such as Beatrix Potter's stories, emerged in England in the early 1900s. Lucy Maud Montgomery's *Anne of Green Gables* and P.L. Travers' *Mary Poppins* published in that same period. The Newbery Medal was established in 1922 to honor distinguished writing for children, and the Caldecott Medal was created in 1938 to recognize children's picture book artists. After World War II, the birth rate experienced a significant increase, and even more parents wanted books specifically designed for children. They could purchase them via mail, at supermarkets, or through Scholastic book programs in schools, further propelling the popularity of children's series. Dr. Seuss, whose real name was Theodor Seuss Geisel, captivated generations of readers with his imaginative and colorful storytelling. By the 1950s, he had published several popular books featuring his trademark writing style. The 1900s saw a notable emphasis on children's education, leading to the creation of books that catered to young readers. Some famous examples include *Blueberries for Sal* by Robert McCloskey, *Charlotte's Web* by E.B. White, and The Berenstain Bears Beginner Books series.

Pura Belpré's *Perez and Martina,* Dhan Gopal Mukerji's *Gay-Neck: The Story of a Pigeon*, and Ann Nolan Clark's *In My Mother's House* brought diversity to children's literature and Arna Bontemps's *The Fast Sooner Hound* and Langston Hughes's *Poetry for Young People*, along with work by Dr. Carter G. Woodson and Jane Shackelford continued to foster diverse themes in children's literature throughout the 20th century (Horning, 2015). Books such as *Brown Girl Dreaming, Last Stop on Market Street,* and *Rain Is Not My Indian Name* show diversity, equity, and inclusion in children's literature.

Transmedia storytelling is when specific media products cross different platforms. In children's literature, transmedia storytelling occurred when filmmakers and game developers turned popular books, like *Beezus and Ramona* and *Charlie and the Chocolate Factory*, into movies and video games. J.K. Rowling's Harry Potter book series and other young adult fiction (YA) also transformed into a transmedia empire of books, movies, and video games. At the same time, Lemony Snicket's A Series of Unfortunate Events became a streaming series. These book series were very profitable for authors and publishers. Bestselling children's book series, such as Percy Jackson, Diary of a Wimpy Kid, and Captain Underpants became popular in the late '90s and 2000s. Books like the Twilight series, *The Hunger Games,* and *Divergent* also helped boost readership and sales. The increasing popularity of YA also spilled over into children's publishing (Meigs, 1969; Post et al, 2000).

YA has its roots in the 1930s but gained recognition in the United States in the 1960s and 1970s. Authors started using realistic titles that address serious subjects, such as death, sex, underage drinking, homelessness, mental health, and drug use. The 1980s saw the genre expand to include horror and adolescent high drama. The genre has become even more popular with the transmedia spread of young adult titles across cinema, video, theater, computer games, television, and comics that incorporate dystopia and science fiction, fantasy, historical fiction, and romance.

Comics and Zines

Comics, a sequential art form, shared a similar trajectory to children's literature. The title of the first American printed comic was *The Adventures of Mr. Obadiah Oldbuck,* an unauthorized translation of the original French publication. Political cartoons, another form of sequential art, became part of the fabric of political unrest in the American colonies (Eisner, 2008). Like film and television, people categorize comics into ages, commonly known as Golden, Silver, Bronze, Dark, and Modern. The first is the Golden Age (late 1930s–1950s), which introduced iconic characters like Miss Fury, Archie, and the Arrow, still around today. National Allied Publications later became D.C. Comics, including Action Comics Superman and All-American Comics's Green Lantern. Timely Comics, later named Marvel Comics, introduced Captain America and the Marvel Universe. In the Silver Age (1950s–1970s), new superheroes like the Flash, the Fantastic Four, and Captain America emerged, along with spinoff characters like Lois Lane and Nelvana of the Northern Lights. In the mid-1950s, famous comic book publishers created the Comics Magazine Association of America (CMAA). The aim was to adopt a regulatory code for comic books because of the growing broadcast and television competition. The Bronze Age (1970s–1980s) added to comic book universes and published new comics. X-Men, Swamp Thing, Daredevil, Howard the Duck, and

Figure 2.3 Comic books from the 1980s.

Photograph by the author.

Jack Kirby's Fourth World Cycle came from the Bronze era. Some comic book historians also note an era called the Dark Age; the 1980s saw the creation of comics like Hell Boy, Wolverine, Venom, and Sonic the Hedgehog. The creators made these comics for adults, incorporating mature themes, sex, and violence.

Throughout comic book history, story plots and themes changed with the times. During wartime, comics focused on patriotic figures and escapist entertainment. Western science fiction, crime, and horror comics gained popularity, requiring the creation of the Comics Code Authority (CCA) in the 1950s to self-regulate and govern content in the comic book industry.

A United States Senate Subcommittee on Juvenile Delinquency pointed to comics, in part, for the issues of the time's youth. Now phased out, this stamp on the front of the comic book deemed it approved to be read by young readers. Comic books were also popular in other forms, in other parts of the world. Counterculture and Underground Comix became a part of American contemporary culture. Japanese Manga and anime share an unmistakably unique storytelling and visual style developed in the latter 1800s and have increased in popularity worldwide, creating a fusion of unique visual styles and storytelling (Arnett, 2007). One outgrowth of the popularity of comic books and their rise in popular culture is the comic convention, often referred to as "Comic Con".

From 1985 to contemporary times, the Modern Age has fostered cross-pollination and transmedia proliferation across all screens. The increased proliferation in transmedia and digital technologies meant comics like *Star Wars*, *My Little Pony* and *Transformers*, for instance, needed additional copyright protection. To protect the First Amendment rights of comic creators and their businesses, the Comic Book Legal Defense Fund was started in the late 1900s. The fund supports the comic book community, including readers, creators, retailers, and publishers, fighting for their rights to parody and fair use (Brownstein, n.d.).

Bookstore Culture Emerges

Suburban bookstores, in cities, then malls, became a place for purchases and social time. Bookstore chains like Borders and Barnes & Noble rapidly expanded. The inventory had a wide range of books, CDs, movies, magazines, and unique, book-related gifts that helped them compete with independent bookstores. Bookstores found it convenient to establish a shop in suburban areas, as more middle-class people moved there. The added square footage made room for small coffee shops in the bookstore. Various bookstores added coffee shops, creating a social atmosphere that attracted customers. In the 1990s, Amazon.com and online bookstores posed a challenge to physical bookstores. However, some physical stores have competed and established themselves in specific communities. And while making content mobile-friendly and using responsive web design has made reading on devices more popular, these developments have also impacted bookstores. Nowadays, the publishing industry combines print and digital formats with various online options for buying eBooks, digital editions, and audiobooks. Smaller publishers and self-publishing have also increased with the proliferation of niche markets. Scholastic, Penguin Random House, and Hachette are prominent children's book sales players. Because of convergence, more people are interested in interactive reading experiences and reading-themed video games.

Script and Fonts

The history and technological trajectory of publishing bring about a transition of the text itself. Printing technologies have evolved alongside writing. The earliest writing systems, such as cuneiform, used pictorial symbols to represent ideas and words. The Phoenician alphabet started being used around 1200 BCE. The 22 characters created represented consonant sounds and impacted writing systems, such as Greek and Latin. Etruscan script and the Greek alphabet moved into the evolution of Latin script, which became the start of many European writing systems. In the Middle Ages, scribes wrote manuscripts by hand in different script styles, such as Carolingian, Uncial, and Gothic. Each was distinct. Initially, the typeface looked like handwriting, but the Gutenberg Bible used a font resembling a Gothic script. In the 15th–16th century CE, new fonts like Renaissance and Humanist emerged. Scribes were influenced by classical inscriptions that led to the creation of Roman typefaces.

Figure 2.4 Wanted poster and broadcast photos from the 1930s.
Photograph by the author.

Type designer Aldus Manutius and others like him played a significant role in refining fonts. Baroque fonts were intricate and decorative, while Enlightenment fonts aimed for simplicity and clarity. Typeface designers like John Baskerville and Giambattista Bodoni influenced font design during the Enlightenment (Krieger, 1987). Numerous foundries emerged in the 1800s, creating a wide variety of fonts.

The 1900s brought the linotype machine and phototypesetting, which made font production more efficient. In the late 1900s, digital typography and the advent of computers revolutionized font design and printed distribution. TrueType and PostScript fonts became widely used and brought increased creative freedom. OpenType and web fonts offer advanced typographic features and cross-platform compatibility. Platforms like Apple and Google created proprietary typefaces only their customers could use. Web fonts, like Google Fonts and Adobe Fonts have created consistent online typography and typeface (Tholenaar et al., 2009). Modern typography allows dynamic kerning, leading, spacing, and color changes. Numerous variations of type foundries exist, and independent designers are creating new examples and uses (Harrison, 2010). The digital age also made easy-to-read web fonts. The Web Open Font Format (WOFF) and the OpenType standard developed in the mid-2010s noted the ability to vary shape, width, thickness, and slant for interface work. In contemporary settings, ADA-compliant fonts are essential for accessibility and individuals essentialized vision. Louis Braille invented the Braille system in the 1800s to help vision-challenged and blind individuals to read and write. Designers developed fonts for increased readability. Many consider San Serif fonts, like Arial and Comic Sans, to be readable typefaces as well as dyslexia-designed fonts like Dyslexie, Opendyslexic, Gill Dyslexic, Read Regular, and Lexia Readable.

Publishing, Transformed

Publishing was revolutionized by the internet, allowing for digital content distribution. In the adult reading sector in the 1900s, paperback books became popular, making books more affordable and accessible. In the late 1900s, digital publishing sped up the digital revolution, changing the publishing industry as other media technologies came together. Ebooks and digital platforms have changed how books are made and read. Another area of change in printing, in more recent years, is a focus on sustainability in printing procedures and paper use. Carbon footprint calculators gauge the environmental impact of printing, from materials to disposal. Sustainable sourcing and water chemical use are part of the calculation. Printing processes that meet sustainable requirements can earn forestry logos for sustainable forest management for product use.

Further, sustainable inks and facilities can impact the carbon footprint of printing processes in all kinds of print-based industries. Initially, companies painted ads on buildings, but with the advent of large-format printing, billboards started appearing in cities and on highways. In many cities, digital billboards have replaced printed varieties, sharing a variety of advertising from one location.

Authors can now bypass agents and traditional publishers by self-publishing online. The contemporary publishing landscape includes conventional publishing houses, independent publishing platforms, and digital media companies that continue to evolve based on consumer preferences. Publishing has played an essential role in shaping cultures and societies. Conventional publishing platforms transitioned magazines to online interactive digital editions. Integrating e-readers, tablets, smartphones, and abundant content illustrates that reading is not going away. Instead, providers are becoming more data-driven in how they provide content. Devices continue to play with e-readers to make them more portable, lighter, and easier to read in bright light, to increase their appeal to consumers.

Mobile apps have integrated digital magazines to reach readers on smartphones and tablets. Near Field Communication (NFC) is a technology that allows people to use their phones to access data, make contactless payments, and tap to pay. Improved digital reading experiences have brought together different media industries. Magazines are integrating augmented reality (AR), virtual reality (VR), and extended reality (XR) technology to offer interactive and immersive experiences for readers. Artificial intelligence (AI) analytics and recommendations have improved personalized content delivery for publishers and consumers. Collecting and analyzing large datasets have helped publishers gain insights into demographics, audience behavior, and tools and platforms to manage digital advertisements and deliver targeted campaigns to readers. Social media has become a part of publishing by producing audio, video content, and podcasts to reach a larger audience. Data security and privacy are essential for protecting reader information and push notifications. Subscription management platforms and interactive content tools, like quizzes and polls, create buzz and engage people. All publishing enterprises use cloud-based solutions for storage, backup, collaboration, and search engine optimization (SEO) strategies to improve and increase publishing strategies. Print-on-demand (POD) is especially useful in the academic publishing industry, allowing books to be printed as needed and reducing inventory costs. Infographics and interactive elements like quick response (QR) codes and geofencing increase reader interactivity, and tracked behavior, and preferences. Additionally, Open Access has made scholarly research freely accessible. Digital rights management (DRM) is a legal way to protect digital content rights and ensure transparent publishing rights and royalties management. Blockchain technology is also being explored to secure copyrights and digital content ownership for books and art.

Research on Effects

Media is considered to alter media consumers differently through its effect on those using a specific media or mediatized experience. Each chapter in this text explores how researchers study media, focusing on effects. "Media-influenced effects are those things that occur as a result—either in part or in whole—from media influence" (Potter, 2012, p. 38). Many studies have been conducted through the years to gauge how much effect there is from media consumption of all kinds, through many different technologies since the first media technology invention. Media effects can occur through engagement with media, overall or specific media consumption, the duration of remembering something heard, seen, or experienced from media exposure, the pleasantness or unpleasantness of a mediated experience, the way someone changes because of a mediated experience, the intention of media and media content toward a specific idea, the level of effect (as in a large or small change), the directedness of the media toward an individual's consumption, and the way a mediated experience manifests in a person's life (Potter, 2012). Media effects on media users can be linked to psychological, belief-based, attitude-based, affective, and behavior-based changes. User effects can be traced to acquiring new ideas, triggering past experiences, altering work or habits, and reinforcing current attitudes and behaviors (Potter, 2012). The following three examples illustrate how researchers evaluate media effects in text-based media. One research group studied readers of YA to examine the impact on readers' social attitudes and gender identity. The findings concluded that, yes, YA stories have an influence on teenagers in ways beyond what researchers initially expected. "The findings also suggest that some narratives in adolescent fiction and their degree of acceptance by readers may reflect some small but significant changes in the construction of femininity, with an increasing emphasis on toughness and independence" (Kokesh & Sternadori, 2015, p. 155). Research findings also note that more recently produced adolescent novels and movies are portraying more independent and emotionally secure girls and women, who now wear pants and boots, but "the genre also continues to enforce traditional femininity in the face of clingy, insecure, and ever-dieting heroines" (Ibid.).

In a different study, researchers reviewed trust in the news and participation in online news. Researchers found that trust in the news differs significantly across countries, with the highest levels in Finland (68.1%) and Germany (60.2%) and the lowest in Spain (34.2%) and the United States (32.2%). Across all 11 countries studied, just under half of all respondents (44.5%) said they had either a high or very high level of trust in the news (Fletcher & Park, 2017, p. 13). The researchers shared that trust becomes a complex idea in the contemporary news environment, where multiple places exist to consume news. Their analysis indicates that media consumers with low trust in news media are more likely to prefer non-mainstream news sources. They are also more likely to engage in online news participation. More specifically, those with low trust in the news are more likely to say that their primary news source is social media, blogs, or news outlets without a print or broadcast legacy. This evidence matches a previous study showing that exposure to non-mainstream news is linked to media skepticism. For instance, for journalists and news organizations, relying on the "'number of shares' to gauge an article's 'success' can be misleading when a considerable portion of shares are driven by low credibility and negativity. Participation may partly reflect distrust or disapproval" (p. 22).

The final study that highlights media effects from print and text-based media is focused on the impact of photo comics media use in elementary education. According to this research, the use of "photo comic media" significantly enhances students' reading interest in elementary social studies subjects. "This is evidenced by a significant difference between the group of students who were given the photo comic media treatment and showed that the group learning to use photo comic media had a higher reading interest" (Senen et al., 2021, p. 2310). The quantitative study further noted that students using photo comic media had higher learning outcomes on their assessments. Media consumers who use text, printed, and comic-styled media are affected by that usage. Media effects research reveals that consumers can experience changes in their sense of self, trust, and participation while increasing interest and learning. Print media use affects media consumers in a variety of ways.

Things to Consider

- Think about the physical process of creating a book before the printing press. How did the physical experience of making a printed document or book change with the invention of the Gutenberg Press?
- The legacy of the early print industry is still evident today, both in physical artifacts and socio-cultural influences. What aspects of this historical period continue to shape contemporary media?
- In what ways did the ancient technologies highlighted in this chapter affect media consumers of their time?
- In what ways did the shift of content creation, separated from funding source interests, change the nature of mass media of the time? Are news media still operating under this separation?

- Which early print and publishing companies and their family names still have connections to the contemporary media landscape?
- Name the different technologies mentioned in this chapter.

Takeaways

- The printing press changed how information and knowledge were distributed, allowing mass communication through the written word, and revolutionized communication models we know today.
- The invention of the Braille-raised print system created a way for the visually impaired to read.
- The evolution of writing systems from symbols to the alphabet set the stage for printing technology.
- The progression of fonts captures the advancements in technology and the creative and cultural energies of many historical periods.
- Technology continuously redefines and molds content consumption habits.
- Many technological inventions became part of the legacy of print media and publishing.
- Name some of your chapter takeaways.

References

Arnett, J. (Ed). (2007). Encyclopedia of children, adolescents, and the media. Sage Publications.

Bell, B. (2021). *Crusoe's books: Readers in the Empire of Print, 1800–1918.* Oxford University Press.

Brooker, P., & Thacker, A. (2015). *The Oxford critical and cultural history of modernist magazines. Volume II, North America 1894–1960.* Oxford Academic Books.

Brownstein, C. (n.d.). Know Your Rights. https://cbldf.org/retailer-tools/know-your-rights-a-retailer-resource/

Doo-Jong, K. (1963). [Until Yi Dynasty] History of Korean Printing. *Korea Journal*, 3(7), 22–26.

Eisner, W. (2008). *Comics and sequential art: Principles and practices from the legendary cartoonist.* WW Norton & Company.

Fletcher, R., & Park, S. (2017). The impact of trust in the news media on online news consumption and participation. *Digital Journalism*, 5(10), 1281–1299.

Harris, M.H. (1995). *History of libraries in the western world.* (4th ed.). Scarecrow Press.

Harrison, J. (2010). *100 GPO years, 1861–1961: A history of United States public printing*/[prepared] under the direction of James L. Harrison. (Sesquicentennial ed.). U.S. Govt. Printing Office: For sale by the Supt. of Docs., U.S. G.P.O.

Horning, K.L. (2015). Milestones for diversity in children's literature and library services. *Children and Libraries, 13*(3). https://journals.ala.org/index.php/cal/article/view/5768

Hyland, K. (2016). *Academic publishing: Issues and challenges in the construction of knowledge.* Oxford University Press.

Johnson, E.D. (1960). *Communication: An introduction to the history of the alphabet, writing, printing, books, and libraries.* (2nd ed.). Scarecrow Press.

Kokesh, J., & Sternadori, M. (2015). The good, the bad, and the ugly: A qualitative study of how young adult fiction affects identity construction. *Atlantic Journal of Communication, 23*(3), 139–158.

Krieger, M. (Ed.). (1987). *The aims of representation: Subject, text, history.* Columbia University Press.

Meigs, C. (1969). *A critical history of children's literature: A survey of children's books in English.* Macmillan.

Post, A., Scott, M., & Theberge, M. (2000). *Celebrating children's choices: 25 years of children's favorite books.* International Reading Association.

Potter, W. (2012). What is a media effect? In *Media Effects* (pp. 33–50). SAGE Publications, https://doi.org/10.4135/978154430850

Senen, A., Sari, Y.P., Herwin, H., Rasimin, R., & Dahalan, S.C. (2021). The use of photo comics media: Changing reading interest and learning outcomes in elementary social studies subjects. *Cypriot Journal of Educational Sciences, 16*(5), 2300–2312.

Sumner, D.E. (2010). *The Magazine Century: American magazines since 1900.* Peter Lang.

Tholenaar, J., Jong, C. de, & Purvis, A.W. (2009). *Type: A visual history of typefaces and graphic styles.* Taschen.

3 Cinema

How we view cinema and the developments of movies, film, and digital images convey important meanings for screened experiences. The cinematic image undergoes many transitions before it is screened. The image undergoes creative processes and technologies before being shown to the audience. Even the idea of screening requires mention of the technology called the screen. Cinema viewing has evolved from town squares to theaters, TVs, and digital screens, like laptops, tablets, and phones. In the history of moving visual work, cinema, film, motion pictures, and movies come foremost to mind. Are they synonyms for the same thing? While they differ slightly, they all describe watching something on a big screen. Like books, cinema has created different genres based on form, style, and subject matter. Many genres have been named; some enduring film genres include action, comedy, documentaries, film noir, horror, drama, musicals, science fiction, and westerns. Some genres have combined through the years, and others have become subgenres. The lines between genres are soft and collaborative; cinema genres continue to evolve as moviegoers' tastes change, and technologies allow for a more creative interpretation of experience.

In this chapter, you'll find essential technologies, historical events, and ideas related to cinema and digital media. It is interesting to consider some early history of cinema when studying screens. What seems most provocative is that it is difficult to pick a specific individual as the inventor of cinema because different inventors were working on cinema technology at the same time across the world. Historians do not claim one as a definitive winner, but brothers Auguste and Louis Lumière, William Friese-Greene, Émile Reynaud, Louis Le Prince, Thomas Edison, and his assistant William Kennedy-Laurie Dickson, are all mentioned. Before the photo camera, the camera obscura was invented. The camera obscura is an instrument that casts a light source 'outside' through a small hole and reproduces it as an 'image' on a flat surface 'inside' a darkened room (Ihde, 2008, p. 385). The flat surface in a darkened room resembles a cinema screen. And the camera

DOI: 10.4324/9781003397588-4

obscura is a perfect technology to kick off a chapter on cinema technologies. The chapter ends with ideas about film theory and narrative story effects on an eager and interested audience.

Cinema as Media

Cinema is a form of media that shares stories, information, messages, ideas, and entertainment with an audience, like television, radio, and text-based materials. The audience of media consumers imbue themselves with cinematic images and sounds that convey meaning. Cinema is also an art because filmmakers masterfully use editing, sound, and visual effects to craft stories and evoke emotions in audiences. Cinema creatively explores profound themes, similar to other art forms like poetry, sculpture, and painting. Cinema was the first visually available moving media that used production values like camera angles, lighting instruments, and editing choices to convey meaning. Screenwriters, directors, actors, and others use their creativity to make scripts come alive with visuals and sounds for audiences to enjoy. This act of interpretation and creative endeavor is artistic. Similar to other artists, movies can profoundly impact viewers through artistic expression. Film techniques and technology are scientific, but their presentation is artistic and has influenced culture, just like other art forms. The artistic creativity of filmmakers affects content creation in the contemporary media landscape. Cinema is also a business enterprise and an industry. Large-scale film projects are designed for intended distribution. Movie studios deliver movies to theaters and streaming platforms for mass consumption, just like other forms of media.

Film Technologies

At the very beginning of cinema, filmmakers used glass plates and paper rolls as technologies to share an image. Celluloid film changed how we capture and store images by printing pictures in synthetic plastic. The invention of celluloid itself predates film. People used the product in manufacturing and decorating before inventing the film product. Inventors created a way to save movie picture images by using flexible and transparent thermoplastic strips called celluloid, coated with light-sensitive chemicals and colors. The combination of the plastic with holes on the side, called sprocket holes, fed through a projector, combined with chemicals sensitive to light, makes film stock that is still used today. Then, the operator loaded this celluloid film into a film camera, with housing that locked into the sprocket holes and a crank and spring to advance the film. While contemporary processes are digital, content creators still go into the world to "film" an image. Those content creators still call themselves filmmakers.

Figure 3.1 Keystone Model A12 16 mm film camera.

Photograph by the author.

Figure 3.2 Cement, oil, and lens shade for film cameras.

Photograph by the author.

Figure 3.3 Piece of film showing the film sprockets at the top.
Photograph by the author.

Cinematography Emerges

In the late 1800s, inventors like the Lumiere Brothers, William Friese-Greene, Émile Reynaud, Louis Le Prince, Thomas Edison, and his assistant William Kennedy-Laurie Dickson were credited with inventing the film or motion picture camera. This technology allowed creators to capture moving images, making it look as though things were progressing. The cinématographe was a workstation system that revolutionized the film industry from start to finish. How cinema leads the visual media experience is central to understanding the larger media landscape. It's hard to say who invented cinema and its technologies exactly, as multiple inventors have made claims. However, the focus of this textbook section is on camera technology. The camera was likely aimed at a screen to capture the moving image. The camera, the moving image, and the screen all play a part in the film experience (Sobchack, 2020).

Early cinematic artifacts connect to modern visual media, showcasing cultural influences and awareness. Cinema, as a topic area, and the film and movie technologies and genres that are tucked into it, balance ideas around film as an art form and industry. So much of cinema history comes from its technologies and techniques. The art, craft, and technique of cinema are part of that story. Instruments have captured visual effects over time, leading to global efforts to save and record these stories on film.

Cinema technologies bubbled into existence in the late 1800s. In these early days, numerous technologies pushed cinema and filmmaking, including the endoscope, the bioscop, and the cinématographe. Early moving images came from the zoetrope, zoopraxiscope, and the magic lantern. These instruments create an illusion of motion by rapidly displaying images one after the other when held up to light, to observe small frames in line. This is the way that the image appears in film. It moves on a projector at a rate of 24 frames per second (fps). Modern digital and cinematic cameras still use the 24 fps rate.

Once filmmakers invented film cameras and film stock, they wanted some way of sharing their work. Many considered Auguste and Louis Lumière the first creators to hold a public screening for their film work in Paris, marking the birth of cinema. Notably, the camera technology predates the birth of cinema. Technology shaped the future of cinema in that manner. At the beginning of cinema, the moving image did not have sound attached to it, as it does now. Silent films were visual images without collected or added sound. These silent films created a fascinating first era of cinema. The "Silent Era", in the late 1800s into the early 1900s, saw many types of films created. In numerous cases, the "silent" film had sound with it as recorded music or live performed music. The piano was a trendy way to lend sound to a film. While the film was screened, a pianist arrived at the theater and performed on the piano. While early cinema recorded visuals only, filmmakers pushed technology to find a way for audiences to listen to the combination of audio and visuals. Well-known early filmmakers from various countries include Indian film producer and director Dadasaheb Phalke, China's actor and film production company owner Anna May Wong, Korean film company owner Yodo Orajo, and Mexico's filmmaker Salvador Toscano Barragán.

Later, inventors developed technology that collects sound. The full-coat magnetic material matched the visual image through sound editing and the entire editing process. In the late 1920s, synchronized sound became more accessible with the invention of the Vitaphone system. This technology allowed sound recordings to be played in sync with the film. This was the birth of talkies or films with simultaneous pictures and sound.

Color Film Stock

Within a decade, inventors and developers created and perfected color film stock, which added a wholly elevated viewing experience for the moviegoer. The Technicolor process became the most well-known product for colorization, but the early processes became antiquated by the 1970s. In the United States, these early days of cinema were called the Classic Hollywood Era. The small neighborhood on Hollywood Blvd burst onto

Figure 3.4 A variety sizes of film reels.

Photograph by the author.

the scene as the mecca of cinema because of the combination of the mild and sunny climate, a variety of readily accessible different geographic settings, and, also, early filmmakers running from patent issues converging to create the perfect early environment for growth. Early European filmmaking introduced different styles, such as German Expressionism, Soviet Montage, and, later, French New Wave Cinema. Films called talkies, with synchronized dialog, soon became popular. Filmmaking grew from an art form into an industry of established studios like Black Maria in New Jersey, and Metro-Goldwyn-Mayer, Inc (MGM), Warner Bros., and Paramount in Hollywood, CA.

Changing Times

Throughout history, mechanical and technological inventions have often occurred during wartime. The push for innovation affected cinema on a global scale. Many countries used cinema technology to produce films that capitalized on war propaganda, employing persuasive political, religious, or cultural messaging tactics and supported films with specific ideologies and wartime messages. From a technical perspective, styles like German Expressionism focused on sets, framing, and lighting connected to film noir. In other cases, like Soviet Montage, film editing became the focus. The technology of its era influenced each style.

The film industry has a variety of professional positions that make a production crew. Many of these positions are also part of other crews in screened media, like television and digital media productions. Some jobs are union-based, some are full-time, and some are freelance. The size of the project determines the variation in cinema crew, and it is common for multiple companies to collaborate in production and distribution. At the movie's end, a list of companies collaborating on production and distribution is displayed. Film companies vary in size, from small to large. Individuals own some companies, while others are publicly traded on the stock market. The first step in making a major motion picture is to develop the script based on an idea. Scripts and story ideas come from various places. Companies can either invest in writing a script or purchase one. Writers in the company's writers' room sometimes write the script in-house; if a script fails to meet its objectives, a producer might hire a script doctor or consultant to revise it. Final screenplays can be original ideas or adaptations of source material, such as novels, books, or comic series. A project adapted from a book or other materials may have a built-in fan base, increasing the chance that the project will make money.

The script stage of a film production often involves multiple revisions and input during preproduction from "above-the-line" producers and essential experts involved in the project. All the planning before principal photography begins takes place in the preproduction phase, including location scouting, set building, planning the shooting schedule, hiring crew, and casting extras. Above-the-line costs occur before the actual production starts. During this process, producers also pitch the film's premise to investors to raise money for financing. Independent filmmakers use funding platforms to raise funds for creative projects. After finishing all above-the-line costs, the crew must be assembled. The production team attaches the lead actors and director early on. As preproduction ramps up, they hire the entire cast and heads of departments like cinematography, production design, costume design, etc.

Numerous professionals are hired on a film set. The director heads the crew leadership on a film set, overseeing the film's creative vision and its connection to the screenplay. Top film producers include Jason Blum, Jerry Bruckheimer, Megan Ellison, Nina Jacobson, Broderick Johnson, and Roy Lee. Producers, directors, and writers have essential roles during preproduction, while cinematographers handle the technical aspects during filming. Often, but not always, the director hires the cinematographer. Some well-known cinematographers, also called directors of photography (DPs), include Dion Beebe, Roger Deakins, Ellen Kuras, Emmanuel Lubezki, Reed Morano, Rachel Morrison, Rodrigo Prieto, Robert Richardson, Nancy Schreiber, Mandy Walker, and Bradford Young. After securing the sound and lighting crew, the DOP sets the rest of the crew. The director leads the cast and crew and works with the producer, who oversees the business aspects of film production, including hiring, production logistics, financing, production schedule, and budget. The DP's crew works closely with the director to establish the look and feel of the film. The production designer is also an essential position for setting the stage for the aesthetics of a production. This role involves creating the film's visual look, including sets, props, costumes, and makeup. The sound mixer collaborates with the director and operates the sound recording equipment on set. Both dialogue and ambient sound are essential parts of the set work. Additionally, grips are on set to handle all the equipment associated with light onset and props when required, and gaffers lead the electrical department and lighting crew. The gaffer executes the DP's lighting choices for the scenes. Once the filming is complete, the production brings on the Editor and visual effects team to assemble shots and create a rough cut and final edit of the movie. The cast and crew work together to bring the script to life on screen.

"Below-the-line" costs occur when production days start. The "line", in this case, is when technical production spending starts and the camera rolls. There can be costly consequences when exceeding the contract and rental window after production. Moving forward with a project after the script has final approval is much easier. The director supervises daily activities and assesses material to ensure sufficient scene coverage in the project. The duration of this phase varies from weeks to months, depending on the project. Next, in postproduction, the film editor and assistants edit the footage together. Then, visual effects, sound effects, scoring, color correction, and audio sweetening occur. The film editor and assistants often edit a trailer or preview to market the movie on social media and in theaters.

The producers relentlessly pursue a distribution deal once the film reaches completion or nears the final stages. Sometimes, the producer and distributor collaborate to ensure that they show the movie in theaters and on streaming platforms. The film often has a full or limited run in movie theaters and possible streaming opportunities. Distribution involves scheduling release dates and organizing promotional opportunities, like fan conventions or events. The producers also work to keep the movie secure, so no one sees a pre-released version. Sometimes, the producers plan a significant event or party while releasing a motion picture. Marketing strives to maximize the film's visibility for a broad audience. The releases of most films are highly calculated, and first-run sales are significant for everyone involved in a large project.

A film has many monetization phases, including ticket sales, theatrical runs, streaming licenses, and possible TV broadcast rights. While many go to first-run, IMAX, and mega theaters, others go to art theaters and are directed to streaming. At one time, filmmakers diverted films to VHS,

DVD, or Blu-ray and made them available at video stores. Now, most post-theatrical runs include time on streaming platforms. Films are also released on television. Another popular form of distribution in the 1900s was the drive-in theater experience. Drive-in movie theaters had big out-door screens and parking lots with rows of spaces that had speakers wired to junction boxes. Sometimes, drive-ins would show a double feature of A- and B-movies, and most locations had a snack bar. Drive-in movie cul-ture spanned from the 1950s to the 1980s, heralding a new cultural phe-nomenon in movie viewing (Levitt, 2016). Some drive-in movie theaters remain, but most have disappeared. Sometimes, an outdoor pop theater is used to evoke the space, sounds, and communal experiences of the open-air movie experience.

Film Editing

A critical aspect of the cinematic experience not touched upon yet is film editing. Filmmakers have made film editing a specialty in the postproduction process, and it has become an integral part of what is ultimately projected on the screen. The process of editing actually begins with the eyes. Every time you blink, your brain edits part of the visual image out and stitches the other parts together. When the filmmaking experience was invented in the late 1800s, people explained editing as cutting a film to a shorter length and then cementing it with another shortened piece. This was called a splice. At first, the process was practical to make the film longer. However, it soon became a narrative device to cut out unwanted sequences and build short new sequences for increased interest. Editing transformed filmmak-ing by shifting its emphasis from practical cutting to creating psychological impact. Technologies like the upright Moviola, Steenbeck, and Mechanik KEM tables, with a lightbox viewer, allowed the filmmaker to review reels, cut with precision, splice an edit, and view the transition. Dutch-American electrical engineer Iwan Serrurier invented the Moviola upright system in the 1920s, and filmmakers extensively used it until the 1960s. The Steen-beck flatbed table and the Keller-Elektro table, both created in Germany, also became main tools for film editing. The new editing flatbeds made editing quieter and more accessible for both image and sound.

Film editors used a grease pencil to mark edits and a guillotine-type splicer to cut the film. Gears on the table aided the editor in moving the film forward or backward through the viewer for an exact edit. Strips of unedited film designating scenes, called film rushes, were labeled and hung in bins for an organized workflow. In the 1980s, digital editing, called nonlinear editing, became the digital standard for editing. Editors ingested visuals and made digital cuts with systems like Media 100, Final Cut Pro, Media Composer, and Adobe Premiere. Moving into the 2000s,

Adobe After Effects, iMovie, Davinci Resolve, and other products became available. Extended reality technologies like artificial intelligence (AI)-assisted editing, virtual reality (VR) editing, and many AI-supported sound technologies have moved editing into an even more sophisticated era.

Film editing has seen numerous transitions, such as cinema directing styles. The changing technology in cinema production, with cameras, lighting, sound, editing, and camera support systems, has altered how film editors approach storytelling. Filmmakers still commonly use continuity editing, which creates a story sequence, today. However, montage editing, parallel editing, and long and quick cuts have become essential techniques. Digital editing makes creating jump cuts and cutaways that enhance the narrative easier. Film directors often work with the same film editors, creating a body of film work with specific director-editor editing styles. Film editors like DeDe Allen, Anne V. Coates, Thelma Schoonmaker, Walter Murch, Andrew Weisblum, and Michael Kahn have become recognized alongside film auteurs, the directors responsible for many iconic movies in cinema history.

Film Movements

Propaganda films are messages designed to sway the audience in specific ways, through a specific agenda. Determining if a film is propaganda can be challenging due to the abundance of opinion-based media. Advocacy documentaries and propaganda films can appear similar, but propaganda employs manipulative messaging to promote misleading and one-sided statements. Media literacy helps viewers understand the difference between what is and is not propaganda. Critical thinking is required for all media message consumption, especially propaganda and political movements. The United Kingdom, Germany, and the Soviet Union all produced propaganda films shown within their own countries. Soviet Film School filmmakers during the wartime propaganda period included Sergei Eisenstein, Lev Kuleshov, Dziga Vertov, Vsevolod Pudovkin, and Esfir Shub (Goodwin, 1993). The Office of War Information oversaw propaganda initiatives and messaging in the United States. During World War II, the Walt Disney Company used their characters, including Donald Duck, to support war effort messaging. Cinema continued to boom during World War II and the post-war era.

After World War II ended in the 1940s, European filmmakers started to gain prominence. Directors like Ingmar Bergman, Federico Fellini, Jean-Luc Godard, and François Roland Truffaut created groundbreaking films that challenged storytelling conventions. Italian neorealism showcased real locations and non-professional actors, starkly contrasting Hollywood's filmmaking techniques and concepts. In the years ahead, Martin Scorsese,

Francis Ford Coppola, Robert Altman, George Lucas, and Steven Spielberg would solidify American cinema in the 1960s and 1970s. At the same time, Claudia Weill, Barbara Loden, and Joan Micklin Silver broke down the cinematic glass ceiling as women entered the workforce. As new cinematic technologies emerged and gained global popularity, film enthusiasts discovered American New Wave and Bollywood movies. In the 1970s, Multi-channel Dolby Stereo gave film viewers a more immersive sound compared to movies that used stereo sound from surround speakers. Blockbusters and B-movies also benefited from these new sound innovations.

The early days of cinema were a time of innovation and experimentation on celluloid material, using cameras, stands, tripods, dollies and lifts, early lighting technologies, sound design, and editing on flatbeds. In the 1960s, inventors created lightweight handheld cameras, allowing directors to move the camera around and make films more dynamic.

This spawned the cinéma vérité style of filmmaking, among other experimental varieties. The Latin American Cinema Novo also became a genre charged with politics, that focused on stories of social equality as an answer

Figure 3.5 Kodak Brownie Movie camera.
Photograph by the author.

to racial and class conflict. Experimental movements, like the Danish style of Dogma 95, Mumblecore, Social Cinema, and Slow Cinema, heralded an age marked by directors Béla Tarr, Lars von Trier, Greta Gerwig, Andrew Bujalski, and Wes Anderson. Advanced camera, lighting, tracking technologies, handheld cinematography and minimalist approaches impact filmmakers' styles and create diverse cinematic approaches that continue to evolve.

Grassroots inventions and experimentation were at the forefront of this new artistic endeavor called cinema. Makeup, costumes, physical effects, and special effects have been part of cinema's legacy for almost as long as its history. In the past, filmmakers used practical effects, such as stop-motion animation and wirework, to create imaginative scenes. As more advanced effects were developed, trick photography increased in sophistication. Makeup artists and scenic designers from theater joined filmmakers to develop new and exciting effects on celluloid. Makeup artistry used grease paints, like theater and circus performers. Still, the ideas improved significantly through the years and became transformative in visual storytelling. An interest in space in the 1950s and 1960s spawned the science fiction genre. Both electronic visual effects and advanced prosthetic makeup were used to push the limits on imaginary creations. In the 1980s, digital visual effects used motion control photography to increase realism in makeup and practical and character generator (CG) effects to give viewers an increasingly exciting and enjoyable cinema experience. The use of motion capture technology continues to add layers to contemporary filmmaking. Advances in computer-generated imagery (CGI) are also creating photorealistic digital effects.

Animation in Film

Animation has also provided cinema with interesting technology-driven material. After the invention of cinema, animation quickly gained popularity. Creative innovators did not take long to combine newspaper comic strips and celluloid to tell a story. The golden age of animation saw the birth of pioneers at Walt Disney Company. They invented things like sound in cartoons, patented Technicolor, and made full-length animated films.

Along with the Walt Disney Company, other major studios, including Warner Bros. (Looney Tunes) and MGM (Tom and Jerry), pushed animation to great lengths in entertainment and realism. As TV became more popular, animated shows like Saturday morning cartoons became cheaper and more common. In the late 1900s, Disney and Steven Spielberg's Amblimation, later bought by NBCUniversal, made famous animated films. Pixar, later bought by DreamWorks, played a significant role in the growth of CGI animation. New animation studios, such as Sony Pictures

Animation, Illumination (now owned by Meledandri) in partnership with Universal, and Blue Sky (acquired by Disney through the 21st century Fox assets deal), emerged. Stop-motion animation, an early form of animation, also saw a resurgence. Advances in computer animation are fueling creativity and bringing captivating stories and characters to media audiences. Anime's Japanese roots and fan culture also make it a distinctive contribution to animation. While animation refers to any type of animated media, anime specifically refers to Japanese-produced animation, with its distinctive visual and artistic style and colorful graphics. Anime's more mature themes and content have been popular among teens and adults.

The ongoing digital revolution has also altered film preservation. The American Film Institute (AFI), the Library of Congress, the National Film Preservation Board, the Austrian Film Museum, the British Film Institute, Cinémathèque Française in France, and the Cineteca di Bologna in Italy, actively dedicate themselves to restoring and preserving the legacy of cinema. Content creation has emerged with a blurring of lines between different storytelling on numerous materials and platforms. In many cases, a person holding a video camera or phone now calls themselves a filmmaker. Today, filmmakers are more interested in the production's artistic process than the recording material. The history of film is now intertwined with the history of material culture, encompassing objects and artifacts created, used, and preserved by society.

One cultural aspect distinguishing a visual image is whether a content creator records it on the horizontal or vertical plane. Cinema, television, video, and art traditions have all played a role in institutionalizing the horizontal video ratio. Vertical video is often seen when a content creator holds the camera vertically, changing the screen ratio. This portrait-style recording creates a visual image that is taller than it is wide. The mobile phone's aspect ratio facilitates this style of recording digital visuals. The mobile-friendly vertical portrait ratio is not going away. Because this ratio does not fit horizontal design, social media has made up for the issue by creating blurred effects on the sides of the image to correct the problem. Despite historical ties to horizontal orientations, the vertical positioning remains increasingly relevant due to mobile phone video specifications. In addition, filters that create a film aesthetic have become one of numerous choices to evoke a look and feel of cinema, regardless of aspect orientation.

High-quality cameras empower independent filmmakers to capture superior images, simplifying editing. They can also crowdfund and share their work with distribution companies. The modern landscape has seen the rise of sharing sites, diverse voices, and freelance opportunities. Union strikes, world pandemics, diversity, equity, and inclusion of voices are part of cinema's current and future landscape. The evolution of new storytelling formats like virtual and augmented reality and immersive experiences are also part of cinema's story.

Contemporary Cinema

Cinemascope's widescreen aspect ratios in the 1950s gave viewers a panoramic, immersive experience on wider movie screens. Digital intermediate (DI) technologies now convert and improve film footage for postproduction and screening purposes. RealD 3D is also a popular projection technology used in theaters. Current cinema experiences depend on digital images and various tools that enhance and sometimes alter those images. Cameras now shoot high-frame-rate (HFR) images that shoot and project films at higher frame rates, typically 48 or 60 frames per second, for smoother motion. Steadicam and gimbal stabilizers help cameras and phones move smoothly while filming. Camera equipped drones are also used to capture aerial shots. The excellent image provides a more detailed and beautiful image projected and screened to an audience. Smaller and smaller cameras pushed these experiences with electronic image sensors—the change from film to digital created more transparent images and improved screen technologies. Digital projection has replaced traditional mechanical film projectors in cinemas, and increasingly enhanced 3D projection systems are standard, allowing for a more immersive film experience. IMAX movie theaters use advanced technology to make movies look clear and realistic. Giant LED screens show movies and ads for a great visual experience. Artistic experiences often use these screens with other technologies to create a more immersive visual effect. Independent filmmakers often move from a compressed file of .mov or .Mpeg-4 to a Digital Cinema Package (DCP) file format for distributing and projecting movies in theaters.

CGI has greatly improved movie visual effects by creating realistic computer-generated images and environments. Green Screen Technology allows filmmakers to replace backgrounds and create realistic composite shots. VR and augmented reality (AR) integrate digital elements into the real-world environment. The increased use of AI has developed into facial motion capture (MO-CAP) and enhanced sound through Dolby Atmos, which continues to push the envelope on cinematic technologies that enhance the viewer experience. Deepfakes are videos that use technology to make fake videos of famous people, like celebrities and politicians. Using the technologies for these efforts is a growing concern for security and public trust and has led to false evidence and misinformation. Holographic displays and facial recognition also play a role in filmmaking. Theatrical experiences could be further enhanced by RealD and other 3D technologies, offering immersive depth-of-field and realistic visuals. Advertising innovations have also capitalized on technologies to market films. Movie previews, called movie trailers, have become a small genre that invokes commercial-style revenues for a film project. Audiences see previews on video sites and social media at the beginning of a theatrical billing. Movies make extra money by featuring products; significant events help fans connect with the people behind them. Licensing deals for toys, games, clothing, and more help boost the financial aspect of movie production. Video-on-demand, streaming, foreign sales, and distribution deals fuel the cinematic economy.

The Metaverse

The metaverse is bringing immersive virtual world opportunities and improved social interaction. Advanced haptics allow heightened viewer experiences. Personalized adventures and virtual theaters are no longer just ideas but realities. People have different ideas about editing when working with 360 degree spherical video cameras in immersive environments. To control the pace and rhythm of these videos, editors stitch visuals together with shorter cuts and increase the speed for more excitement. A slower-paced grouping of visuals gives viewers more time to explore and absorb the immersive environment. For example, editors guide the viewer's attention within a 360-degree space, when editing more traditional content, by creating transitions between scenes and perspectives or providing audio cues. Cuts and transitions in 360 degree spherical videos are designed to feel more realistic. Products like Google Glass, Oculus, and Apple Vision Pro take the cinematic experience to a virtual level. Maintaining continuity and avoiding disorientation in an immersive experience is essential because consumers become disoriented or feel dizzy using VR goggles. Editors are an integral part of well-designed immersive experiences. They can provide essential touchstones in scenes to foster engaging "360 video" narratives and stories that build tension, excitement, or serenity. Audio editing is also crucial for 360 videos. Soundscapes cue viewers to action outside their field of vision and set the mood and atmosphere. Branding in immersive experiences, by adding 2D graphics, logos, text, subtitles, and audio descriptions improves navigation and captions in 360 videos to enhance the experience. Video editors can enhance the immersive experience by color-correcting or grading the footage.

Narrative Effects

Philosophical thinkers like Henri Bergson, Sergei Eisenstein, André Bazin, Roland Barthes, Gilles Deleuze, Mary Ann Doane, and Bracha L. Ettinger developed film theories to bring scholarly attention to the numerous effects of the film viewing experience (Stam 2017). One way to study media effects in cinema is through narrative influence. Several models, like the Extended Elaboration Likelihood Model, which notes that attitudes and behaviors are a function of a consumer's immersion into the experience and perspective of story characters, and the Model of Narrative Comprehensive and Engagement, where users position themselves to experience the perspective of story characters, can be useful. These two models and other theories and models help us understand how narratives influence media consumers (Green et al., 2019).

Other research focuses on immersive film experiences, like the point of view (POV) perspective. Research shows that people who watched POV content were more engaged in the story than those with a traditional narrative structure. The viewers also had a more extended gaze fixation for longer amounts of time (Cannavò et al., 2023). Immersive and VR narratives are also becoming more popular in media effects studies. Attentional synchrony is when a viewer focuses on a media clip from start to finish, a crucial immersive concept. In this study, researchers used heatmaps to track and collect data on how people interact with immersive media. The researchers found that viewers paid more attention to the characters who spoke faster and for more extended periods in the VR environment compared to the non-VR environment. Researchers also noted a deeper understanding of the importance of the nuanced rhythm of editing in the film production process. They observed that immersive media production can apply many practical techniques from traditional filmmaking, such as directing and editing. Filmmakers can influence the audience's perception by recognizing its influence. They can deliberately use aesthetic techniques to manipulate audience awareness, giving them the freedom to engage viewers in specific ways. (Bender, 2019, p. 18). Recently, film theory has focused on how digital visual effects change our experience and genres (McClean, 2007).

Things to Consider

- Study how cinema technology has reshaped and molded all visual industries.
- Brainstorm the technological inventions in the legacy of cinema.
- Contemplate some of your favorite movie genres.
- Name the different technologies mentioned in this chapter.

Takeaways

- Studying cinematic history highlight the revolutionary path of cinema's inventions and technologies.
- Cinema is a multifaceted business and art form encompassing numerous media areas.

- Cinema affects audiences in varying ways.
- Editors are essential in constructing a film's story.
- Propaganda films have been part of media history on a global scale.
- The rising popularity of anime and the use of CGI demonstrate the ever-expanding and diverse nature of animation in cinema.
- Many different kinds of professions and technical positions are involved in making cinema.
- Cinema has proliferated many different kinds of genres based on form, style, and subject matter.
- Name some of your chapter takeaways.

References

Bender, S. (2019) Headset attentional synchrony: Tracking viewers' gaze watching narrative virtual reality. *Media Pract Educ, 20*(3), 1–20.

Cannavò, A., Castiello, A., Pratticò, F.G., Mazali, T., & Lamberti, F. (2023). Immersive movies: The effect of point of view on narrative engagement. *AI & SOCIETY*, 1–15.

Goodwin J. (1993). *Eisenstein, cinema, and history.* University of Illinois Press.

Green, M., Bilandzic, H., Fitzgerald, K., & Paravati, E. (2019). Narrative effects. In *Media effects* (pp. 130–145). Routledge.

Ihde, D. (2008). Art precedes science, or did the camera obscura invent modern science? *Instruments in Art and Science: On the Architectonics of Cultural Boundaries in the 17th Century, 2*, 383–393.

Levitt, L. (2016). Hollywood, nostalgia, and outdoor movies. *Participations: Journal of Audience and Reception Studies, 13*(1), 218–233.

McClean, S.T. (2007). *Digital storytelling: The narrative power of visual effects in film.* MIT Press.

Sobchack, V.C. (2020). The address of the eye: A phenomenology of film experience. Princeton University Press.

Stam, R. (2017). *Film theory: An introduction.* John Wiley & Sons.

4 Television and Broadcasting

Television and broadcasting connect to printed text, cinema, and radio through their technologies and business models. This chapter explores the early evolution of television and how it developed with a particular emphasis on the innovations that shaped content creation and distribution through broadcasting. Top news stories, election results, and entertainment and sports events were witnessed live by people in their homes because of broadcasting technologies. The impact of this visual experience was so profound that it transformed the culture. Watching global events on TV has brought people together through sports, music, comedy, and entertainment. This chapter discusses the early days of television and how it evolved, with a focus on technology and programming. The chapter also shares information about networks, public television, and ends with research that studied generational viewing and audience engagement patterns. A separate chapter focuses on video and streaming contributions.

Birth of a Medium

The cathode ray tube (CRT) was a screen technology and an important one in the history of television. It was invented by German engineer Karl Ferdinand Braun in the late 1800s, around the same time as cinema technologies were developed. The CRT, a photoelectric cell that converts light to electricity and screens it, made the first television image. German engineer Paul Nipkow and Scottish inventor John Logie Baird also created necessary scanning and broadcasting devices which combined with the CRT to build the mechanical television. Several inventors from different countries are connected to the first television broadcast with this new technology, including American inventor Philo Taylor Farnsworth (Kisselhoff, 1995).

Television stations popped up nationwide to become the organizational and programming mechanisms for the first televisions, which screened programming in a colorless monochrome fashion on a tiny screen. The National Broadcasting Company (NBC) and the Columbia Broadcasting

DOI: 10.4324/9781003397588-5

System (CBS) in the United States (US), and the British Broadcasting Corporation (BBC) in the United Kingdom were the first to broadcast television shows regularly in the 1930s and 1940s. However, in the early 1940s, news coverage sharply decreased because most technical media staff had joined the military service during World War II. Television eventually became a viable communication medium, creating media markets nationwide and a habitual activity for new media consumers (Edgerton, 2009). Black and white broadcasting transitioned to color in the 1950s when the primary colors of red, green, and blue were integrated into the television set mechanics through electron beams onto phosphor stripes. CBS soon began broadcasting in color at several stations on the East Coast of the US.

Figure 4.1 Amperex 8179 amplifier tube used in broadcasting.
Photograph by the author.

By the mid-1950s, most Americans had access to a television. Radio talent transitioned to television, resulting in a mix of well-known personalities. News became one of the first kinds of programming to fill the schedule, along with variety and serial dramas. Viewers loved shows like *Wild Kingdom*, which aired for 18 seasons and featured documentaries about animals and nature worldwide. People became used to hearing and seeing radio voices on TV in their homes. Coverage of wars and politics became part of that news coverage, taking a generation of viewers who had never flown on a plane into other parts of the world. Lowell Thomas, Edward R. Murrow, Dorothy Fuldheim and Walter Cronkite achieved fame in broadcast news, but others became popular over the years. The nightly newscast became a significant fixture in the daily lives of Americans. Like the fancy furniture-style boxes for the first radios, TVs were also encased in large cabinet boxes that were part of home furnishings in the 1950s when they became widely available in the US. Later on, remote control "clickers" replaced dials and TVs got smaller because of transistor advancements. They also became more energy-efficient and more portable (Bianculli, 1996). The living room cabinet encasing televisions made way for smaller sets and moved into kitchens, bedrooms, dens, and basements. Television viewers continued to make daily "appointment style" space in their day for their favorite programming until the 1980s when cable television services, syndication, and video rentals and purchases created 24-hour visual programming.

At the start of the cinema timeline, film cameras were mechanical and either on location in a specific locale or in a film studio. They used hand-cranked mechanisms to move both the motor and the film. The video camera revolutionized how media was made and became another vital piece of television equipment. Once video cameras were invented, the industry placed them in the television studio during the early days. Television cameras were heavy and mounted on pedestals for movement. Their Vidicon tubes converted light into electrical signals to broadcast an image that went on air. Television shows were primarily recorded in studios during this early era. In the 1950s, charged-couple device (CCD) sensors were invented, allowing cameras to become smaller and more portable compared to the large vacuum tube cameras of the time. The image sensors in the cameras were much smaller than tubes, creating lighter and more portable cameras. These image sensors improved image quality and contributed to the growth of electronic newsgathering and field production. Jerome Lemelson patented one of the first small cameras. As cameras shrank in size, manufacturers produced tape cassettes in smaller sizes to record video. In the 1980s, manufacturers combined the separate equipment into one camera unit, forming the name "camcorder" by combining the words camera and recorder.

Figure 4.2 Broadcast studio control room during a news show.
Photograph by the author.

Integrating camera stabilizers into the camera body is common, but different production scenarios still rely on various tripods, support systems, and stabilizers. Lighting, too, has transformed from the early days of television. Lighting ideas came from film, photography, and theater in early television studio settings. These strategies did not always work with early television cameras. Still, eventually, lighting designers created lighting suitable for the large, stationary tube cameras designed for the television studio. Lighting grids were initially on studio ceilings for camera mobility. Essential tungsten lights illuminated the news set, the anchor and talk show host, and guest. Lights were manually mixed until grid systems were designed to program specific lighting setups.

Lighting technicians and lighting instruments underwent many changes with the introduction of color video. The lights were bright and generated a lot of heat on set. A minimalist lighting design grew more sophisticated as studios shifted from essential news and information to elaborate sets for fiction and nonfiction programming. In the 1950s and

1960s, a 3-point lighting approach used a key, fill, backlight, and incandescent bulbs to produce a warm, yellowish light that transformed into creative and dramatic effects using colored gels that mirrored a production's overall mood and impact. Quartz halogen lights were invented to provide brighter and whiter light, causing most lighting professionals to switch from incandescent bulbs to softboxes and reflective boxes around the light for softer lighting effects. Lights also became more portable as camcorders became smaller.

TV and video lighting technology changed in the 1990s with the introduction of LED lighting. This new lighting technology did not develop heat. It provided lighting professionals multiple opportunities to mix different lighting temperatures for the optimal lighting color and intensity based on all available light. Studio computer-generated imagery (CGI) and green screen technologies also needed specific lighting instruments and techniques. Contemporary grid systems are lighter and mostly use LED lighting instruments for the best brightness efficiency, and DMX-controlled systems make it easier to automate lighting and create presets in studios. Smaller lighting fixtures also make it simpler to design lighting for different areas. Mobile phone cameras have also been altered for optimal lighting for recording video. Besides cameras and lighting, more miniature microphones and sound collection also became essential advancements. Large desk microphones transformed into small lapel mics as talent moved from behind the desk to the reporting field. Camera microphones have improved and now use a mounting device called a "hot shoe" to connect to power. Content creators have used advanced technology to make media for consumers since the beginning of the broadcasting industry. This led to the growth of a new industry focused on media, broadcasting, and digital technology.

Creating Consumers

People scheduled their day around TV and radio shows. Some called this phenomenon making an appointment with the news. Breaking news, that at one time occurred on the radio, quickly moved to television; Networks broke into regularly scheduled programming to share urgent news. Viewers dedicated time to Morning, Evening, Nightly, Late-Night, and Breaking News. During the years of concentrated television viewing, starting in the 1950s, people began their day with radio or TV news. TV networks made their morning shows to keep viewers interested and attract specific audiences. Examples include NBC's *Today Show*, ABC's *Good Morning America*, and *CBS Morning News*. Networks also had noon newsbreaks, but the most focused news programming occurred during the evening news hours.

Programs like *CBS Evening News*, ABC's *World News Tonight*, and NBC *Nightly News* became branded evening shows. People watched the news around the dinner table or in the living room, sitting at a "TV tray" eating a "TV dinner". Late-night news also provided additional news breaks for avid news followers. Late-night TV talk shows followed right after the late news.

As programming grew, networks made a place for sports and sports "news" as a daily report feature. Early in broadcasting history, coverage of the Berlin Olympics in 1936 set a precedent for sports coverage. Sports news, live broadcasts, and streaming of sports events, including Esports, are still successful economic and programming models today. This topic is covered more thoroughly in a chapter on sports media. Another area of programming was called weather reporting. Meteorologists became an important aspect o news coverage, giving weather forecasts and other information. This led to a new genre and a dedicated cable channel for weather. In the 1960s, news and information programming gained in popularity. At its inception, news coverage was designed to keep the public informed and provide information on current events and issues so that citizens could stay informed about what is happening in their world on a local, national, and international level, hold leaders accountable, and act as a public watchdog to prevent abuses of power across political spectrums.

The birth of the internet occurred in the 1960s when the US Department of Defense Advanced Research Projects Agency (DARPA) invented the ARPANET network to connect computer networking between military researchers. This private network was decommissioned in the late 1980s, and soon after that, the World Wide Web became available to all who had connectivity. The internet became a significant tool for news gathering. Military technologies, like global positioning systems (GPS), satellites, and digital photography, aided newsgathering.

American media is a revenue-generating industry. However, the news industry, a central part of American media history, is charged with providing a public forum for exchanging ideas and promoting transparency of those ideas. As the media industry grew, public broadcasting was established to promote transparency in programming. In 1967, the government funded the Corporation for Public Broadcasting (CPB) to provide Americans with free, high-quality media programming. Public Radio and television stations benefit from these funds, and nearly 100 percent of Americans can access CPB programming (CPB, 2023). A combination of government funding, listener and viewer support through fundraising drives, and corporate sponsors funds the radio and television stations affiliated with CPB. Public Broadcasting Service (PBS) and National Public Radio (NPR) are two well-known programming groups that benefit from CPB funds. Viewer donations and corporate sponsorships now play a more significant role in public broadcasting and are replacing a more extensive government funding model due to declining support, competition, and political concerns. In contrast, in many countries, most television networks are owned by the government.

Shifts in Programming

The history of television programming is long and storied. In the beginning, radio shows were used to develop television show programming. TV created its style of programming, drawing on its technological strengths. For years, variety shows, talk shows, comedies, dramas, detective shows, soap operas, and news programming dominated media. At that time, television cameras were too large to leave, so programming was brought into the studio. As cameras got smaller, shows changed to single camera style and focused on procedural dramas, like hospital and police shows. Miniseries also became a new style of limited-run programming. The invention of Ampex's videotape recorder (VTR), the Betamax brand of recorder and videotape, and shortly after, the VHS brand of recorder and tape affected

Figure 4.3 Electronic News Gathering (ENG) camera.
Photograph by the author.

broadcasting in the 1970s. These machines allowed viewers to time and record programming to watch later. This was the first opportunity for the consumer to move away from timed video programming and appointment viewing, and also allowed consumers the ability to purchase movies and other original and recorded content to view.

The DVD and the Laser Disc were also both used to record programming for a time. Later, the DVR moved the recording to a digital hard drive for on-demand viewing. Afternoon talk shows and soap operas also provided years of entertainment programming. Late-night shows lasted until broadcast stations signed off the air for the night, the The Star-Spangled Banner was played, and the station test pattern was aired. This ritual was stopped sometime in the 1990s. Television programming also continued to foster studio sitcoms, game shows, and talk shows, but also an influx of reality television in the 2000s. Increasingly, broadcast primetime shows are moving to network-affiliated streaming after their initial air. The 2000 Screen Actors Guild strike, concerning pay for actors in TV commercials that aired on cable TV and streaming, illustrates how a new technology or format can shift resources, stakeholders, and economics while finding a space in the media consumption environment.

In 2009, amid the Writers Guild of America (WGA) and the Alliance of Motion Picture and Television Producers (AMPTP) strike, reality television, also called unscripted entertainment, became a consistent and prevalent contributor to television and now streaming programming. Reality TV didn't need writers for unscripted shows, so networks used it to fill their programming schedule. While some reality shows have been seen since the 1940s, reality programming flourished in the 2000s, and a long list of shows continues to be featured in the contemporary media ecology. Family-friendly reality shows on TV brought families together to watch live or recorded programming. Along the way, one-hour dramas continued to anchor evening television viewing. Broadcasting companies still cover sports like football, basketball, and baseball, as well as significant events like the Super Bowl and the Olympics.

Programming Blossoms

Along the way, countless comedies, dramatized fiction, nonfiction, and live televised media have made an indelible print on viewers. Cable and satellite TV services expanded viewing options by broadcasting TV signals over wide areas. Cable service companies didn't produce the shows, but they installed the cables to deliver the content to subscribed homes. Some houses lacked cable wiring, so alternative technologies were used to attract consumers. Some consumers subscribed to satellite television and its variety of programming options. Not all communities had coaxial cables, so satellites provided alternative programming to them. Satellite services work by sending content from a satellite to a ground dish. Programming had to be purchased by production companies, syndication libraries, or secure rights to broadcast. As a result, different TV channels were created to serve various audiences, offering various programming options like news, music, sports, movies, and more. This also opened the door for diverse programming cable channels like Black Entertainment Television (BET), now owned by Paramount Global, Telemundo, now owned by NBCUniversal, Univision, now owned by TelevisaUniversal, and Oprah Winfrey Network (OWN), now owned by Warner Bros. Discovery.

Contemporary media consumers have devices that provide visual programming from many services, including broadcasting, cable, satellite, and streaming platforms. Increased use of devices like phones and tablets for individual viewing means fewer shared viewing experiences. This has resulted in a culturally fractured media landscape. Still, contemporary streaming platforms can create shared media experiences when they release a show to audiences once per week which points back to appointment viewing.

Screen Innovations

Inventors have developed many different television screens, including the flat panel display screen, liquid crystal display (LCD), and plasma display technologies. These advancements have created thinner and more energy-efficient television sets. The cost of these sets, combined with the rise of big box electronic stores, created an expanded market for electronics. High-definition TVs improved picture quality and introduced the concept of the home theater. Screens transitioned from being larger and integrated into furniture to becoming smaller, and then once again larger, as viewers adapted to changing viewing habits and improved technologies. Cinema screens are also much more sophisticated than TV or computer screens and are designed to fill the viewers' entire field of vision for the fullest cinematic experience.

The size of television screens and monitors can be limited, typically reaching a maximum of 80 inches. In the beginning, TV screens had a 4:3 aspect ratio, which gave them a square shape rather than a rectangular one. However, with the advent of digital technology and the widespread use of computer screens for viewing, monitors now come standard in the 16:9 aspect ratio. Cinematic wide-screen aspect ratio can be 21:9 or greater. TVs and computer monitors feature HD to 4K quality, mobile phone screens often have Full HD quality, and TV and video screens are designed to reduce motion blur. Movie projectors show a more comprehensive range of colors, making the colors look more vibrant. TVs and

Figure 4.4 Radio & television console from the 1950s.

Photograph by the author.

monitors have less vibrant colors and aren't as accurate. The viewing conditions also make a difference. TV and video screens are also designed for daylight brightness, and cinema screens are designed based on dark theater viewing.

The early 2000s heralded the era of the smart TVs, which shifted the screen to a monitor-style device with internet connectivity and app capabilities. Streaming platforms and internet TV services are gaining popularity, causing traditional TV stations, satellite technologies, and cable TV to lose revenue. This has continually disrupted and altered traditional television broadcasting, giving viewers on-demand content. Just as cable and satellite pushed into the broadcast market, streaming companies entered all of these previous industries to take a share of the media consumer market.

The contemporary media environment is shifting. Consumers continue to be interested in news, but news is now accessible 24/7 in the modern news cycle. And the definition of what makes up news content has also shifted. Essentially, news is a mix of facts and timely information that impact people's lives on different scales. When the broadcast environment was formed, and for numerous years afterward, news broadcasters designated specific periods during the day, such as 5, 6, or 11 pm, to deliver news. Some networks shared morning news or a noon news break. As technology grew, newsgathering options also grew—global media outlets partnered with local stations to share international news. Contemporary news comes from a much more decentralized place. The consumer must find the most ethical news source that fits their needs. Canada's Online News Act, also called Bill C18, prohibits sharing news on social media to aid traditional media companies. This legislation calls for a "link tax", meaning that companies who share news through social media must pay for the labor that went into creating that news story. Canadians will not see news on their social media accounts and must use the Canadian Broadcast Corporation (CBC) and CTV for news.

Oversight History

The Federal Communications Commission (FCC) is a government agency founded through the Communications Act of 1934. The commission is still operating today to regulate radio, television, cable, satellite, and wired communication to ensure competitive markets and practices. The government started overseeing the use of airwaves with the Radio Act of 1927. This act created a licensing system for media stations that extended to television. Through the years, many FCC rulings have guided the history of legacy media and contemporary media foundations. The FCC, however, does not regulate any online content, and there is no single law regulating internet privacy. Different countries across the globe use other tactics for media oversight. Some pivotal FCC acts include: copyright protections for creative works, including media; regulations for media ownership in the cable industry; internet, and other communication mediums, protections; and rules for copyrighted content distributed digitally or online. FCC oversight includes rules on truth in advertising, national communication policy, and cable TV regulation.

Several organizations created and later revoked various children's media protections through deregulation. The FCC governs how websites and online services collect data from children under 13. The Children's Internet Protection Act (CIPA) is still in effect, along with the Children's Television Act, in which US broadcast television stations air programming specifically designed to serve children's educational needs while limiting the time for advertisements during children's programs. Cable programming is not under the FCC's jurisdiction, so programming can address children's and young adults' content and themes not allowed on broadcast television. In the US, other laws overlap the internet, like privacy laws or copyright laws, and they affect how business is conducted on the web. Other legal restraints can also be used for some internet activity, including suing individuals for defamation of character or bullying. Consumers cannot, currently, sue internet social media companies. They are considered "not libel". Copyright disputes over music licensing, fair use of clips, and intellectual property theft have occurred. Networks are concerned about government control, censorship, indecency, media ownership, and children's programming.

Lawsuits against networks and media conglomerates aim to pressure and regulate consolidation, advertising sales, cable bundles, and media mergers to prevent unfair competition. The first notable labor-organized strike for media-related employment started in 1962 when the American Federation of Television and Radio Artists organized a strike against radio and television networks, involving broadcasters and announcers over residuals and jurisdiction of programming, among other issues. Unions now include compensation, residuals, licensing rights, and other disputes in their negotiations. TV development and production have struggled with intellectual property problems like plagiarism and copyright infringement. The concerns have arisen from management's use of technologies. Programming itself has come under significant scrutiny because of various cheating scandals. In the 1950s, scrutiny fell upon one specific US show when it was found to be rigged, bringing the game show and quiz show genre programming under scrutiny. Producers gave answers to contestants to create more drama and impact, leading to stricter rules for quiz shows. Other shows, through the years, have fallen victim to a variety of cheating manipulations. Investigations have been conducted on talent shows to determine if the voting is rigged and manipulated and if producers are showing favoritism.

Leadership in Media Organizations

Managing a television organization can be complicated. Technology is pushing boundaries, which requires management to stay aware of the industry, the technology, and the staff. Television ownership rules have also changed over the years. In the early days of television, most stations were owned by individual companies or families. These owned and operated (O&O) stations are known as networks and affiliates. No specific limit exists for the number of stations an individual or company can own, as long as the total reaches less than 39 percent of US households with televisions. The FCC made Broadcast Ownership Rules that they review every four years to make sure they're consistent and to consider new technologies. This 39 percentage will ensure that the top networks do not merge. Radio ownership is different.

Networks did not invest in the ownership model in the early days of the technology. During the 1970s and 1980s, as well as today, big companies bought various forms of media, like movie studios, radio and TV stations, and newspapers. This caused media ownership consolidation to increase. Different media companies merged under one larger company. These giant media groups used vertical and horizontal integration for a more significant impact in a less expensive way. Vertical integration occurs when a company owns a group of companies that produce different products or services that combine to satisfy a standard product need up and down the supply chain. Horizontal integration occurs when a company purchases other companies in the same industry that produce similar products or services. This helps increase production and grow the company's size. Media conglomerates can function as monopolies, oligarchies, or monopolistic companies with fierce competition. Many big companies control most major media outlets in the contemporary ownership environment. While the top ownership constantly shifts, Comcast (NBCUniversal), Disney (ABC), ViacomCBS (CBS & Paramount), AT&T (CNN, HBO), Fox Corporation, and Sinclair Broadcast Group control much of the national media in the 2020s. Media ownership is merging, making individual and family-owned TV stations rare.

Mediated Effects

One of the most desired types of research on television viewing, whether on legacy platforms or digital and streaming platforms, is identifying generational viewing and engagement patterns. This helps predict future directions in both technology and programming. Some programming takes years to produce, so trying to nail down these patterns is essential for certain kinds of media content investments, especially in series television, and movies. Contemporary generational guidelines shift individuals into approximately twenty-year cohorts, from oldest to youngest: Traditionalists, Baby Boomers, Generation X, Millennials & Generation Z (Drugas, 2022). The next generation, beginning in 2010, has not been specifically named, but some media and researchers are floating around the label Generation Alpha for this highly wired and technologically adept group not yet of voting age. One research project on generational political participation found that various political media influence different generations. "When it comes to mobilization through political information exposure, more clear-cut, generational differences become visible. We see a clear sign that the youngest generations benefit most from news exposure" (Andersen et al., 2021, p. 131). The researchers share that political media engagement has risen for most generations. The study shows that Gen Z is more widely active through social media participation than through more passive legacy and terrestrial media use.

Another interesting finding was that the more older generations are exposed to political information on social media, the more strongly they participate in activities. In contrast, youngest generations are the most active in short-term, case-oriented campaign activities and participatory social media (Andersen et al., 2021; Xenos, 2014). Some of the longest-running research studies on media effects and media influence have occurred on television platforms. As early as the 1960s, media theorist George Gerbner was studying media influence (Gerbner, 1977; Gerbner et al., 1996; Dennis 1991).

> George Gerbner matters to the history of media scholarship as one who introduced the idea that media actively creates social reality. . . . While it is important to study in some detail his arguments over why media violence was such a problem, it is equally crucial to remember that the violence question was a variation on a theme, and it is the theme that matters most in applying cultivation theory today.
>
> Ruddock, 2020, p. 1.

The idea behind cultivation is how media shapes viewers' perceptions, beliefs, attitudes, and values. This sociocultural theory addressed the role of media in shaping culture, and television was initially the sociocultural phenomenon to be studied (Shrum, 2017; Ruddock, 2020). One 2018 study completed in India focused on public health awareness through media. The aim was to investigate how mass media, such as television, radio, posters, social media, and other platforms, spread awareness of infectious diseases. The study emphasized that timely information could stop the spread of some diseases and reduce the economic costs of medications. "It may be noted that the change in human behavior towards the diseases through print media, social media, and the internet are limited only to educated people, but TV ads can impact large population (less educated people too) in a very short period of time and thus are more effective" (Misra et al., 2018, p. 1316). The researchers used a mathematical model to study the impact of TV, print, and social media ads on the spread of an infectious disease. The study found that TV and social media ads can help reduce the number of infected people. Still other efforts, like treatment and sanitation, are also important for eliminating the disease in the community (p. 1330). Researchers found that "older adults may watch television for many reasons, including social bonding with a spouse, as well as for companionship and entertainment when alone, but unfortunately, this may lead to health problems because of its negative associations with physical and emotional well-being" (Fingerman et al., 2022). A different study evaluated viewing, but this study focused on eating while watching television. Researchers used a questionnaire and online diary or called someone on the phone to record information for data collection. This study found that "eating while watching TV may contribute to increased immediate and overall food intake, possibly by drawing attention away from eating" (Alblas et al., 2021, p. 756). Their study shares evidence that both resonates with prior similar studies for validity but extends the idea that eating while watching TV can be a factor in cultivating obesity habits. Other recent media effects studies involving television deal with children's viewing habits (Vadathya et al., 2022), children's exposure to alcohol brands (Gabrielli et al., 2022), and a study by Hwang & Borah (2022) which suggested, based on study findings, that those with anxiety disorders refrain from viewing emotionally ambiguous entertainment television programs involving sadness, suffering, and pain.

Each year, on November 21, the world celebrates World Television Day. On this date, the impact of television is considered a tool for educating, informing, and entertaining viewers across the globe. The technology, as well as the programming, has shaped a large swath of the contemporary media environment. Analog has switched to digital, and electronic media converged to digital media. In the modern television and broadcasting landscape, it is about casting to digital platforms and technologies.

Things to Consider

- Consider the idea of the 24-hour news cycle and how that effects consumers.
- Reflect on how original TV programming has transitioned from legacy media to streaming. Could you provide a list of a few of these shows?
- Explain how cameras have become smaller over the years. How has this change in technology altered content creation?
- Discuss the cultural concerns of streaming old programming.
- Brainstorm ways that broadcasting, as an industry, is still part of media in the contemporary media market.
- Which historical events interrupted regular programming instead of being shared through a newscast or cable news?
- Consider some of the media effects studies discussed in this chapter. What media related topics would you study?

Takeaways

- Even in contemporary media making, ideas, formats, processes, symbols, and workflows from early audio and video are still used.
- The transition from black and white to color TV sparked technological advancements in television. The switch from black and white to color also led to the innovation of the standard television and the smart TV. Television began switching to flat-screen TVs, projectors, and more.

- The innovation of cameras continues to occur. With the invention of the CCD, cameras were lighter. They switched from mechanical with a hand crank to electronic, then the camcorder, and now all kinds of digital cinema and 360-degree capture cameras.
- The legal ownership of television has changed from being held mainly by individuals and families to being dominated by corporations.
- Name some of your chapter takeaways.

References

Alblas, M.C., Mollen, S., Wennekers, A.M., Fransen, M.L., & van den Putte, B. (2021). Consuming media, consuming food: Investigating concurrent TV viewing and eating using a 7-d time use diary survey. *Public Health Nutr*. doi:10.1017/S1368980021002858

Andersen, K., Ohme, J., Bjarnøe, C., Bordacconi, M.J., Albæk, E., & De Vreese, C.H. (2021). *Generational gaps in political media use and civic engagement: From baby boomers to Generation Z*. Taylor & Francis.

Bianculli, D. (1996). *Dictionary of teleliteracy: Television's 500 biggest hits, misses, and events*. Syracuse University Press.

CPB (Corporation for Public Broadcasting). (2023, May 1). *About CPB*. https://cpb.org/aboutcpb

Dennis, E., Gerbner, G., & Zassoursky, Y. (1991). *Beyond the Cold War: Soviet and American media images*. Sage.

Drugas, M. (2022). Screenagers or "Screamagers"? Current Perspectives on Generation Alpha. *Psychological Thought, 15*(1), 1.

Edgerton, G. (2009). *The Columbia History of American Television*. Columbia University Press.

Fingerman, K.L., Kim, Y.K., Ng, Y.T., Zhang S, Huo M, & Birditt K.S. (2022). Television Viewing, Physical Activity, and Loneliness in Late Life. *Gerontologist, 62*(7), 1006–1017. doi: 10.1093/geront/gnab120. PMID: 34379115; PMCID: PMC9372884.

Gabrielli, J., Corcoran, E., Genis, S., McClure, A.C., & Tanski, S.E. (2022). Exposure to Television Alcohol Brand Appearances as Predictor of Adolescent Brand Affiliation and Drinking Behaviors. *J Youth Adolesc. 51*(1), 100–113. doi:10.1007/s10964-021-01397-0

Gerbner, G. (Ed.). (1977). *Mass media policies in changing cultures*. Wiley.

Gerbner, G., Mowlana, H., & Schiller, H. (1996). *Invisible crises: What conglomerate media control means for America and the world*. (Critical studies in communication and the cultural industries). Westview Press.

Hwang, J., & Borah, P. (2022). Anxiety Disorder and Smoking Behavior: The Moderating Effects of Entertainment and Informational Television Viewing. *Int J Environ Res Public Health, 19*(15), 9160. doi:10.3390/ijerph19159160

Kisseloff, J. (1995). *The box: An oral history of television, 1929–1961*. Viking.

Misra, A.K., Rai, R.K., & Takeuchi, Y. (2018). Modeling the control of infectious diseases: Effects of TV and social media advertisements. *Math. Biosci. Eng, 15*(6), 1315–1343.

Ruddock, A. (2020). *Digital media influence: A cultivation approach*. Sage.

Shrum, L.J. (2017). Cultivation theory: Effects and underlying processes. *The International Encyclopedia of Media Effects*, 1–12.

Vadathya, A.K., Musaad, S., Beltran A, et al. (2022). An Objective System for Quantitative Assessment of Television Viewing Among Children (Family Level Assessment of Screen Use in the Home-Television): System Development Study. *JMIR Pediatr Parent*, 5(1), e33569. Published 2022 March 24. doi:10.2196/33569

Xenos, M., Vromen, A., & Loader, B.D. (2014). The great equalizer? Patterns of social media use and youth political engagement in three advanced democracies. *Information, Communication & Society*, 17(2), 151–167. DOI: 10.1080/1369118X.2013.871318

5 Video

So where does television "end" and video "begin"? Or did video technically precede television? The screens diverge in their uses despite being based on similar technologies. Video is a broad term for a technological output. TV combines video with industry and programming. Television is one way to watch video content. This chapter discusses how video differs from other media, including how it can be compressed, how video chats and videoconferencing work, and how social media has affected video production. The chapter ends with ideas about the effects of binge-watching streamed videos.

Video is an encompassing medium recorded from many devices and stored in various compressed formats. Video cameras used many kinds, shapes and brands of videotape. Now different kinds devices record video. Most moving images are captured and digitally stored on a card, hard drives, or in the cloud. Video, as a kind of content, comes from broadcast or live transmission. VHS and S-VHS cameras and video tape were cheaper alternatives to professional equipment, leading to their adoption in prosumer, consumer, and home video markets. People started recording home videos to capture memories and share them with family and friends. This opened an entirely new area of content called home videos. TV shows like America's *Funniest Home Videos* used VHS recorded media to feature some of the first amateur and user-generated content consistently aired on broadcast television.

In the mid-1980s, the Sony D1 digital video format was among the first to record uncompressed standard-definition component video. The D1 format was not exclusive to Sony cameras and worked in various professional broadcasting environments for recording, editing, and playback. Cameras became smaller and sported a lighter Electronic News Gathering (ENG) field style design. The electronics and mechanics of the cameras influenced the design of the tape cassettes. Models using analog pro and consumer cameras needed VHS, Super VHS, and 8mm

DOI: 10.4324/9781003397588-6

Figure 5.1 Film reels, U-matic, VHS, Beta, DV cam, 8mm, and DV tape formats.
Photograph by the author.

style tape called Video8, Hi8, Digital 8, and Mini-DV tape. Before D1
tape, professional cameras used 1-inch tape, U-Matic ¾, and Betamax
for recording.

When recording formats switched from analog tape to digital formats
in the late 1980s and '90s, the entire industry slowly started to integrate
the new format. TV stations have used analog and digital video technologies for many years. The migration from tape to SD cards and other digital recording devices revolutionized videography. There was a substantial
difference in quality between film and video. In the past, film and video
had different ways of recording images. Now, they offer the same digital
quality shooting, editing, and mastering options. The shift from tape-based
systems to digital storage significantly changes digital video creation.

Video Stores

One fixture of the 1970s and '80s was owning a video play deck to watch movies. The Betamax and S-VHS decks fit tape formats for a variety of films. Later, DVD rentals and ownership sales flourished as the home play and record technology shifted from VHS tapes to DVDs. The mid-1980s saw the founding of Blockbuster, the most well-known media rental chain, with thousands of locations at its height. Customers carried a membership card and could rent from a chain store near their at home or when traveling. Even though Blockbuster had competition, it still managed to dominate the video rental market for a significant period. Among others, Hollywood, Family, and Showtime Videos sprung up to feed the need to watch films. At one time, Netflix had a DVD rental model that allowed users to reserve and receive DVDs of films by mail as one of their subscription models. Customers logged on to their webpage and entered DVDs into the queue for distribution. The company then sent the discs through the mail when they became available. These movie rental models have been mostly closed down because of the popularity and ease of digital streaming services. Consumers can still rent and return popular films through Redbox kiosk vending machines. Video game rentals are available online and at some Redbox kiosks, but they're becoming less common.

Screens and Projectors

The home video market also changed the home viewing experience for media consumers. In the days of early radio and then television, people gathered around their devices, often in the living room. Initially, the cabinets that housed radios and televisions were often ornate and beautifully carved out of wood. In the 1950s, manufacturers embedded TV and music devices in furniture like consoles. As the technological interworkings got smaller, radios and televisions became more portable. The increased video quality and the ability to bring films home in VHS or DVD form required improved viewing screens. The 1980s saw a rise in popularity for home theaters due to easy film access and affordable digital screens.

Another problem related to sound became a significant concern. Designers created specialized surround systems for the best home viewing and listening. Sound speakers continue to be used as monitors become thinner and the internal speakers become smaller. Most times, Bluetooth sound bars and speakers are used to boost sound and audio quality.

Way before video, when art, cinema, and photographic images were the only visual media, consumers wanted a way to project an image for viewing. The magic lantern, known as lanterna magica, projected images onto a screen or wall and transcended the world between picture and moving image. Before electricity, the device used candles or oil lamps as the projection light source. Producers, called "lanternists", projected the slides on the wall for audiences to experience. Magic lanterns became more sophisticated, with moving slides and other abilities to shift images for visual effect. This technology was developed in the 1600s and provided entertainment and education for many years. As cinema became more popular, the magic lantern moved into obscurity and obsolesce. Nevertheless, the principles of early projection technology can be observed in cinema and slide projectors.

Several late 1800s and early 1900s inventions, including the Zoopraxiscope, Cinématographe, and the Projectoscope, paved the way for many different projectors. These significant technologies were frequently transported on a dolly or cart from one room to another. Large film spools were also heavy. By the 1950s, homes, businesses, and schools started using smaller film reels, film projectors, slide cartridges, slide projectors, and portable screens. In the 2000s, Liquid Crystal Displays (LCD) and 4K and 8K projectors replaced Digital Light Processing (DLP) projectors to provide wide viewing angles and high-resolution images.

Projectors need screens or large blank walls, and the trajectory of projection and screens has taken similar paths through the years. Improvements in TV screens, projectors, and video player equipment have enhanced home viewing. Screens have evolved from rolled-up paper to interior video mapping and high-definition mechanisms with successful sound options.

Film cameras have maintained a 16:9 aspect ratio throughout their history. When making films, filmmakers use the entire elongated screen space for action and visuals. Film compositional theory aims to use that whole space, pulling the viewers' eyes from one place to the next as part of the experience of discovering the story. When copying those films for television viewing, which has a 4:3 aspect ratio, distribution companies would either cut off the two sides of the screen or letterbox the movie. Adding a black bar at the top and bottom of the screen during that time altered the aspect ratio so the image was not clipped for the viewer. Digital opportunities increased an interest in 16:9 again as screens got larger. Cameras and editing software have guides to assist content creators in capturing action in the appropriate aspect ratios. Technological advancements have transformed how people view media and changed consumer preferences.

Sizes Shift

Screens are also becoming smaller, more portable, and attached mainly to their devices. Mobile phones and smaller pad devices are now used for entertainment viewing on screens that can flip, fold, or roll and are propped up by various differently styled holders. Social networking and social media in the 2000s changed how we view screens. It also created a separation between broadcast television and uploaded videos on Vine, Vimeo, and YouTube. This created a market distinction for media consumers and the actors, celebrities, and media personalities who made content for them. New photos, videos, and interviews were easily shared across many platforms. Verified accounts, spoilers, and Easter eggs are all ways to engage fans and get them talking about new content. At the same time, celebrity stalking, cyberstalking, and heightened paparazzi attention are facilitated by cell phone use and social media uploads. Fans share videos of celebrities on the streets, and celebrities share behind-the-scenes (BTS) experiences on set and in their personal lives. Social media users identify their experiences of missing these events as FOMO—fear of missing out. Privacy becomes more public, and what was private becomes contested, legislated, and debated.

Television is a device plus programming. Television primarily aims to broadcast video and audio to a large audience using a digital antenna. Broadcast stations, cable providers, or streaming services often schedule and transmit TV content at a specific time, but monetization and digital technologies have brought on-demand options to viewers. Analog broadcasts stopped in 2019 when transmissions went digital. People who used antenna television needed a converter box to transfer the analog signal to digital. Digital-ready televisions have mostly replaced analog televisions. Video content can be watched on many devices besides TVs, such as computers, phones, tablets, and smart TVs. Streaming services, video on-demand (VOD), and over-the-top (OTT) content revolutionized how people consume visual content.

High-definition (HD) made a sharper and more detailed video image for both broadcasting and home video possible. For digital technologies to communicate effectively, video cameras had to transition to HD resolutions, like 720p and 1080p. In 2007–2008, the Writers Guild of America (WGA) went on strike to demand better pay for their work online and on new media platforms. They reached a new agreement that gave the WGA control over new media, required streaming platforms to hire WGA writers for higher-budget shows with specific rules, and created a new payment system for digital distribution earnings.

Video Devices

Modern video devices have voice recognition, touch screens, and intelligent features to make navigation and content selection effortless. Consumers can use different devices to view current video content, which could have originated from broadcast platforms cable, or streaming outlets. The media industry uses the term TVAnywhere to describe the technology that lets you stream TV shows and other types of content. CloudTV is one way to distribute interactive content on different screens, so consumers can watch their favorite shows and movies whenever they want. OTT TV is similar, but uses the internet to push content to the consumer so they can access programming on a smart TV app. OTT stands for over-the-top, a separate digital distribution from traditional broadcast and cable media content.

Better video compression will improve the quality of streaming visuals. One significant type of content is live content that can be transmitted on television channels, streamed on network-related legacy streaming apps, or sent on other streaming apps not connected to legacy broadcasting. The competition over content is pressing television to compete for viewers differently. Anyone can "broadcast live" with a click of a button on several social media platforms. The TV industry fights to stay relevant because many shows are on different platforms. The legacy model is struggling due to competition, consumer preferences, and investments in digital operations. Advances in technology, higher production costs, changing advertising methods, and an aging population have impacted media producers and consumers. As mentioned earlier in the chapter, video is tied to different visual platforms, and language has evolved to focus on *digital* media.

While proof-of-concept content was streamed in the 1990s, most streaming services, like the live-streaming company Twitch, and Netflix and YouTube, became embedded into a media culture in the 2000s with compression and Macromedia flash technology. Integrating virtual reality and augmented reality technologies into video options has also popularized immersive viewing experiences. This is where the consumer is transported into a media experience. When people consume media, they consider different options, such as the content and device on which it can be viewed. People multitask on multiple devices like phones, tablets, laptops, gaming consoles, and monitors. This has led to new marketing and advertising approaches. As streaming moves into the 2020s and beyond, more and more streaming services will become available to the public.

Video Goes Mobile

Better visuals require a pricier, more sophisticated camera when using a videotape for recording. In numerous cases, only large television stations had the funds for the high-quality technology. Every TV station had specific delivery requirements for incoming content, such as commercials, public service announcements (PSAs), and other completed content, as well as for programming produced in-house for broadcasting. Because of the low compression rate and low (1g) bandwidth cellular networks early in mobile phone development, mobile journalism was not seen as a viable way to create professional or "broadcast quality" content. But all of that has changed. For many decades, the signal used to record a video picture with 525 lines of information. The vast improvement in clarity and sharpness came with a HDTV signal of 1080 lines, 4K at 2160 lines, and 8K at 7,680 lines. By improving the dynamic range, the blacks became darker and the colors brighter, resulting in a more precise and detailed picture. Go to any archive of older videos to see the difference. In contemporary streaming sites, video and audio need to meet specific compression levels to meet quality needs. In a nutshell, a newer mobile phone model's quality has a superior image to many video camera devices. This is one way phones record at much higher levels than "broadcast quality".

Video streaming, video conferences, and live video chats have entered the digital media scene. Multimedia combines software, hardware, images, audio, text, and other elements that are accessed in real time. This technological shift produced a media boom, as users began attaching (and creating) pictures, videos, emojis, and links to text messages. One of the most significant phone technology innovations occurred with the debut of the smartphone in the 2000s. The Blackberry, iPhone, and Android revolutionized digital communication by combining calling, texting, and computing into a small device. Blackberry phones with a QWERTY keyboard became especially popular for business use. A prosperous environment of mobile applications, app stores, and file sharing created a new digital ecosystem. The advent of long-term evolution (LTE) saw increased speeds and the ability to share HD video streaming, gaming, and the Internet of Things (IoT). Smartphones had features like note-taking apps, a calendar, music, personal email, and internet search. Each phase brought on increasing media use and content creation. Touch screens and better cameras have opened up new job opportunities for multimedia journalists, who use their phones to shoot and edit videos. After LTE came 5G networks, which offer significantly faster data speeds, reduced latency, and the potential for transformative applications like autonomous vehicles and augmented reality. GPS has also helped with location-based services for investigative reporters and data triangulation. Artificial intelligence (AI) assistants and AI apps help journalists and content creators research stories on the go. More recent tools, like biometric authentication and gesture controls, have quickened phone usage on the go and increased ease in content creation. One of the main ways the mobile phone has changed media production, also called content creation, is through the many tools added to the device and the various apps available.

Conferencing

With the invention of the first television, videoconferencing was conceived. It was called videotelephony. In 1927, AT&T made the first television videophone, called the ikonophone. It had 18 frames per second and took up half a room of equipment. The problem right from the early days was the tremendous amount of video data and the networks' limited capacity. Video calling, video conferencing, voicemail, text messaging, cloud storage, and faxing are all part of this concept, facilitated through traditional fixed-line telephones, internet protocol (IP) networks, and cellular technology to transmit sound and data wirelessly. The objective has always been to decrease data usage for video, optimize bandwidth utilization, and improve network capacity (Brey & Furht, 2019).

Alexander Graham Bell received the telephone patent in the mid-1870s, but numerous inventors, programmers and engineers helped bring about contemporary video. In the late 1920s, inventors started discussing the idea of interframe compression, but it wasn't until the 1980s that the H.120, the first video compression standard, was introduced. In the intervening years, a technique for doubling the perceived frame rate of a video display without consuming extra bandwidth, called interlacing, set the stage for video communication. New technologies developed during that time set the foundation for modern compression methods. Developments created other standards, such as MPEG-2/H.262 and MPEG-4/H.263, and the most widely used contemporary video format, the H.264/MPEG-4 AVC (Jacobs & Probell, 2007). Video coding formats continue to evolve with the development of H.265 (HEVC), H.266 (VVC), and AV1. Each generation gives another factor of two compression over the previous. Two of the ways contemporary compression works involve lossy or lossless video compression. Lossy compression reduces file size (bandwidth) by eliminating some data but simultaneously sacrificing some quality. Lossy compression can significantly decrease bandwidth by 200x–300x, but the question is how much degradation is tolerable. Lossless compression keeps all original data and reconstructs the exact original file but can only reduce bandwidth by 2x–10x. For many media business needs, broadcast productions, and content created for large screens or very high detail, sacrificing quality is a significant concern, so lossless compression is preferred. However, lossy compression is used widely for streaming, YouTube, and videoconferencing worldwide. Both kinds of compression have their place in media production and distribution. The US Patent Office shows over 100,000 patents for video conferencing.

Media Containers

Video compression for screening requires media containers, like the MP4, MOV, and WebM standards, for best use. In the 1970s and '80s, as other areas of video and content creation increased, such as affordable prosumer and consumer technologies, nonlinear editing and compression emerged as digital components of the production workflow. Streaming services like Skype, Zoom, and FaceTime were made possible by online conferencing and video compression standards. Similarly, video platforms such as YouTube, Vimeo, TikTok, Vine, and Periscope also benefited from these advancements.

These file formats allow many data streams of audio, video, closed captioning, and multiple soundtracks to be combined and matched in one file. Because many data streams are bundled together to be sent as a single entity, the process of moving digital programming is called streaming. This standardized way of storing and moving compressed media determines the compression and decompression process for sending and using media for listening, watching, and experiencing. The ability to upload, convert, store, and playback video content online requires an online video platform (OVP). After the internet became a viable place to send and receive digital audio and video, companies launched user-generated content streaming services like Vimeo and YouTube. They also introduced programmed television and film streaming services, like Netflix in the early 2000s before introducing numerous social media sites with streaming capabilities. Video transcoding and compression technology enable content creators to stream user-generated content from anywhere online.

Calls and Chats

One additional significant way to communicate is by video phone calling. While people often used Skype and Zoom for business, now all these apps, including FaceTime and video chats, are available for personal communication. Skype was first introduced in the early 2000s for audio calls. After eBay purchased Skype in 2003, the company announced its video calling service and expanded Short Message Service (SMS) that people can send and receive on mobile devices. They also used the same infrastructure for voice calls. In 2011, Microsoft acquired Skype, and also bought a free group messaging app GroupMe. A year later, Skype became widely available and released a free video messaging service. Zoom, in contrast, was founded a decade later, in 2011, under a different name. In 2012, the Zoom Video Communications product launched a beta version that allowed 15 video participants to be part of the conference. Zoom grew in prominence and became the top video conferencing choice at the start of the March 2020 Covid-19 pandemic. In the mid-2000s, Apple Inc. introduced FaceTime with their iOS 4 phone. Shortly after that, Apple released the Mac computer and iPad versions. Google Meet, Microsoft Teams, Webex, and Whereby also became available.

Consumer Effects

Effects from consuming videos mirror many of the impacts of television. Streaming is one of the factors that differentiates this. The act of "binge" watching video programming came into prominence when it became clear from platform algorithms that viewers were watching an entire series of video programming back-to-back in one sitting. This new viewing habit was counter to prior viewing, requiring the viewer to watch weekly programming called "appointment viewing". The introduction of DVDs and box sets for VHS and DVDs, to some extent, suggested continuity viewing, which could be considered binge-watching. The use of DVRs has transformed broadcast viewing from appointment viewing to potential binge-watching. Viewers can now record broadcast and cable programming at a specific time on a hard drive. Viewers could also watch syndication, cable, or broadcast "marathons" when available. Still, the option to pick from a plethora of choices on various streaming platforms was a new consumer experience.

While some platforms release an entire series or season simultaneously, other streamers "drop" shows at a specific time each week to mirror prior viewing experiences with broadcast television, to build interest, and create show hype. Either way, the episode list grows, allowing the consumer to view it immediately or wait until episodes accumulate. One study on binge-watching notes the discrepancy in research about when viewing moves into the "binge" category (Starosta & Izydorczyk, 2020). Some researchers state that after two episodes viewed at one sitting, a show is being binge-watched. In other cases, completing three episodes of the same show in one sitting notes binge-watching. Some research emphasizes the need for more studies on binge-watching (Jenner, 2020). It suggests that theories such as uses and gratifications, media system dependency, and mood management could help researchers understand more about bingewatching (Merikivi et al., 2020).

A separate study looks at binge-watching as a media ritual. A study found that people's viewing habits for binge-watching are often influenced by technology. "Most binge-watching occurs at home, during weekday evenings and weekends, for those who work Monday to Friday. Some people said they like to binge-watch shows while on vacation, especially ones they didn't have time for during the work week. Viewers motivated by the sense of completion often held off on starting a show until they had downtime because they were aware that they would not want to stop watching" (Steiner & Xu 2020, p. 92). Viewers also noted the difference between high attention binge-watching and low attention "background noise" viewing and share that "to appreciate its nuances, we must understand that binge-watching cannot be either positive or negative, cultural or structural, but an evolving human experience driven and energized by contradiction" (Steiner & Xu, 2020, p. 96).

Binge-watching is one habit of consumer visual media that will continue to be on the radar of researchers and scholars.

Things to Consider

- Think about ways video telephones have altered communication.
- Study the ways camera sizes have changed content creation.
- Mull over the way habits have shifted as content has become more "on-demand".
- Brainstorm how video and television intertwine as technologies.
- Name the different technologies mentioned in this chapter.

Takeaways

- There has been a change in the many recording formats, from film to tape to digital.
- Introducing box sets for VHS and DVDs, video stores, and DVRs changed the way people watched media content before streaming and created the term binge-watching.
- The technological creation of video calls and chats and the origin of those technologies as forms of media have altered communication.
- Including compression as part of media history makes sense for streaming and explains why videos are compressed today.
- Name some of your chapter takeaways.

References

Brey, S., & Furht, B. (2019). Videoconferencing systems and applications. In *Handbook of Internet Computing* (pp. 451–484). CRC Press.

Jacobs, M., & Probell, J. (2007). A brief history of video coding. *ARC International*, 1, 6.

Jenner, M. (2020). Researching binge-watching. *Critical Studies in Television*, 15(3), 267–279.

Merikivi, J., Bragge, J., Scornavacca, E., & Verhagen, T. (2020). Binge-watching serialized video content: A transdisciplinary review. *Television and New Media*, 21(7), 697–711. https://doi.org/10.1177/1527476419848578

Starosta, J.A., & Izydorczyk, B. (2020). Understanding the phenomenon of binge-watching—A systematic review. *International Journal of Environmental Research and Public Health* 17(12), 4469. https://doi.org/10.3390/ijerph17124469

Steiner, E., & Xu, K. (2020). Binge-watching motivates change: Uses and gratifications of streaming video viewers challenge traditional TV research. *Convergence*, 26(1), 82–101.

6 Journalism

Journalism is two things in contemporary society: a practice and a discipline. Journalists must follow rules like telling the truth, being accurate, and staying objective. At the same time, there is evidence that journalistic products reach back in history to a daily ancient Roman bulletin called the *Acta Diurna*, the Tang Dynasty's daily *bao*, and Germany's *Weekly News* and *Daily Courant*. Journalism, as a practice, dates back to the 1800s. This chapter discusses journalism as a practice and the impact of technological advancements in the field, the 24-hour news cycle, watchdog approaches, and economics. At one time, journalism was referred to as print journalism because of the material nature of the process. After the invention of television and newsrooms starting to produce broadcasts designed explicitly for news, the term broadcast journalism was added to the journalism vocabulary. Then, with online publications, the term digital journalism was coined. Moving this journalism chapter to the back of the book in the synergies section might make sense. Still, the discipline's link with legacy media has landed it in the front third in the screened section.

Journalism's future is intertwined with the technologies noted in the earlier chapters that transform how news and information are consumed and produced, requiring journalists' organizations to adapt and incorporate digital platforms and processes to reach wider audiences. Information provided by journalists helps media consumers make better decisions. Early French filmmakers Aguste and Louis Lumière invented the first newsreels on film at the end of the 1800s, converging cinema and journalism in new ways and including visual images in journalism earlier than you might have thought. Journalism's primary purpose is to provide truthful news that informs people about what is happening, through traditional and modern media. In recent years, indelible journalistic stories, such as Rebecca Skloot's award-winning work in *The Immortal Life of Henrietta Lacks*, illustrate how technology is used by journalists to "get the news out". This chapter explores journalism through technologies, including legacy media.

DOI: 10.4324/9781003397588-7

The topics covered include embedded journalists, the 24-hour news cycle, journalistic practice, and the effects of journalism on consumers.

Technologies of Journalism

Studying journalism in the 21st century is challenging, notwithstanding the tools and technologies used to convey journalistic information. This chapter focuses on the tools used to share the news because the tools and technology are closely related to what journalism "is" as media. However, the distinction remains clear: journalism is not specifically media but a way to create news shared throughout media history (Barnhurst & Nerone 2009). While ancient Italy may have early claims on journalistic activity using a form of pen and paper, the invention of Gutenberg's printing press was a catalyst for newsgathering and distribution. The press, a technology, later became synonymous with the contemporary name for the journalism industry, "the press".

Newspaper Era

Newspapers became a regular form of global media in the 1600s. Periodicals and newspapers gained popularity, providing a wide audience with news, information, commentary, and entertainment, including English publications like *The Tatler* and *The Spectator*. Before the American Colonies became the United States, Benjamin Franklin published the *Pennsylvania Gazette* in 1723. While newspapers were becoming an established form of legacy media, others used pamphleteering and "papers" to get printed information out in other ways. Uprisings and wars like the French Revolution share evidence that pamphleteering was used to incite unrest. The move from the sizeable movable type to the smaller press emerged in the early 1800s. Embedded journalists also appeared in the mid-1800s, when correspondences reported on the American Civil War.

Thomas Paine's "Common Sense" pamphlet greatly influenced public opinion during the American Revolution. Universities and libraries started collecting more books, which made academic journals more popular. In the 1700s, scholars began publishing their research, forming the "publish or perish" mentality. Early encyclopedias and dictionaries created references available to general audiences. The brands and volumes of encyclopedias grew significantly through the years. One of the significant shifts in movable type came when Ottmar Mergenthaler patented the Linotype machine in the late 1880s. While typesetting was a slow process, even with movable type, the Linotype involved casting an entire line of text at once instead of using individual lettering. The Linotype operator used a keyboard to type words and spaces into a mold cast in liquid metal, creating a line of type called a slug. These slugs were lined up to create printed pages of text. This method remained popular until the invention of the offset printing press. People primarily used this method until computers were used in the 1960s, when screened technology gained prominence.

The printed word faced copyright and licensing concerns as the newspaper and publishing industry grew. The legal concept of copyright started in the 18th century. Copyright laws allow authors and publishers to protect and profit from their written works. England's Statute of Anne is one of the first copyright laws, passed in the early 1700s. The United States passed its first copyright law in 1790, creating legal guidelines for intellectual property rights. Another pivotal technological boom occurred with the mass production of goods during the period, primarily regarded as the Industrial Revolution. Early newspapers in the United States were still printed using movable type until the steam engine printing press was invented a few decades later. Inventors Friedrich Koenig and Andreas Bauer built the steam-powered cylinder printing press in England in the early 1800s. The steam-powered two-cylinder rotary press made it easier and cheaper to print newspapers which cost the consumer only a penny. This mass production model significantly increased newspaper industry development in the US beginning in the 1830s: for example, see Frederick Douglass's newspaper *The North Star*. Printing also found a widespread use in wartime. During the American Civil War, soldiers focused on newspapers and political cartoons, using portable printing processes that the troops carried and printing facilities commandeered during the war. The cost and the technology combined to become known as the "age of the penny press."

The first newspaper photograph was printed in 1880, but the press did not start featuring photographs routinely until the 1920s. Lighter cameras and quicker lens mechanisms were introduced in the 1920s, ushering in the age of photojournalism with the invention of the first 35 mm camera. While newspapers routinely used photos, magazines focused on a style of photojournalism that allowed for the combination of photography with the printed word, with photographs becoming a predominant medium for imparting important and striking material. The invention of film on rolls in the 1850s popularized amateur use, and by the mid-1900s, black-and-white and color photos were prevalent. Magazine photos enhanced news stories' visual impact and changed reporting style. Halftone printing and photogravure improved the printing process. They made photographs look better by showing a more comprehensive range of shadows. Using photos in print media enhanced the visual appeal of stories and provided an impactful way to report events.

The penny press distribution model, along with the telegraph, spread the news to mass audiences nationwide. The mass-production shift developed a media model that made all kinds of local, regional, and national news products reasonably accessible to broader audiences. This shifted the business model and economics of the news business and news production. Because of the low price of the newspaper itself, the print industry needed increased revenue beyond circulation and newsstand sales. Newsstands brought in revenue as well as privately funded or subscription-based circulation. Still, advertisements soon became a significant revenue boon for print companies.

Access to low-cost news content that the masses could afford shifted stories and coverage more toward entertainment. The newspaper industry also fostered the idea that the press is independent of politics. Until this point, political figures funded the newspapers distributed to the public. This new shift to developing independent news content, separate and disconnected from the funding sources, changed the nature of mass media. Many media models fostered independence and division between content and ownership. News organizations worked to separate advertising from editorial content. The term editorial can be confusing and is often connected to op-ed or opinion content. In actuality, all content created to entertain or inform in a news context is considered editorial content. In the history of journalism and news, the ideal has been to keep advertising and funding interests separate from editorial content.

The ideas of the press pass, the press box, and the press room came from journalists' use of the printing press technology. The Associated Press (AP) was launched in the mid-1800s by a group of newspapers as a way for the press and professional journalists to cooperate and form a more national identity for newsgathering and distribution. The company was called a "newswire" service because newspapers leased telephone wires to transmit information to them through a subscription deal that paid for the timely and continual access to content. In the 1950s, radio teleprinters, then satellites, were used to transmit facts and story information. Today, the "wire service" still represents groups that research and write national stories for journalists to localize and use for a subscription fee. However, most information comes through digital means. The Associate Press (AP) started as a news resource for journalists in the mid 1800s. Other news distribution groups like United Press International (UPI) and Reuters came later. These subscription services primarily cover national and international stories. Local news reporters often work with wire services to share local stories with more people.

Printing color photos, while expensive, was used to spark interest in newspapers and placed "above the fold", which means the top half of the newspaper where the photo would be visible on the newsstand—both color and black-and-white images showcase important news and ongoing stories. Using photos in print media enhanced the visual appeal of stories and provided an impactful visual way to report events.

Figure 6.1 Broadcast journalism single camera interview set up.
Photograph by the author.

Broadcast Journalism

The invention of radio and television technology further opened the doors of news and information to the public. Radio announcers on the news and in sports became household names as their voices became more distinct. Live reporting and broadcast journalist entered the vernacular of the day. The cultural phenomenon of millions of people viewing an event live, all together, by radio or television, cemented a generation and further changed the nature of communication. The National Association of Broadcasters (NAB) was founded in 1923 and made up mainly of radio station owners, because broadcasters saw the viable nature of the media business. The American government created the Federal Radio Commission (FRC) to develop policies and laws regarding the proliferation of media. The FRC was transitioned to the Federal Communication Commission (FCC), which is still in power as a government entity today.

People enjoyed the intimacy and immediacy of radio news, making it a popular way to get information until TV came along. In the 1950s and 1960s, televisions became a central technology in many people's homes in the United States. Adding color to the picture further enticed consumers to purchase a television set. News division reporters and TV anchors gained fame and influence as on-air talent and news hubs formed in major cities, with affiliates owned in smaller towns throughout the country. Flagship stations transmitted national and international news which became the standard in nightly TV broadcasts. The 1960s also saw the birth of the underground press, which provided alternative perspectives.

News gatherers use various technologies to gather the news they share with the public. Small reporter pads have given way to digital audio recorders and small digital cameras, also called camcorders. In turn, journalists are often called multimedia journalists (MMJs), video journalists (VJs), or backpack journalists (BPJs). A mobile phone acts as a camera, and they can also access wire service subscriptions like AP, Reuters, or UPI for news, data, and press releases. Newsgathering involves culling social media, using web monitoring tools, and web scraping to gather information, especially for in-depth data journalism.

Social media content creators have also become highly popular on platforms like Instagram, Snapchat, and TikTok, producing videos for many topic areas. Drones, satellite images, and news bots also help cull story information and provide aerial visuals to audiences.

Also, data scraping, transcription software, and other artificial intelligence (AI) tools help with note-taking, crowdsourcing, research, and analytics. Video chat tools provide easier methods to interview experts. The First Amendment protects freedom of speech, press, religion, assembly, and petition. In 1949, the Fairness Doctrine was passed as an FCC policy that required broadcasters to cover controversial issues in a balanced manner. The policy was terminated. Other laws include the Privacy Protection Act, the Equal Time Rule, Shield Laws, Reporter's Privilege, and Sunshine Laws. Important televised news events in American history were broadcast, including elections, crime, politics, strikes, marches, and demonstrations. News cultivates cultural values and popularizes trends across many topics. How consumers find news and the make-up and structure of the news environment will continue to impact consumers who attempt to be informed.

The 24-hour News Cycle

The Cable News Network (CNN) was launched in 1980, introducing television programming to the 24-hour news cycle. Satellite technology allowed live remote broadcasts to reach anywhere worldwide with satellite coverage. As cable television gained prominence, so did the cable network. Ted Turner, founder of CNN, also launched other well-known channels like Cartoon Network, Adult Swim, and Turner Classic Movies.

The next big fundamental technological jump for journalism occurred when the internet became standard in the 1980s and '90s. The domain name system (DNS) gave journalists a web location to find verified information. Education adopted the .edu website name, and the government labeled their sites as .gov to sift out potentially credible domain name hierarchies and provide top-tier news and information-gathering sites. Pressures of the cable industry popularity and the internet brought increased economic pressures and competition for advertising dollars to the newspaper industry, which ushered in the era of newspaper conglomerates, changing the nature of the local newspaper industry. It became more cost effective for owners to create big newspaper companies with a single owner, like E.W. Scripps, Pulitzer and Gannett. Email became a popular form of communication, and digital technologies changed how news information was made and consumed. Dial-up technology got quicker, and digitally published news briefs, White Papers, and newsletters were shared online.

Citizen journalists and media consumer participation increased the available information on many events and topics. Legacy news models shifted toward a proliferation of independent news sources. The internet revolutionized the news and shared news globally. Soon, legacy media, independent startups, participatory journalists, and media consumers started using social media platforms to push news out to many individuals and other sources. Aggregate websites worked to categorize news and offer it to consumers. The ease of website creation saw the emergence of more news sites. Content management systems (CMS) became more user-friendly as visual What You See Is What You Get (WYSIWYG) technologies and rich text editors enabled novice users to publish digital content.

News consumers contributed to the commentary on blogs and social media posts. This environment decentralized the news. Contemporary news reporting and the entire business model are founded on the speed and immediacy created by digital technology like the internet and mobile technologies. Access to increasing amounts of information available through digital books, public records, databases, and data repositories in the cloud, make fact-checking and fact-finding easier. Embedded video and multimedia, interactivity, data visualization, infographics, augmented virtual reality, and AI give journalists tools to tell the story in increasingly compelling ways. Data journalism and computer-assisted reporting, as a way of fact-finding, have become synonymous with journalism. These data-driven insights have brought challenges like misinformation, surveillance, fake news, and clickbait into the spotlight. Social media also distributes news, which allows journalists to monitor algorithmic trends.

Algorithmic journalism involves using specific software to create parameters that automatically monitor algorithms to generate news stories. These algorithms select news for readers on aggregate sites—those that specifically gather and present news in website format—and social media. Machine learning and natural language processing have been used more readily to identify data points, scrape and extract information from documents, and analyze data for investigative journalism. Specifically, algorithmically driven platforms that push specific kinds of news and information have been studied, and media literacy is encouraged when reading all forms of journalism. Photo and media editing apps give mobile journalists tools to turn around visual materials quickly and report news on the go. Geolocation tools help with location-based reporting, facial recognition, and image analysis technologies. Drones, podcasting tools, and live-streaming platforms are now mainstream, and automated content creation, data analysis, and immersive storytelling experiences continue to be at the forefront of contemporary journalism. Surveillance and secure communication tools that protect sources, cloud storage, and sensitive and personal information are increasingly being discussed because of international hackers and espionage working to steal and leak information. Additionally, cybersecurity solutions are increasingly needed to protect against data breaches.

Watchdog Approaches

From the late 1900s through the contemporary media landscape, digital journalism has paved the way for a technological transformation of journalistic enterprises involving news production, distribution, and consumption. But even as far back as the beginning of journalism, the aim has been to inform the public accurately and thoroughly about issues, developments, and events that affect them in a fair and ethically unbiased way. Journalists have also been charged as professional media makers who serve as watchdogs for governmental powers and hold them accountable for their actions. Factual news and information can be challenging to parse transparently in a politically devised world. Illegal recordings of phone hacking have been used to manipulate news stories (Pettegree, 2015). Media technologies have fostered a watchdog approach to journalism and news. "Of all of the established functions of the press in American public life, the watchdog role is among the most hallowed and, at the same time, the least securely institutionalized in the daily mission of the contemporary news organization" (Bennett & Serrin, 2005, p. 169). The independent examination and analysis of government, business, and public institutions is at the heart of watchdog journalism. Journalists document, investigate, and question activities important to public concern and life. At some points, journalists find hidden deceptions. While this style of journalism is practiced daily, there are gaps in processes guided by various digital surveillance and investigative-style technologies. While many concerning items may be uncovered and shared, contextualizing the significance in meaningful ways may occur less often for multiple reasons. Watchdog journalism and investigative journalism are very similar. Watchdog journalism is a kind of investigative practice that precisely fact-checks public figures to increase accountability and transparency in democratic governance. Watchdog journalism is impartial and not political in ideology, and bias and reliability are to be considered by media-literate consumers. The uncovering of the Watergate case, the Roman Catholic church's cover-up of clergy sex abuse, and the Flint Michigan Water Crisis were all aided through watchdog journalism initiatives.

The digital revolution continues to transform journalism across all media platforms with real-time reporting, interactive storytelling, and data-driven journalism. Journalists can report, edit, and publish information faster, leading to live shots by television stations, live internet and social media reports, and contributions of the work of citizen journalists— amateurs who share information through their phones to the public. Technology with better connectivity and more sophisticated mobile phones has made this landscape possible. Media outlets now solicit user-generated content for media coverage. The development of online internet platforms and digital media technology, like social media sharing, allows anyone to participate in recording and creating information. Citizen journalism influences information distribution worldwide, reporting from the scene of disaster zones and political upheavals. However, the lack of verification of facts proliferates fake news, confuses the objectivity of reports, and puts others in danger. When citizens post visuals from other countries to websites like YouTube, those in power can seek and find those individuals and stop them.

For this reason, YouTube allows its content creators to blur out faces to protect the identities of the individuals in those videos. The democratization of the reporting process, combined with the participatory nature of the media landscape, means it is more challenging to identify facts because the technological tools can create a professional aesthetic. Artificial intelligence, robotics, virtual and augmented reality, participatory realities, blockchain, and non-fungible tokens (NFTs) have further reshaped news media.

Embedding Journalists

In the 1990s, the Gulf War was extensively covered on television, introducing 24/7 war reporting. This was also a time of innovation in the technical standards of televised content, as high definition television (HDTV) dramatically improved the quality and resolution of the viewing experience. Embedded reporters, journalists, and photographers, on-site during conflicts, reported on what they saw. Embedded journalists can access military leaders and the front and back lines of experience and strategy. Research has shared more about this experience for journalists and the sentiments or frames they share in their reporting (Buchanan, 2011; Pfau et al., 2005). Integrating embedded journalists has been precarious in military conflicts, including those in the 2020s. There is always a balance between the obligation to provide information to the public and the military's responsibility to keep the public and the soldiers safe. Social media and geotags can quickly identify the locations of journalists and the military. Some journalists are captured and tried as spies. The launch of the smartphone revolutionized how journalists report news and how viewers consume it both in the United States and abroad. For example, in the early 2000s, the 24-hour news cycle became saturated during the 9/11 World Trade Center and the Pentagon attacks and the Flight 93 crash in Western Pennsylvania. National disasters like the Hurricane Katrina Category 5 storm, and wild fires in California received constant coverage. The Covid-19 pandemic accelerated streaming service use, pushing the 24/7 news cycle coverage even further and to new platforms. The Russian invasion of Ukraine and Middle East conflicts push cell phone networking and internet access in new ways to track drones and missiles.

The Economics of Journalism

In a newspaper office and other kinds of news organizations, the content creators and the sales and revenue departments work to remain separate to maintain the integrity and promote independence of the news content from the company's commercial interests. While this might seem an old-fashioned concept in the contemporary political partisanship environment, the main goal of a news-related enterprise is to report the news accurately and in a reader-friendly way. Separating a news enterprise from the interests of advertisers is essential to preserve the credibility and trust of the organization to its public.

Aside from the partially government-funded American Public Media (APM), news organizations are largely for-profit companies in the United States. They make money from advertising, subscriptions, and, sometimes, philanthropic funding. Recent declines in legacy media advertising revenue have shifted the economic landscape of advertising, and media management has leaned more on new technology for efficiency and automation. The financial sustainability of journalism is essential for maintaining the integrity and independence of the journalism and newsgathering profession to maintain its credibility and provide the public with accurate and reliable information.

Freedoms and Ethics

The American Constitution protects freedom of the press in the First Amendment to the Bill of Rights of the US Constitution. The Amendment allows the press to report ideas and information without government interference as part of freedom of speech. Technology has significantly altered the freedom of the press through advances in media and information technologies that affect these platforms. As computers and data storage, electronic messages, and information services continue to grow, concerns about invasions of personal privacy have also increased. Technologies that restrict access to public information and censorship are also a concern. However, new technologies are also being used to expand access to information and limit the power of the government to control media. Threats to press freedom, such as online harassment, surveilling critics, and the deliberate spreading of misinformation, continue. Telecommunications regulation that undermines the creative and participatory possibilities are also scrutinized.

American laws regarding a journalist's ability to record someone without their knowledge vary by state and the circumstances of the recording. Federal wiretapping laws consider one-party consent sufficient for recording a phone call. This means that as long as one person in the recorded conversation agrees, the recording is a legal enterprise. The rules have become more complex when recording in-person discussions. It is generally illegal for journalists to record phone conversations between other people. This standard also applies to in-person communications that are expected to be private. There is no reasonable expectation of privacy in public, so it is usually not illegal to record someone without their consent, as long as they can be seen and heard. But, in private settings, like bathrooms or changing areas, recording is illegal. The ability to record someone depends on several contextual circumstances, location, and applicable state laws. Journalists need to be aware of the legal aspects of journalistic work.

In early television, news was formed to report news and information to the public as a mass media service using radio and television. Most broadcast media organizations had a news bureau or newsroom. The Freedom of Information Act (FOIA) was designed to create ways for journalists to access government information more easily, for improved, transparent, and factual news reporting. Journalist organizations made ethical codes to remind journalists of their duty to the public. Codes of ethics came from organizations like the Radio Television Digital News Association

(RTDNA), and the Society of Professional Journalists (SPJ). The 1947 publication *A Free and Responsible Press*, from the federal government's Hutchins Commission on the Freedom of the Press, came after several years of study on print, broadcast, and film and on the researched owners, managers, and pressure groups involved in journalism. The commission wanted to know if the First Amendment's freedom of the press was in danger. More printed content meant more extensive newspaper staff, more writers, and experts with specific roles. The affordability of information through the connection of technology and economic availability, which created the penny press, affected journalism in many ways, including changes in technology, distribution, profits, format, and content models. Media consumers wanted an independent press that was not tied to specific political ideologies and funding. The Hutchins Commission discovered that freedom of the press was at risk due to the many voices in the media that did not meet ethical and journalistic standards. The report threatened regulation or control of the press if their practices did not change (Shedden, 2015). The report helped foster a code of ethics for journalists and the print media industry. The commission asked the press, as an industry, to focus on truthfulness, comment, and criticism, represent without stereotypes, clarify the goals and values of American society, and reflect the public's right to know (North Dakota State University, n.d.).

Journalistic Practice

Good journalistic practice involves honesty, fairness, impartiality, and accountability. These components are considered to be part of the ethical side of journalism. The Society of Professional Journalists' code of ethics emphasizes seeking truth, minimizing harm, acting independently, and being accountable. Not surprisingly, new technologies, including digital technologies, create new challenges. The blurred lines between objective and personal have become central to this debate. Even fact-checking has limits. Using technology to verify the authenticity of sources is one way to strengthen the authenticity of facts. Still, humans are fallible, and they often program the technology. In the case of viral breaking news stories, components of the story come fast and furious, and it is difficult to pinpoint precisely what is going on in a specific situation. Even describing what someone is explicitly seeing can be difficult, as each view is seen differently. The democratization of media has muddled what constitutes journalism, which raises questions about journalism ethics. Journalists must be equipped to navigate and maintain the integrity of their work.

These technologies have essentially altered how journalism, with its people and business models, has operated and been made available to media consumers. The 1890s were a time of yellow journalism and yellow press, when newspapers used eye-catching headlines and sensationalized stories to increase sales. Contemporary examples of this include clickbait with sensational story examples, fake news, and the proliferation of misinformation and disinformation. The emphasis is on how, when, and if media consumers seek and use the information. It is also essential for journalists to work with a variety of community members to collect information. It is generally an accepted requirement that journalists refuse gifts, free travel, tickets, reimbursements, special treatment, and favors, because it may compromise their integrity and raise questions about their impartiality in a story and the integrity of their profession. This historically significant concept stems from the idea that accepting gifts compromises journalistic integrity. Another area of concern for journalists is citing sources of information. Many newsrooms require several interviews in a news package, which involves contacting multiple voices about a news topic. Journalists, when needed, protect informants through source confidentiality, also called reporter's privilege. The aim of this practice is to prevent authorities from forcing a journalist to reveal the identity of an anonymous story source. In many cases, a strong guarantee of anonymity means sources are more likely to share information of public interest with journalists. Authorities and courts cannot coerce a journalist to share a confidential source.

The United Nations International Covenant on Civil and Political Rights (ICCPR), created in the 1950s and still in use today, commits nations to, among other things, respect an individual's freedom of speech and expression. However, this protection is not ironclad. Journalists can be required to give up protected sources under certain circumstances or face legal consequences, including imprisonment.

Journalism Effects

News media plays a vital role in constructing pictures of reality. McCombs and Shaw (1972) explored Walter Lippmanns' 1922 theory that news sets the agenda for what is essential in society—that idea in their research focused on the presidential 1972 election. While much has happened in media and news production since the 1920s and even the 1970s, their research still bears weight in its findings and the idea that researchers were forming media effects theories more than 100 years ago. McCombs and Shaw found that people learned factual information from watching a broadcast and started to understand the relevance of a specific story based on the coverage. If the story was breaking news, or shared in the first few minutes of the broadcast, it was deemed a more important story. Setting the agenda for the news rundown affected the audience.

Over the years, this is contrary to other effects theories that noted minimal consequences from media use. McCombs and Shaw called this influence agenda setting. They surveyed a sample of randomly selected undecided voters in North Carolina to test this hypothesis that the media agenda can set the public agenda. In the survey, these undecided voters were asked what they thought were the day's critical issues, regardless of what the candidates might say. The problems in the survey were ranked according to the percentage of voters recalling each one to describe the public agenda. In short, the researchers share that mass media can set the agenda on issues for voters. This was just one study in hundreds that focused on journalism's agenda-setting probabilities.

Things to Consider

- Take into consideration the experiences of embedded journalists. What kinds of ethical dilemmas might journalists face in current conflicts?
- Ponder the history of journalism. What specific technologies quickened the profession of journalism?
- Deliberate on the ideas from the Hutchins Commission. Did the commission's work affect contemporary journalism?
- Consider the ways Yellow Journalism tactics are still used today.
- Brainstorm ways AI and new technologies might alter the journalism profession.
- Consider the current economic model of journalism. How might that change in the future.
- Can agenda setting occur in other types of media besides a broadcast? Consider how.
- Name the technologies used in this chapter?

Takeaways

- Gutenberg's Printing Press is ultimately the source for mass publication and the proliferation of journalism and literacy.
- The low cost of the penny newspaper, called the penny press, provided inexpensive news and information to a mass readership.
- Examining how technology affects journalistic freedom highlights the importance of maintaining legal protections and exercising caution regarding privacy and the fine line between protecting fundamental rights and advancing technology.
- Technology use in journalism creates moral dilemmas because of technology's dual roles as a source of false information and a tool for verification.
- Name some of your chapter takeaways.

References

Barnhurst, K.G., & Nerone, J. (2009). Journalism history. In *The handbook of journalism studies* (pp. 37–48). Routledge.

Bennett, W.L., & Serrin, W. (2005). The watchdog role. In *The Press* (pp.169–188). Oxford University Press.

Buchanan, P.G. (2011). Facilitated news as controlled information flows: The origins, rationale, and dilemmas of 'embedded' journalism. *Pacific Journalism Review, 17*(1), 102–118.

McCombs, M.E., & Shaw, D.L. (1972). The agenda-setting function of mass media. *Public Opinion Quarterly, 36*(2), 176–187.

North Dakota State University. (n.d.). Hutchins Report. https://www.ndsu.edu/pubweb/~rcollins/431ethics/hutchins.htm

Pettegree, A. (2015). *The invention of news: How the world came to know about itself*. Yale University Press.

Pfau, M., Haigh, M.M., Logsdon, L., Perrine, C., Baldwin, J.P., Breitenfeldt, R.E., . . . & Romero, R. (2005). Embedded reporting during the invasion and occupation of Iraq: How the embedding of journalists affects television news reports. *Journal of Broadcasting & Electronic Media, 49*(4), 468–487.

Shedden, D.S. (2015, March 27). *Today in media history: 1947, the press reported on the Hutchins Commission report*. Poynter. https://www.poynter.org/reporting-editing/2015/today-in-media-history-in-1947-the-press-reported-on-the-hutchins-commission-report/

Part Two

Sounds

7 Music Recording and Foley

Capturing sound with a recording device through various methods, including generating Foley, is the crux of this chapter. Music recording and Foley are integral technology-focused areas of media creation and production that introduce the section on sound. These overarching topics fold into cinema, television, video, and audio but have their own technological story to share. Music is essential in many media and mediated experiences through screens, sounds, and contemporary synergies. Music recording producers are a specific technical career position involving recording music with precision and clarity, using various technologies. Music recording and Foley are used in all kinds of content, for streaming audio and video platforms, cinematic soundscapes, recorded sound for diverse mediated experiences, and naturally collected sounds or actualities. Music's influence in media, through the music-making technologies and, then, the music-playing technologies and artifacts, provide much to consider. This chapter starts with a historical context of sound technologies. It discusses vinyl and radio's role in music recording, mixing, and online distribution. It ends with some ideas about the effects of research. Chapter 8 delves explicitly into radio technologies.

Historical Grooves

The study of recording and Foley art can center around what is real and realistic. Specifically, are sound effects always better than authentic sounds in a movie? Researchers considered ideas around audio creation through Foley art and audio from the actual action. They studied whether their interview subjects knew the difference. The study concluded that there was no difference in perception as long as Foley met the expectations of sounding *like* the action. The researchers wanted to know if Foley sounds are always a better experience for the viewer and listener than actual sounds. The study shared that there was no difference for the viewer as long as the sounds were natural and made sense. Researchers noted, "The

DOI: 10.4324/9781003397588-9

lack of important differences between Foley sounds and real sounds might be related to the fact that each sound expresses the action that it represents, even if it has a different source" (Trento & De Götzen, 2011, p. 6).

Humans have been creating, manipulating, and transmitting sound through the ages, and instruments or technologies have been part of the process. Humans also have acoustics, echoes, and vocal amplifications that push sound. In early cases, artifacts were used as an instrument of some sort. Most times, a sound does not travel far from its source. It travels from the source, across airwaves, and into our ears. Sound needs to be manually projected if there is a lack of amplification. This could occur through acoustical amplification using the cupping of your hands to create a horn, an acoustic horn, or a megaphone. In all cases, the flared side of an instrument amplifies and projects the sound. In our contemporary world, sound-making and recording involve technology. Tradition and cultural differences in the craft of mediated storytelling create descriptors or dividing terms that separate one kind of content creation from another. Specifically, the term sound is used by film music composers and video game composers to address the work's historical and current nature.

Music composers collaborate closely with the management and staff of media projects to create and enhance the listener's experience. They use collaborative digital audio workstations (DAWs), collaborative platforms, cloud collaborators, and online digital organizer programs, that include group chats, file management, voice messaging, video chats, and other tool integration, to organize projects digitally. The composer and their team work together to create original music that compliments narrative, character, and atmosphere. Even music reused from an artist's media catalog is often reworked by the composer for a renewed but still nostalgic experience. Understanding the creative vision of the overall project is highly important, along with accentuating emotional beats through story integration. Essential elements include focusing on the beginning, middle, and end of the project, the branded sound, a franchise connection, character development, and overall project integration. In a changing media environment that focuses on extended reality projects for instance, composers must provide many tracks or music elements for in-game play.

In most cases, composers create demo tracks, receive feedback from the team, and then record and produce the music using many different technologies. Then, composers—such as Hans Zimmer, Rachel Portman, and John Williams—work with others to integrate the music into all project phases. Danny Elfman, Howard Shore, Bear McCreary, Jeremy Soule, Phil Boucher, Anne Dudley, and many others have made critical technological strides and contributions to how music is recorded and experienced. Viewing a film scene with sound off and then sound on, shows significant differences in the experience.

Sometimes, specific terms bind to a tradition, regardless of current usage. In many cases, filmmakers will discuss sound, and broadcasters will discuss audio. This distinct difference comes from early cinema history. In early filmmaking, sound was collected during the film production process. The emphasis was on the sounds on the set at the time, including the music, effects, ambient sound, and dialogue. The emphasis was on the acoustics and original sound occurring on the set. Acoustics studies the mechanical waves in solids, liquids, and gases that create sound and vibrations and focuses on the production, effects, transmission, and reception in electroacoustic communication, among other areas. Acoustics are essential for designing media spaces that ensure the best sound when filled with live sound. Recording and sound engineers understand acoustics in a variety of spaces.

Once all ideas about sound and acoustics are considered and recorded, the collected film sound is synchronized to the images on the screen. In filmmaking, this is called synced sound. For filmmakers, the sound was tied to the visual representations; for broadcasters, audio is a separate signal, as in music or radio. This sound is not married to visuals. Audio has historical roots in legacy broadcast media, and broadcast audio is transmitted separately. Audio, in broadcasting, refers to a specific audio signal being transmitted or manipulated. Film sound and broadcast audio require different techniques and expertise that provide clarity within each industry.

The first recorded sound is thought to have occurred in the mid-1800s, before cinema, television, and video media. Frenchman Édouard-Léon Scott de Martinville invented and patented the Phonautograph. He was inspired by understanding how a photograph could be taken using a Daguerreotype photographic process. The sound device worked to capture and record sound waves and vibrations as they passed through the air but the device could not directly play back the sounds to hear them. The first successful record and playback came through Thomas Edison's phonograph. Shortly after that, in the 1920s when radio was gaining popularity, cinema sound was integrated into filmmaking. Warner Bros. produced one of the first talking films in 1928.

Cinema uses sound in a variety of ways. One of the main ways sounds are collected in a film is through dialogue. Sound editors record, edit, and mix dialogue so it sounds clear and matches the visuals. Many mics and pick-up patterns are used to enhance the collection of sound. Sound effects are another part of the film's soundscape. These were not added during filming. They can be ambient sound that fills up an environment. Still, in most cases, they focus on specific effects like explosions, gunshots, or other movements or significant scenes. One specific integral part of realism in cinema sound and radio dramas is film Foley, also called sound effects. Foley sounds gained prominence when Universal Studio's sound effects editor, Jack Foley, started experimenting with creating sounds for films after shooting was complete. Foley studios and stages employ gravel pits and props to recreate footsteps and other needed movements and sounds to match the visuals. This experimentation also moved sound work to the postproduction phase of creation. This work used reel-to-reel tape to edit, increasing the timing, precision, and experimentation of sound effects creation, as opposed to working on a live production during the screening, along with the music composition (Burgess, 2014). Postproduction sound editing, including the addition of Foley artists, became an established and well-known practice in filmmaking. Background sound, called ambient sound, captures the environment and sets an immersive feel to the film experience (Ament, 2014).

Cinema sound can also incorporate silence, a manipulative way of playing with the viewer's emotions. And lastly, cinematic music has become a genre and specialty for some composers. A film's score is a collaboration with the film's director to heighten emotion and movement during a specific scene or part of the film, as well as to set the mood and emotional tone of the film. The most well-known scores come from films that evoke a sense of excitement and adventure. Sometimes, the film score becomes a hit and lands on top popular music charts. Prolific composer John Williams has used a large symphony orchestra with specific musical strands or elements for main characters, iconic singular riffs, and percussion and strings into motifs that capture adventure and awe. He won five Academy Awards (Oscars) and 24 Grammy Awards, Golden Globes, BAFTAs, Emmy Awards, and many nominations from all award organizations. Film composer Rachel Portman is known to compose lyrical scores that evoke emotional and lyrical elements. Film composer Anne Dudley's work has focused on many musical influences like jazz and pop with strong, memorable melodies at their center. Dudley also used electronics and synthesizers in her film scores. Both have also won Academy Awards for their film scores. Film composers create orchestration, tone, and musical motifs to create lyrical themes that become intimately linked to their movies.

Film composers use a variety of technologies to create their soundscapes. While some cross over from other audio uses, some have specific components and nuances designed for film scores and live music compositions for visual creations. All contemporary film composition work uses DAWs to record, edit, and mix music on a computer. Virtual instruments, plugins, and advanced digital editing capabilities make the job easier. Digital sample libraries are also used to emulate the sound of real instruments. Musical Instrument Digital Interface (MIDI) keyboards and controllers help composers play and record MIDI information to control virtual instruments and performance enhancement information, such as pitch and length. Microphones with preamps also enhance live instrumental and vocal performances.

Scoring stages as a location for an orchestra or live music performance started shortly after the birth of cinema, and large recording studios, with isolation booths that cut ambient noise, are a more recent invention. Film scoring stages now feature digitally controlled acoustic systems and motion control rooms with computers, monitors, and audio interfaces to handle audio processing, and innovation continues to evolve.

Video games also use sound elements in their creation. Like a film score, video game score music is written to enhance the visual and interactive elements for gamers, and designed with immersive aspects of the game's world and dynamics. Composers for video games keep interactivity in the forefront when composing for games. The music must be adaptive to heighten players' actions and activities in-game. While early video game music contained more elemental sound chips with an individual bank of sounds or short jingles, contemporary video game developers employ full orchestras in score development to heighten both the narrative and aesthetic experience. Memorable riffs leave an indelible impression on players, evoke nostalgia, and become the beginning of dance moves and full dances.

Some video games release soundtracks for fans based on the music highlighted in the game. Video game music composers are specialized artists who have to understand each games' trajectory, narrative structure, and adaptability of game scenarios, along with more traditional music theory and compositional skills. Music also cues changes to the narrative and invites interactivity. Music sets a game's mood and emotional tone, reinforces game themes, which often help with geographic or historical-based scenarios, and establishes specifics about a character or personality in-game. A music score can also help the gamer move between different areas of the game world and in-game plot points by providing repeated motifs. Increasing use of algorithms and adaptive artificial intelligence (AI) means that music can link to core gameplay, to heighten interest, excitement, and pace for the player, and have an integral role in the video game industry. Video game composers like Christopher Tin, Stephanie Economou, Charlie Rosen, and Jake Silverman have won Emmy and Grammy awards for their work. Many major entertainment awards have music categories. An environment of increased synergies, transmedia connections, and vertical integration in media business models means that music can more easily bridge traditional media genres and interactive game products.

Mixing It Up

Another aspect of music recording is mixing. Recording, also called tracking and mixing, don't require the same skills as composing. Recording music focuses on capturing music tracks while combining tracks to create different sounds. Mixing using multitrack technologies creates a master for distribution.

Like many other media, music recording and Foley use AI tools for their creative work. Machine learning techniques help recording professionals generate compositions, and analyze patterns. AI can identify suggestions and harmonization of compositions and can be used to create and enhance lyrics and recording workflow. Sampling in music recording has also been enhanced through AI tools. In addition, AI can identify riffs that might suggest copyright infringement. One term often used when a pre-existing sound is required for media use is a "needle drop". These can be used for advertising or jingles in television, film, and streaming programming. The term "needle drop" originally referred to playing a track on a vinyl record. Still, the name has continued to persist in explaining the need to purchase a previously produced song. The music is singularly purchased to enhance a specific scene or sequence in a variety of media products.

Technological Wonders

Music developed over the last century has been profoundly changed by the technologies it is inexplicably linked to. Consider that even a music box uses sound technology. The Phonautograph and Phonograph are early sound technologies from the later quarter of the 1800s. Inventor Emile Berliner's gramophone used a flat disc shape and an adjacent cutting motion to record and play sound. Sound recordings used acoustic horns and mechanical styluses as mechanical production machines. Recording artists sang or played into a giant megaphone-like horn, to be recorded by etching sound waves into the groves of the disc. In the 1920s, electrical recording was invented with the birth of radio and various other technologies. This new technology improved the recorded sound quality significantly, and microphones replaced horns as the conduit of sound and finer fidelity of recordings. Early prototypes formulated the idea for the vinyl record. As soon as the technology to record became standard, record companies created "labels", based on specific genres of music. Columbia and RCA Victor are two early companies that produced, recorded, and distributed records. This twofold ability made music more widely available and commercially more acceptable. Media consumers purchased gramophones and then, later, record players and records to hear music on demand. This was the beginning of a new and highly influential industry.

Vinyl was a breakthrough for recording development in the 1930s. Vinyl records were made from polyvinyl chloride (PVC) and created and amplified better sound quality and a more durable music recording than previous wax cylinder recordings. Innovation for better quality in recording and sound capture continued, and inventor Fritz Pfleumer's magnetic tape recording was introduced in the 1930s. This invention allowed recording to be edited together in high fidelity, creating the first magnetic tape editor position. The 1950s saw a boom in radio music and recording, proliferated by the recording industry's integration of stereo and Hi-Fi. Les Paul and Ampex Corporation's multitrack recording enabled layered recording and mixing. These systems continued revolutionizing the audio experience for music artists and lovers. Even floppy discs were used as music recording material for a time. Vinyl—in the form of 78s, Long Plays (LPs), and 45s—8-track tapes, cassette tapes, compact discs (CDs), and MP3 players have all played a part in the history of recorded music because these technologies allowed the consumer to bring the music home to play, solidifying consumers' role in music recording history and popular culture (Millard, 2005).

The mid-1970s saw the most significant single-technology change in the history of music recording. The birth of digital recording carried high-fidelity capture of the complete sound spectrum, forever altering how sound is collected, processed, reproduced, distributed, and stored. Where analog technologies transfer the original sound wave onto a physical medium like tape, digital processes convert sound waves into a mathematical sequence of 0s and 1s for processing and storage in near-perfect replication. Minimal distortion and background noise, aided by microphones and other computer filters and isolation software advances, created a new experience for listeners, consumers, and the music and recording industry. For a period, as in other media industries, technologists and creatives worked in the space between analog and digital.

The analog-to-digital transformation in the late 1990s brought digital audio recording (DAT) technology to the forefront. Digital recording has many advantages, including ease of editing, reproduction, and storage. The popular AutoTune audio processor software and programs that measure and alter pitch in vocals and other isolated areas within a music composition have also become a standard mixing component. Suppose a musician has a pitch issue during a studio performance. The audio processor software alters that vocal track to fix pitch in real-time using algorithms to interpret sonar data. Sony and Philips jointly created the CD, which additionally revolutionized the music industry. The CD's digital audio quality and durability replaced vinyl records and cassette tapes as the dominant recording and listening format until file-based formats like MP3 became standard for recording, sharing downloads, and purchase. From the artist and creator side, computer-based DAWs created an easy workflow to record, edit, mix, and manipulate audio. Digital compression codecs like.MP3 led to a new world of music distribution and streaming, changing how consumers made, bought, sold, and listened to music. AI-driven algorithms designed to suggest tailored music selections made prominent playlist contributions. Genres, styles, and sounds of music took precedence over specific track selections.

Music recording embraced digital technologies, using MIDI controllers, that help musicians interact with software instruments, plugins, and effects that enhance sound, and cloud-based collaboration, that allows musicians to connect remotely on recording projects. AI intelligence assists with music composition and arrangement, mixing and mastering, and audio analysis of content, like genre classification and vocal detection. New virtual reality and spatial audio technologies and techniques create immersive soundscapes. The economic model of music recording has also changed. Digital technologies now embed blockchain into products to ensure fair royalty distribution. Above all, streaming technology has brought advancements to music streaming platforms and protocols. The Internet of Things (IoT) has connected smart devices for interactive music experiences throughout any space.

Economic Shifts

Technological advancements and consumer taste and behavior have mutually altered the economic structure of music production. Early profit models were straightforward because consumers visited music stores to physically buy material media. This process was trackable and profitable for record labels. Shortly after the Great Depression ended, people started buying records again. Before that time, consumers were purchasing records of various kinds of music popular at the time, from jazz to classical music. Still, the financial severity of the depression altered purchasing patterns of non-essential goods. By the 1930s, four American major record companies, namely Radio Corporation of America (RCA), American Record Corporation (ARC) (which owned the Columbia and Brunswick labels), Electric and Musical Industries (EMI) and Decca controlled most of the music market.

The economic model in the early 1900s was reasonably straightforward, with record labels collecting revenues from record and jukebox sales. Bars, diners, and arcades purchased jukeboxes for music entertainment in their establishments. The owner would buy or lease a jukebox from a supplier or manufacturer, and customers would insert coins to play their choice of record available in the jukebox. The revenue was shared between the venue and the jukebox owner. The jukebox created a pay-to-play environment that brought revenue to the venue without the hassle of flipping the record.

Jukebox owners of the 1940s to 1960s did not share performance revenues with record labels. In the late 1970s, the ruling changed. Jukebox owners paid a flat performance fee that was transferred to record labels. The music royalties for songwriters, composers, and music publishers and producers involved in that song were paid through them. The flat

Figure 7.1 Beetles vinyl LP album cover.
Photograph by the author.

fee system for jukeboxes ensured that music creators and rights holders received compensation for their music being used in public venues,
which recognized the value of recorded music. Internet and digital distribution platforms transformed the economic model as consumers valued
music differently, significantly impacting the traditional revenue model
for record labels. Free digital downloads and bootleg recordings were
part of this shift. The preference to download a single song instead of an
album affected the economic structure. Piracy led to a decline in physical
sales, forcing the industry to create new content delivery models. Streaming is one of those models. Streaming services are a significant source of
revenue for music labels, driving growth after years of decline. Another
considerable revenue stream involves music licensed for television, radio,
video games, and online platforms.

Figure 7.2 45 RPM (Revolutions per minute) record on the Columbia label.
Photograph by the author.

Radio's Music Programming

Another area that radio technologies invented was radio programming. When radio broadcasting started in the early 1920s, programming consisted of news, live music performances, radio dramas, and variety shows. Radio stations also played a variety of music genres and styles. This was termed the "block programming" era because a specific radio announcer played a particular kind of music for a block of time. Interestingly, college radio continues block programming at many universities today. When it was clear that radio had become a highly popular mass entertainment medium, with the rise of national networks, radio serials, also known as "soap operas", became hugely popular during this decade. In the 1940s, radio quiz shows became a widespread phenomenon. Popular programs, such as *The $64,000 Question*, and top music radio formats, like the Top 40, played popular "hits" in pop music. This shift from block programming to branded genre styles is still used today.

In addition, the role of radio announcer shifted to disc jockey or DJ. This announcer played music on the air. The term combined "disc", referring to the disc-shaped record, and "jockey", "riding the gain" on the radio board to fade the song in and out or cross-fade on two record players in the radio studio. Audience members would use cassette tapes and a tape player to record songs between DJ banter, coining the phrase mixed tape.

Local DJs built a notoriety, appearing at 1950s "sock hop" dances, where they would spin music live and talk between songs. Sometimes, they would be the master of ceremonies (MC) at events and publicly appear as local celebrities in parades. This kind of radio announcer developed into the professional party DJ and club DJ positions, away from radio station environments. More recently, shock jock personalities and morning zoo formats have altered the DJ's role from announcer to branded personality. Stations played the top 40 most

Figure 7.3 60-minute TDK audio cassette tape.

Photograph by the author.

popularly charted songs based on revenues, and often from the *Billboard* magazine charts, repeatedly throughout the day. This trend dominated radio through the 1960s and 70s.

As FM radio became more popular, stations began carving their programming into specific formats that targeted specific demographics. The MOR (middle of the road) format played popular songs from various genres. AOR (album-oriented rock) gained traction in the late 1960s, playing album cuts, rock, and progressive rock. Classic rock focuses on rock hits from the 60s and 70s. Country music formats became popular in the 1970s and 1980s. Rhythm and blues (R&B) urban contemporary formats playing hip-hop also emerged in the 1970s and 1980s. Niche formats have continued to target demographics from the 1980s, and these niche stations continue into contemporary radio business models. FM radio fostered the current music industry business model by updating how music was broadcast and consumed. A broader range of programming also enlarged the recording music industry, supporting more stations than AM radio and promoting better audio quality. AM radio did broadcast music, but when FM stereo became focused on music because of its better sound, AM radio switched to news and talk formats. New music genres like rock, punk, disco, and later, AOR flourished.

In the 1950s, television replaced radio as the most popular home entertainment medium. As music, talk, and news became more prevalent, Top 40 and rock and roll music dominated radio programming. When FM radio was introduced in the 1960s, offering Hi-Fi sound, FM radio stations tended to have more specialized formats like AOR and public radio. All-news radio formats became popular to stay relevant because most radio listening was done in cars. Deregulation in the 1980s and '90s led to growing media consolidation, while satellite and internet radio emerged as competition. Talk radio also grew during this decade.

A portion of a record company's time on a musical artist is spent on promotion. Contemporary digital media can be a prominent link to promotion, but bootlegged and leaked digital copies have also become a problem. While a record company, or label, was required until recently, musicians and bands can now release their work online and re-release their music under their label to increase their profit margin. A lot of this has to do with any record label contract they signed. Current promotion strategies include digital platforms and streaming services, social media, vinyl releases, innovative and interactive immersive experiences, and independent promotion companies, where artists retain rights when the music is distributed for sale. Automation, satellite radio, streaming, and digital tools, such as Discord for podcasting and other programming, led to more consolidated ownership and less variety in formatting for all kinds of programming.

Industry Scandals

The radio industry also had scandals that shaped the nature of the industry and its continued popularity. The radio adaptation of HG Wells' play *War of the Worlds* (1938/1997) was narrated by Orson Welles and broadcast in 1938. The realistic radio drama about an extraterrestrial Martian invasion caused panic among radio listeners across the country, who thought it was an actual news broadcast because it was produced as a series of news bulletins interrupting a regular program. Eventually, most listeners realized that it was a fictional story. The effects of this show on media consumers gained the attention of government regulators, researchers, and marketing executives, and initiated an enduring conversation about the power and influence of the media and media effects. Another scandal was called the Payola Scandal (1950s) where radio DJs were caught accepting bribes to play certain songs on air. When a DJ plays a song they were bribed to play, they illegally participate in "payola". This persistent practice still happens in the contemporary music industry. Record executives and DJs have received fines and jail time for participating in payola-focused crimes. The practice of illegal pay-for-play is also seen on streaming platforms, where undisclosed payments are shared to promote an artist or song. The ethical implications include suggesting a song is more popular than it is, based on promotions and voting for specific songs. Record companies also try to pay for precise placement on the stream. Influencer marketing and stream playlists can be manipulated by AI algorithms by "upvoting" a song on a streaming app.

As the music moved more into digital media, companies like Napster, with its peer-to-peer (P2P) file-sharing application, allowed users to download and send media to each other, violating copyright. Napster originated as a free file-sharing service, but after mounting legal fees from copyright infringements for unauthorized uses of music, they filed for bankruptcy in 2002. The company has been reorganized several times since its inception. Even though they had significant issues from the company's P2P file sharing, Napster made an indelible imprint on media and altered the music industry. P2P threatened the traditional music business model and paved the way for the consumer distribution model of the contemporary music environment (Dowling, 2022).

Another scandal facing music was the idea of sampling, which also increased when music became more digitally produced. Combining the ease of duplication without quality loss, coupled with the constant creation of new content and the limited musical combinations available, creates an environment of easy replication. While sampling parts and riffs of songs has been around for some time, AI use has proliferated unauthorized use. In the same ways that deepfakes can misrepresent people, AI can recreate voices and add them to songs. AI can slightly alter songs so the original artist sounds somewhat different, perhaps more energetic or melancholy. AI sampling can affect accuracy, security, and bias, changing someone's voice with filters. Legal issues of public and private use, intellectual property, and consent for use have become more central in a digital environment. Sending anonymously produced songs using lyrics of someone singing, generated by AI, continues to float through social media, and the issue becomes increasingly problematic when those producers try to monetize the work. While someone's singing voice is not copyrightable, a name is copyrighted, and appropriation of identity can also be proven. The work and performance of musical artists and singers are copyrightable material. Copyright, security, privacy, and identity/branding guidelines are not currently set for all areas of AI use in the entertainment and media industry, and legal precedent has not been established in many areas of AI use.

Online Distribution

In recent years, the main boost to recording and consuming music has come from online distribution sites like Pandora, SoundCloud, and Spotify. Most distribution streaming sites have audio platforms with free services, commercial revenue, and pay-to-listen subscription services. The platform allows musicians to record and share their music and podcasts easily. The sound-related work can be shared publicly or privately, and uploads and online listening are free with commercial breaks, similar to the radio monetization model. Musicians can also monetize and distribute their work through these sites, with third-party integrators employed to help monetize. Music distribution sites are global, bringing in music and pulling in listeners from all over the world. Unique features to the digital experience of these sites involve commenting on tracks, reposting songs, connecting and networking with other musicians and content creators, and using hashtags to promote songs, which brings the listener into the experience as a participant in ways beyond paying for a product.

Sound in Social and Mobile

Sound is increasingly being integrated into social media and on mobile phones. At one time, consumers purchased ringtones for their phones. Social audio and voice-based social media communication have continued to provide media consumers with exciting ways to receive information and engage audiences. Content creators use live audio to personalize the customer experience and foster meaningful interactions. Some social users keep the sound off, so this additional sensory experience is not experienced by all customers.

In some cases, on TikTok mainly, sound can gather users into a community of like experiences like duets, where participants can browse the app to sing with a specific creator. Other trends include the Sea Shanty trend, the Daily Dice Roll Walk trend, and a variety of dance challenges based on particular songs. TikTok's algorithm also specifically isolates popular sounds on the platform, identifying the most used sounds and songs on TikTok and focusing on current music trends. Music streaming services also publicize TikTok trends that users like discovering and listening to. Social media also curates compilations of viral songs and the latest emerging trends. As shared in many chapters, legal issues around data privacy, copyright, and security are becoming increasingly important because of digital technologies. ByteDance, a private Chinese company, owns TikTok. China's 2017 National Intelligence Law compels any organization, including private ones, to assist or cooperate with investigations that might expose sensitive information from millions of American users and provide surveillance data and trends. Tiktok's owners have shared that China may have accessed TikTok data from US users, that a former employee claimed that the Chinese Communist Party accessed TikTok user data for political purposes, and that China-based employees can access European and American user data under certain circumstances. TikTok has confirmed that US user data that involves monetary transactions are stored in China. TikTok's privacy policy shares that it allows the transmission of user data outside the United States (Ke, 2023).

Things to Consider

- Brainstorm how specific artists have used digital technologies to capitalize on their brand and sound.
- Develop a list of artists who have become successful through exposure on TikTok.
- Deliberate on security and data privacy in the contemporary digital landscape.
- Contemplate ways that artists and musicians can further protect their creative work from illegal downloading and use without financial ramifications.
- Study some specific legal cases involving music sampling and illegal likeness usage.
- List the different technologies mentioned in this chapter.
- Consider the global impact of current music and the digital reach and footprint of specific music styles. How does this impact culture?

Takeaways

- The technology it is inexplicably linked to, has profoundly affected the music that developed and became popular over the last century.
- Film composers use a variety of technologies to create their soundscapes.
- P2P file sharing was an essential step in contemporary streaming.
- Technology is used when creating music. Technology and equipment go into making, producing, and playing music.
- Having a significant digital media presence throughout one's life means it is easy to forget what life was like before digital media existed.
- Name some of your chapter takeaways.

References

Ament, V.T. (2014). *The Foley grail: The art of performing sound for film, games, and animation.* Routledge.

Burgess, R.J. (2014). *The history of music production.* Oxford University Press.

Dowling, S. (2022, February 24). *Napster turns 20: How it changed the music industry.* BBC News. https://www.bbc.com/culture/article/20190531-napster-turns-20-how-it-changed-the-music-industry

Ke, S. (2023, March 24). *Asia fact check lab: Can TikTok share US user data with China's government?* Radio Free Asia. https://www.rfa.org/english/news/afcl/fact-check-tiktok-03242023144611.html

Millard, A. (2005). *America on record: A history of recorded sound.* Cambridge University Press.

Trento, S., & De Götzen, A. (2011, July). Foley sounds vs real sounds, in *Sound and Music Computing Conference (SMC2011).*

Wells, H.G. (1938/1997). *The war of the worlds.* Dover Publications

8 Radio, Audio, and Podcasting

Audio is the electronic representation of sound; energy that travels as waves to a receiver and is perceived in the ear and felt in the body. Sound travels through audio, the electronic pathway. In the history of media, sounds are recorded, transmitted, or reproduced through technology to become audible frequencies. Listeners hear programmed audible frequencies through radio, podcasts, and other media and technologies. Not all sound frequencies are audible to humans. Some are only heard by animals, and other technologies tune in to specific frequencies. This chapter focuses on the history of radio and audio and its digital transformation into internet and satellite radio and podcasting. The birth of AM (amplitude modulation) and FM (frequency modulation) radio, the government oversight of the medium, the proliferation of different kinds of programming, noncommercial radio, and transformational modes of delivery, like podcasting, are reviewed in this chapter.

Origin of AM

A convergence of concentrated work on sound recording and transmission in the late 1800s and early 1900s solidified the beginnings of audio through the invention of radio. In the late 1800s, Guglielmo Marconi achieved progress by experimenting with wireless telegraphy, which created Morse code. Heinrich Hertz and Nikola Tesla were among the first to conduct sound experiments with electromagnetic waves. Marconi's transmission from England to Canada marks the first recorded transatlantic wireless transmission, and Reginald Fessenden successfully created the first broadcast of voice and music. Lee de Forest created the Audion tube, which made radio waves better. This early increase in sound quality through improved technology is a thread of media innovation still seen in our contemporary world. These early inventions paved the way for radio broadcasting and all that would come during and afterward in audio design, transmission, and recording. The first radio

DOI: 10.4324/9781003397588-10

station, KDKA, was launched in Pittsburgh, PA in 1920. This also kicked off the link between media and politics, when the results of the 1920 United States presidential election were broadcast live on KDKA. Like all the ones after it, this station's call letters identify the station and a frequency where listeners could tune in on their radio. No specific governmental entity had jurisdiction over this new medium at the time. In 1927, the Federal Radio Commission (FRC) was created to manage radio media. The FRC became the Federal Communication Commission (FCC) in 1935. The Commission designated that radio stations west of the Mississippi River start their call letters with the letter K and East of the River, the letter W was used.

AM is the first kind of radio to be consistently used. The technology for AM is based on a system of wireless transmitters and receivers. AM stations occupy the frequencies of 540 kHz to 1700 kHz on the radio dial. Each radio station is granted a license to broadcast a specific range of power. An AM radio station has a specific amplitude frequency that connects with a radio when the radio dial is tuned to that station's frequency. The wavelengths of AM radio signals vary in size but are larger than FM radio signals. The radio station encodes music or information into radio

Figure 8.1 Zenith Wave Magnet radio.
Photograph by the author.

waves through modulation. The wave is broadcast onto a particular frequency number on the electromagnetic spectrum picked up by the radio antenna. The broadcast's carrier wave stays at the same frequency while sound waves change its strength. This is how AM radio works.

Commercial radio took off from that first broadcast and moved into what historians call the Golden Age of Radio. Radio stations created new broadcast programming for consumers, like music, comedy, drama, news, and comedy. The timed daily or weekly schedule was integrated into people's daily habits. The Golden Age is known for many breakout programs; producers and radio programming became a central focus of many people's homes. While it was sometimes joked that the radio became the new hearth of the home at that time, even the furniture changed to accommodate the electronic equipment, it was most often placed in a living room so many people could gather around and listen. Early radios were relatively large technological pieces that were not moved around and could be very ornately designed. Radio "furniture" paved the way for music consoles and entertainment systems, which were also styled and integrated into furniture. As radios became increasingly small and mobile, they were officially added to cars in the 1950s, at the height of radio popularity.

Figure 8.2 1940s Collector's Edition Radio CR-3 Crosley Radio.
Photograph by the author.

Formation of FM

Next came FM radio. Edwin Armstrong's 1930s invention of FM radio increased audio quality and static resistance in a technological underpinning still used today. FM commercial stations are authorized on frequencies 92.1 MHz to 107.9 MHz, which match channels 221 through 300 on a radio dial. FM differs from AM because FM uses frequency modulation, and AM uses an amplitude modulation style. FM has a straight line of waves within a parameter, and AM waves look like hills of waves. FM uses a different signal than AM, which carries more information and gives clearer sound with less static. From a physics perspective, AM radio waves have lower frequencies and much larger wavelengths that can move through solid objects. FM radio waves have higher frequencies but smaller wavelengths that cannot travel through objects. This is why listeners can sometimes receive AM radio programming from quite a distance at night. Listeners would stay up later, turning the dial to find stations in towns and cities far away from them. This helped spread a variety of different musical styles throughout the country. The FCC website shares the engineering history behind AM and FM radio and spectrum licenses.

Radio Technologies

Radio stations have used a variety of technology over the years. Radio boards have seen many upgrades, from pots to sliders to digital buttons, and transmitters and antennas have become increasingly more sophisticated. An antenna is required to carry the audio signal to the audience through their radio. Receivers in the form of radios used to be the only way to hear radio programming, but in contemporary broadcasting, computers and mobile phones can receive a radio signal. Some stations push programming to air and also to digital audio broadcast (DAB) technology for internet radio. Computers and automation systems help station managers organize and control music and commercials. Radio Data System (RDS) encoders send text and metadata like names of songs and traffic alerts to various in-home and in-car receivers. Station malfunctions can lead to dead air. Stations use silence detectors to notify management of missed programming and to start automated programming (Bottomley, 2020).

Operations and Management

The structure of a radio station has changed over the years with growing regional and national network ownership. However, there are still more than 15,000 radio stations across the country. Companies like Audacy and iHeartMedia Inc. own many stations, and others own one or two. Radio stations are also in over 250 countries (Central Intelligence Agency, n.d.). In general, a radio station has a variety of management, including a station manager, operations manager, programming director, chief engineer, and sales manager, as well as sales and office staff. The on-air talent includes Disc jockeys (DJs), hosts, and announcers. Stations profit primarily through on-air and website advertising and sponsored content.

Radio stations often have a promotion department that arranges giveaways, content, and public promotional events. They may also populate and edit the webpage and communicate with station fans. Other times, news staff write stories and update information materials on a radio website. Another important unit is the production department. This department is responsible for creating and overseeing the audio content produced before it goes on the air or on the web or other platforms. Examples of production content include local commercials, promotional stories, and comedic bits. The audio and content producers work with station talent to produce all content. Independent radio stations complete the same tasks as large radio stations, but the staff is smaller, and

Figure 8.3 1960s Zenith transistor radio.
Photograph by the author.

employees may do several jobs. Radio station management generally involves understanding radio operations, proficiency in audio editing and other technical skills, content creation, the ability to conduct interviews, a sense of FCC regulations, and communication and organization. Small stations may have three or four staff, and large stations may have over 30 employees. The number of staff depends on the market size of the station and the station format.

Programming and Formats

Technology drove radio's development, but programming and formats also greatly influenced radio's popularity. These formats were a technology in themselves, ensuring content was provided for the listener at regularly scheduled intervals in a broadcast hour. Radio shifted to music formats, and talk shows through the latter half of the 1900s. From a programming perspective, music has played top billing on radio for many years. Historically, radio programming focused on live music performances in the classical, jazz, big band, and swing music genres. When Top 40 radio became popular, it connected record companies and radio music play. This kind of music attracted young audiences with rock, pop, country, and rhythm and blues (R&B) hits. DJs became the name for the announcers who introduced songs and, in some cases, became local or national talent if the radio program became syndicated programming. DJs like Dick Clark, Jack Leroy Cooper, Alan Freed, Wolfman Jack, Casey Kasem, Annie Nightingale, Martha Quinn, and Robin Quivers gained recognition. The power of the DJ to break new acts at large radio stations opened a new era for radio talent. The morning and late afternoon radio slots were considered "drive time", when most consumers listened to the radio as they drove to and from work. This allowed DJs to share new and popular musical acts, slotted in between news, sports, weather, and traffic reports. For many years, DJs formatted their hours using a clock model. At the top of the hour, DJs were required by the FCC to share the station ID and call letters. Commercials occurred at specific times across the hour, and then music and perhaps public service announcements (PSAs) were shared.

Government Oversight

More than 100 years ago, the United States government instituted the Wireless Ship Act of 1910, to get a handle on the new media technology called radio. This act made it mandatory for ships with 50 or more passengers, traveling over 200 nautical miles from US ports, to have radio equipment and a radio operator for safety. This was the first governmental requirement designated for radios and radio operators. The act also supported the idea that ships could communicate via radio, regardless of their communication system. This was also an issue because radios were designed differently and did not share the same signal components. The stakeholders had to collaborate. The FRC Act of 1912 made operating a radio station without a federal license illegal. Additionally, it required ships to be on constant alert for distress signals. Two years earlier, flaws in the 1910 Act created an environment that prevented the Titanic's SOS distress signal from being heard because of radio signal interference.

Once the FRC transitioned to the FCC, interstate and international communications regulations were created for radio, television, wire, satellite, and cable. Media oversight started with the Radio Act of 1920. One main issue included who could own a license to run a radio station. Individuals need to apply to the FCC to obtain a license—the Communication Act of 1934 regulated telephone, telegraph, and radio communication. The FCC needed to give more opportunities for spectrum-based services to small, women-owned, and minority-owned businesses. This act opened the door to varied and equitable ownership programming across the United States.

The 1960s saw an increase in diverse ownership. The 1965 FCC Policy Statement also included diversifying control of mass communications media. Many of these policies were based on court rulings that reversed comparative hearing results. In 1978, the FCC specifically outlined the use of minority ownership policies and introduced other programs to increase minority interest in the secondary license market. The Telecommunications Act of 1996 was designed to improve and promote competition and reduce regulation. The 1996 Act was an amendment and extension of the 1934 Act. The overarching goal was to open competition to allow any communications company or business to compete in any market against another. The act: led to media mergers and the vertically and horizontally integrated environment in contemporary media; reduced regulations on the cross ownership of media outlets in local markets and created less competition within media-related industries; and shared provisions to prevent monopolies, but the industry also saw consolidation ownerships.

The Emergency Broadcast System (EBS) was created in the 1950s to address the American people during a national emergency. The system was redesigned in the 1990s, and the name was changed to the Emergency Alert System (EAS). Emergency authorities can use this system to share information with the public through different media platforms. Stations are required to broadcast national alerts. The FCC, Federal Emergency Management Agency (FEMA), and the National Oceanic and Atmospheric Administration each play a part in the contemporary EAS national warning system. The system also shares important National Weather Service alerts and AMBER alerts. Mobile integration has also moved the Wireless Emergency Alerts (WEA) forward. Mobile phone users can receive federal, state, local, tribal, and territorial public alerts broadcast from cell towers to any enabled device (FEMA, n.d.). In 2023, a national WEA test alert message was conducted to capture data on the alert's geographic reach to the public. Information will help many safety-related groups, including public safety officials, expand the alert system (Shukla, 2023; Gill, 2020; Romo-Murphy et al., 2011; Birowo, 2010; Moody, 2009). The FCC and FEMA will work together to analyze the reporting system data. The Commission has jurisdiction in all 50 states, the District of Columbia, and US territories. The FCC promotes competition, innovation, and investment in broadband services and facilities and supports the nation's economy by ensuring an appropriate competitive framework for communications technology, keeps the best use of spectrum domestically and internationally, revises media regulations, and provides leadership to strengthen US communications infrastructure. In contemporary oversight, the independent US government agency is the primary authority for communication law, regulation, and technological media innovation. The commission also shares information through social media, YouTube, and GitHub. Consumers can share concerns that shape federal enforcement and consumer protection related to media through the complaint center available at the FCC.

Military Media

The Armed Forces Radio Service and American Forces Network (AFN) have been part of military life for close to one hundred years. In the 1940s, the Voice of America (VOA) radio station, part of the United States Information Agency (USIA) and its programming, broadcast over 3200 programs to 40 countries each week (VOA, 2023). The programming was designed to promote American democracy and values. VOA is still available today, reaching a weekly global audience of more than 326 million people through radio, television, mobile and social media, and the internet (VOA, n.d.). Later, in the 1950s, Radio Free Europe/Radio Liberty (RFE/RL) was "established at the beginning of the Cold War to transmit uncensored news and information to audiences behind the Iron Curtain" and played a significant role in the collapse of communism and the rise of democracies in post-communist Europe (RFE/RL, n.d.). Their programs are broadcast in 27 languages in 23 countries through various methods, including the digital television network. Along with these radio-based communication innovations, American-owned pirate radio stations were set up in certain areas to broadcast music and information from offshore locations.

During the 1950s and the Cold War movement—which was the label for high tensions between the US and capitalism, and the Soviet Union and communism—RFE/RL began operating to broadcast information and news across geographic boundaries into communist countries in the area they could not enter, known as the Iron Curtain. This was where the Soviet Union blocked satellites and all Western materials, media, and otherwise. Radio Free Europe focused on Eastern European countries, while Radio Liberty focused on the Soviet Union and its surrounding satellite states. American broadcasters based in Munich, West Germany, transmitted their radio signals toward these geographic areas to counter communist propaganda and censorship and share uncensored news and political analysis to heighten diplomacy efforts and influence foreign public opinion. The effort was primarily funded openly through the US Congress's Board for International Broadcasting. Later, RFE/RL expanded broadcasts to central Asia and other areas, and the programming continues to operate and be funded through the US Agency for Global Media.

Pirate Radio

However, not all media had an interest in following the FCC Act. In the US, operating pirate i.e. illegal radio stations, are under the perview of the FCC (FCC, n.d.). Unauthorized or "pirate" radio stations are when someone runs a radio station without a license from the FCC, and they go beyond the emission limits set by the Commission's rules. "From their vessels, they broadcasted rock-n-roll music, which could scarcely be heard on public radio stations at the time" (Hoeven, 2012, p. 928) Some early and pirate radio actions are seen in the current internet radio movement (Melchior, 2019).

Sound Qualities

FM Radio had better sound quality than AM radio, and album cuts or album-oriented rock (AOR) formats became a popular music format, separate from the Top 40. This allowed exposure to more extended album-oriented and progressive rock. The 1970s added the appeal of the drive-time morning shows that capitalized on DJ personalities, duos, and team or crew that entertained with comedy and call-in banter between music selections. Media consumers tuned in to hear increasingly outrageous comedy bits and prank phone calls from their favorite media personalities. Some programs were purchased for national syndication when national radio networks became a new business model. Syndicated shows of famous on-air personalities strengthened unified branding and popularized shock jocks, political talk radio, and sports talk radio personalities who could be heard daily across the world as part of network programming. The 1996 Telecommunications Act allowed companies to own multiple radio stations, leading to consolidation and big companies buying many stations. After this shift, the radio industry became more corporate and focused on niche audiences. In the 2000s, satellite radio, such as SiriusXM, and online streaming gave people more media options and encouraged new ideas. Radio companies have tried to find a balance between the local advertising needs and the national needs of the corporation that owns them. Some stations have syndicated morning and afternoon shows, with local news, sports, and weather peppered throughout, to give a local feel to the programming while curbing staff and management costs.

Streaming Audio

Now, many listeners use a mobile phone device linked through Wi-Fi to a streaming app for on-demand listening, with or without commercials, depending on the consumer's chosen subscription. Spotify "radio" is a feature that provides listener subscribers with the opportunity to gather a group of songs or artists and mix them into a program of "like" music in the same vein as traditional radio. Contemporary radio has continued to provide music on-air while internet radio and streaming apps invent new ways to duplicate many components of traditional radio, just not over airwaves. The National Association of Broadcasters (NAB) has discussed difficulties in managing the magnetic spectrum, which is responsible for transmitting signals to radio and TV stations. For legacy or terrestrial radio, as it is sometimes called, additional regulatory issues with ownership, licenses, and content standards have plagued broadcasting. The FCC has designed spectrum auctions and allocations to give permits to companies and potential owners. Traditional media had to adjust to meet the changing demands of consumers due to increased competition from online streaming services. The industry is working to balance local consumer needs with national needs. If radio becomes less popular, concerns about emergency response at both local and federal levels will increase. Legacy media has different restrictions because of FCC oversight, affecting economic and business models and revenue from broadcasting platforms. Broadcasters must also continually pitch the viability and usefulness of radio and television and engage audiences on new tech and platforms. Several European countries, like Norway, have turned off FM signals and FM broadcasting for an all-digital system called Digital Audio Broadcasting (DAB+) (Jauert et al., 2017).

The NAB is working on ways to preserve the viability of local radio amid continued station consolidation. The NAB Depend on AM Radio campaign was designed to heighten awareness about the importance of radio use in cars. An estimated 82 million monthly listeners listen to AM radio for news, weather updates, sports, traffic, talk shows, world language programming, and emergency communication (Inside Radio, 2023). Several automakers have proposed the removal of radios in cars, which prompted the AM for Every Vehicle Act, which requires manufacturers to have AM radio available devices. Reasons to keep AM radio in cars include access to timely public safety and information. Another concern for the radio industry is the possibility of additional performance fees. Local radio stations pay music royalties to songwriters, publishers, performers, and record labels based on the number of times it is played. Royalty groups include performing rights organizations like the American Society of Composers, Authors and Publishers (ASCAP), Broadcast Music Inc. (BMI), the Society of European Stage Authors and Composers (SESAC), and Global Music Rights (GMR). At one time, stations reported music on paper logs, but now automated software is used to note songs and commercials played on the air. A new performance act proposes that radio stations may have to pay extra fees for broadcasting music or go through a process to determine rates based on economic, competitive, and programming factors (Stroink & Edwards, 2021).

Wired for Sound

Microphones with varied ranges of sound collection, called pick-up patterns, helps record the best and most appropriate kinds of audio. Analog and, more recently, digital audio recorders collect sound directly into digital formats, which removes the step of collecting through analog means and then transferring to digital. The invention of amplifiers and synthesizers also significantly impacted sound creation and manipulation completed on digital audio workstations (DAWs). Sound effects and synthesizers are commonly used to improve the overall sound quality. Artificial intelligence is increasingly used in apps and software to match algorithms, fix mistakes in recording and sync, and alter sound using automatic dialogue replacement (ADR) before completion. Once the audio finds its final destination, it might be formatted in Dolby Atmos or other surround formats, allowing for an immersive sound experience that matches the cinematic visuals.

The original economic model, and most models today, involved commercials placed in radio programming. Some commercials were 30 seconds, and others were 60 seconds long. Radio announcers learned to back-time their music and banter to account for commercial breaks. Local commercials were sold by the local sales team and created in-house by the production director, and national commercials were sent by mail in a reel or downloaded by satellite. A radio station's business office accounts for items broadcast during the day by requiring the on-air operators to sign logs noting content aired. These logs serve as affidavits, documenting that specific content was actually played. This process may also be automated through broadcast management software. Missed commercials should be aired at a similar time. Selling commercial time is the basis of radio economics and radio viability as a business. Radio stations also simulcast sports and other programming for a fee paid to the station. The flagship stations collaborate with local stations for news, sports, and public affairs reporting. Satellite radio, internet radio, and podcasting have all adopted radio's economic model and current radio programming, and are also growing many new genres. On-demand access moved the consumer away from timed habitual listening, which altered the technology and the habit. At one time, legacy stations had radio talent, production managers and staff, sales managers and staff, promotion departments and staff, business staff, and traffic/sales compliance staff. In contemporary legacy media, several radio stations owned by one company may share staff, and programming from a flagship show can air on all other stations. Syndicated radio shows have also been adopted throughout the radio business. This involved talent leasing the rights to their show to other radios for a fee without going through a network structure.

Podcasting

One of the most significant segment shifts in radio and audio is the popularity of podcasting, which has become a popular medium in the 2000s. This new way of packaging audio programming started as audio blogs, available for file sharing download in the 1980s. The free audio files downloaded through a Really Simple Syndication (RSS) web feed were later made available on the website in real time and loaded to product service repositories for a fee, like the Apple's iTunes business model. This monetization for on-demand niche content was more convenient than scheduled radio broadcasts. Once podcasters could find sites to gain exposure for their content, podcasting became very popular (Bottomley, 2015).

During the pandemic, the early 2020s saw a significant boost in podcasting for entertainment and educational purposes (Nee & Santana, 2022; Grunow, 2020). Long-time MTV video jockey (VJ) and radio announcer Adam Curry's *The Daily Source Code* podcast, an independent podcast initially, became one of the early podcasts downloadable to an iPod in Apple's podcast catalog directory. Another product, RealAudio streaming, was slow to be used because of the early download speeds but eventually became popular. The generation of RSS feeds was a significant milestone in podcast development, and before long, consumers were finding, listening, and subscribing more efficiently, which encouraged and drove growth (JRE Clips, 2020). Some podcasts were amateur in sound; others followed the well-known, highly produced radio-style format. Radio talk shows and serialized dramas influenced podcasts, and podcast apps and hosting websites supported creators, strengthening the audio platform. Podcasts cover various topics, including sports, society, comedy, culture, lifestyle, and true crime. They also explore unique subjects not found elsewhere. The popularity of podcasts is still increasing, and podcast hosting and producing are now considering new ways to monetize programming.

Noncommercial Radio

Another radio entity initially funded by the government is public broadcasting and public radio. In 1970, National Public Radio (NPR) was created to produce and distribute radio news and cultural and children's programming nationwide to NPR member stations specifically. The Corporation for Public Broadcasting (CPB) is a nonprofit organization that helps distribute government funds to local public media and promotes public broadcasting. Corporate sponsors, foundations, membership drives, and state and local governments provide the most funding. Critics of American public broadcasting note that public broadcasting is not a necessary organization with expanded consumer media choices and should not receive federal funding.

College radio stations, run by educational institutions, provide essential training for broadcasters. Some college radio stations serve as partially syndicated hubs for NPR. College radio stations train students for careers in broadcasting and radio and are affiliated with a college or university, often broadcasting an alternative music format. Some are commercial-free, and student fees, fundraising, and advertising fund others. The first college radio station began broadcasting in 1920 in upstate New York. College radio gained popularity in the 1980s for playing diverse genres like punk rock, alternative rock, grunge, jazz, hip hop, indie rock, and local or underground acts. Early airplay on college stations helped launch musical careers. Because of the nature of student management and leadership, DJs often had total control over their playlists and their block programming while still following FCC regulations. Each October, World College Radio Day brings awareness of college radio and its importance for new music discovery.

Tech Trends

Radio is an accessible, inexpensive medium that reaches broad global audiences, and the technology that makes radio work is inexpensive. The receivers (radios) are mobile and do not require internet connectivity. People can listen anywhere within a station's broadcast range, adding flexibility, reach, and accessibility. After initial infrastructure investments, broadcasting over the airwaves is an inexpensive way to reach listeners and is incredibly accessible to individuals. Radio is essential for emergency broadcasts, news updates, live reporting, and safety information. It also helps create a sense of community with listeners. Local radio provides locally focused content that has helped radio forge a local identity and bond with listeners. Radio creates a relationship between listeners and local on-air talent and can continue as a viable resource in the contemporary digital world. Short-range wireless technology, called Bluetooth, started in the late 1990s, using radio waves to connect technologies (Bluetooth®, n.d.). Dutch engineer and inventor Jaap Haartsen holds the patent for Bluetooth technology. While working at Ericsson corporation in the mid-1990s, Haartsen worked on connecting electronic components without cables through low-power radio frequencies (EPO, n.d.).

Another technological trend central to the radio industry is automation. These systems, created in the 1950s and used through the 1990s, were designed to provide automated programming without a person standing by to act as talent. First, reel-to-reel and cart systems were invented to record prerecorded news and information at a specific time. Automation decreased the number of talent and board operators required to be in a radio station. That, along with satellite transmission of programming, reduced costs for radio. Automation was also used to simulcast the AM and FM stations simultaneously, providing programming for both at the cost of one kind of programming. Artificial intelligence (AI) continues to increase radio automation. Using AI-powered radio hosts and voices saves money by reducing the need for human talent, but also leads to job losses. Radio continues to look for ways to streamline operations and reduce manual labor. Audio, the carrier signal of radio, and the digital continuation of radio programming in the form of podcasting illustrate an interesting analog-to-digital transformation that shares connections back to the early days of radio. Innovators and inventors of early radio provided technologies that are still relevant today.

Aural Effects

Podcasting has become an increasingly popular way to communicate information. While many podcasts are created and then loaded onto platforms like Soundcloud or indexed on Spotify through the anchor hosting platform, others create podcasts for digital education platforms to foster collaboration and interaction for learners. In one study, researchers used the

Instructional Materials Motivation Survey (IMMS) to quantitatively assess the effects of podcast integration on learning. The study results indicated that students were positively motivated by the addition of podcasts in their online courses. Specifically, they found the information necessary and relevant to their learning (Bollinger et al., 2010). Multimedia and website content have also benefited from audio components (Spinelli & Dann, 2019). Another increasingly important focus area is immersive media experiences, including immersive audio through virtual, augmented, and extended reality. One study used semi-structured open-ended interviews and online surveys to gather data using qualitative analysis software to identify emergent themes centered around distance perception, multi-sensory access, and emersion factors, specifically: "The ability for a user to become fully immersed within an IME was intrinsically linked by participants to the quality of all aspects of the production, both technological (e.g., ability to replicate accurate sensory information) and non-technological (e.g., quality of narrative)" (Turner et al., 2021). The study concluded that collaboration with professionals in the sound industry is an integral part of future effects research and that personal user experience is very individual and varies from consumer to consumer.

Things to Consider

- Name the different technologies mentioned in this chapter.
- Trace the connections between radio and other early media and create one timeline for radio, television, and cinema.
- Deliberate over the future of radio and its importance in emergency preparedness.
- Create some case studies of popular radio shock jock hosts.
- Brainstorm ways in which the consolidation of station ownership has affected the viability of radio.

Takeaways

- Radio technology is an accessible device for scheduled entertainment and military and emergency purposes. It has gone through many eras, and inventors have reinvented it through digital media, internet radio, and podcasting.
- Radio is an influential media communication method that soared in popularity over the 20th century. People connect with its simplicity, versatility, and variety of programming, from music to news, sports, and talk radio.
- Radio is free.
- Name some of your chapter takeaways.

References

Birowo, M.A. (2010). The use of community radio in managing natural disasters in Indonesia. *Bulletin of the American Society for Information Science and Technology, 36*(5), 18–21.

Bluetooth®. (n.d.). *Origin of the Bluetooth name.* Bluetooth®. https://www.bluetooth.com/about-us/bluetooth-origin/

Bolliger, D.U., Supanakorn, S., & Boggs, C. (2010). Impact of podcasting on student motivation in the online learning environment. *Computers & Education, 55*(2), 714–722.

Bottomley, A.J. (2015). Podcasting: A decade in the life of a "new" audio medium: Introduction. *Journal of Radio & Audio Media, 22*(2), 164–169.

Bottomley, A.J. (2020). *Sound streams: A cultural history of radio-internet convergence.* University of Michigan Press.

Central Intelligence Agency. (n.d.). *The world factbook.* Central Intelligence Agency. https://www.cia.gov/the-world-factbook/countries

EPO. (n.d.) *Jaap Haartsen.* European Patent Office. https://www.epo.org/en/news-events/european-inventor-award/meet-the-finalists/jaap-haartsen

FCC. (n.d.). *Pirate radio.* Federal Communications Commission. https://www.fcc.gov/enforcement/areas/pirate-radio.

FEMA. (n.d.). *Integrated Public Alert & Warning System.* FEMA.gov. https://www.fema.gov/emergency-managers/practitioners/integrated-public-alert-warning-system.

Gill, G.S. (2020). When all else fails, amateur radio becomes the lifeline of communications during a disaster. *International Journal of Emergency Services, 9*(2), 109–121.

Grunow, T.R. (2020). Podcasting during the pandemic and beyond. *Teaching About Asia in a Time of Pandemic,* 131–139.

Hoeven, A. van der. (2012). The famous music heritage of the Dutch pirates: Illegal radio and cultural identity. *Media, Culture & Society, 34*(8), 927–943.

Inside Radio. (2023, June 2). *Here are the markets with the largest proportion of AM radio listeners.* https://www.insideradio.com/free/here-are-the-markets-with-the-largest-proportion-of-am-radio-listeners/article_83a95ef8-0117-11ee-be56-63d806f6c01d.html#:~:text=244).,U.S.%20AM%2FFM%20radio%20listeners

Jauert, P., Ala-Fossi, M., Föllmer, G., Lax, S., & Murphy, K. (2017). The future of radio revisited: Expert perspectives and future scenarios for radio media in 2025. *Journal of Radio & Audio Media, 24*(1), 7–27.

JRE Clips. (2020, March 4). *Adam Curry was the first podcaster | Joe Rogan.* YouTube. https://www.youtube.com/watch?v=VFOQk5pz2fo

Melchior, V.R. (2019). High-resolution audio: A history and perspective. *Journal of the Audio Engineering Society, 67*(5), 246–257.Moody, R.F. (2009). Radio's role during Hurricane Katrina: A case study of WWL Radio and the United Radio Broadcasters of New Orleans. *Journal of Radio & Audio Media, 16*(2), 160–180.

Nee, R.C., & Santana, A.D. (2022). Podcasting the pandemic: Exploring storytelling formats and shifting journalistic norms in news podcasts related to the coronavirus. *Journalism Practice, 16*(8), 1559–1577.

RFE/RL. (n.d.). *Our History.* Radio Free Europe/Radio Liberty. https://pressroom.rferl.org/history

Romo-Murphy, E., James, R., & Adams, M. (2011). Facilitating disaster preparedness through local radio broadcasting. *Disasters, 35*(4), 801–815

Shukla, R.K. (2023). Radio for Disaster Management. In *International Handbook of Disaster Research* (pp. 1517–1526). Springer Nature Singapore.

Spinelli, M., & Dann, L. (2019). *Podcasting: The audio media revolution*. Bloomsbury Publishing USA.

Stroink, D., & Edwards, E. (2021). Radio and Audio in 2020. *Journal of Radio & Audio Media*, *28*(2), 344–354.

Turner, D., Murphy, D., Pike, C., & Baume, C. (2021). Spatial audio production for immersive media experiences: Perspectives on practice-led approaches to designing immersive audio content. *The Soundtrack*, *13*(1), 73–94.

VOA. (2023, September 20). *VOA through the years*. Voice of America. https://www.insidevoa.com/a/3794247.html

VOA. (n.d.). *VOA History*. Voice of America. https://www.insidevoa.com/p/5829.html

9 Phones

Communication methods have transformed humans. The telephone is one of the technologies that launched communication into the electronic and digital age. In many cases, communication switches from voice to text. The digital version of the phone is an integral part of communication in contemporary society. This chapter discusses how the telephone started with sound and how the digital phone's screen has become a communication and content creation hub. The chapter shares the history of the telephone and moves on to ideas about mobile phone networks, multimedia, and texting. The last section of the chapter digs into participatory culture, the digital divide, and the effects of digital connection.

Tele-history

Throughout history, long-distance communication occurred through written communication. People started using writing tools and paper instead of carving on stones and walls. They then sent messages through messengers, carrier pigeons, and postal systems. In the early days, messages were delivered by walking, riding horses, and using various modes of transportation, such as railways, ships, airplanes, trucks, vans, cars, bicycles, camels, and even pneumatic tubes. It was a slow and indeed "snail mail" process, with different mishaps. In the mid-1800s, someone patented the telegraph, creating the first telecommunication innovation. This technology was the first nearly instantaneous communication over long distances. However, it is still far from the technology that delivers the e-mail we receive in our mailbox.

The telegraph worked by encoding messages into electric signals sent over wires. As many media technology stories go, the telegraph heralded a new technological age, and before long, Alexander Graham Bell patented the telephone in 1876. This real-time two-way voice communication over wires gave people the experience and opportunity to have conversations across long distances to any place the cables were

DOI: 10.4324/9781003397588-11

available. In the early days of the telephone's development, and similar to the beginnings of other technologies in the history of media, other inventors were also working on communication technologies. Antonio Meucci and Elisha Gray sent caveats to the US office before Bell's patent, indicating their plans to apply for the telephone (Bargellini, 1993; Hounshell, 1975). The "talking telegraph" replaced dots and dashes in Morse code with electric signals. These signals were sent over a wire to the receiver and played back as audible sounds. Alexander Graham Bell later invented variations using microphones and speakers, like landline telephones which are still used today. In the early days of telephones, before they were considered a "utility", individual companies invested in wiring cities for phone service. With ownership of the cables came ownership of the communication in that region. Service fees were attached to the phone services, and the company was called when a line went down or stopped working.

Phone service was globally available in most countries by the early 1900s. Networks of phone wires were pulled across cities and countries and underwater to reach other continents. The process also heralded a new age of innovation and experimentation, and illustrated the process of electronic communication reaching mass audiences in real-time. The invention of transmitting information electronically through the airwaves rather than wires, in a broader scope to a mass audience, invented broadcasting, first through radio and then television. Broadcast stations used telephone lines to transmit their signals. Automated switches and telephone infrastructure allowed mobile phones and the internet to be developed. The telephone was the primary one-to-one communication over distances throughout the 20th century.

The landline telephone was perceived to represent a more intimate, personal, and secure form of media interaction than mass media. In the early days of telephones, employees patched wires into different lines, and these workers could stay on the line to listen, betraying that idea of privacy. The ability of phone operators to eavesdrop on conversations sparked concerns about privacy and security in the industry. As technology advanced, area codes and telephone numbers made line patching unnecessary, allowing calls to be directly routed. Even though human intervention is not required for a consumer to be "patched" through anymore, privacy and security are still paramount (McCormick, 2004).

Into Homes

Homes across America integrated a phone, and eventually several phones into everyday living. The telephone's Top Box wall set model transitioned to more stylish models in the late 1800s. Rotary telephones in the early

Figure 9.1 Wooden wall phone from the 1920s.

Photograph by the author.

1900s turned to push button phones, and designers fashioned specific models for use. Telephone companies printed and shared telephone books with American households, giving everyone a directory of personal phone numbers and business lines. The *Yellow Pages* was one such phone book, published by Reuben H. Donnelley, with additional advertising for local businesses. Apartment buildings and colleges put a phone at the end of the hallway for easy pick up, and job sites mounted them to poles in the streets. Public telephones, housed in phone booths for privacy and a shield from noise, were available in many cities.

Individually owned telephone companies popped up as well. Alexander Graham Bell's phone company owned much of the phone industry. The company grew nationally, producing the nickname "Ma Bell" for its vertically integrated telecommunications monopoly. The split of Bell Operating Companies, owned by AT&T, did not happen until the 1980s. Soon, these regional systems, called "Baby Bells", popped up nationwide. AT&T was formed in the late 1800s to connect all local companies, creating a regulatory monopoly. The Federal Communication Commission (FCC) allowed this monopoly as long as they approved policies and pricing. Telephone services remained primarily unchanged, growing and saturating all corners of America until mobile phone service became so prevalent that customers no longer wanted to pay for home wired phone services and a home phone number. Landlines were no longer necessary for phone communication. Mobile phones became more prevalent than landlines by the early 2000s. The phone book, however, is still around and shared for a fee with customers who request one from their landline provider (Agar, 2013).

Federal Laws

In the late 1960s, lawmakers created federal laws that required one-party consent when recording phone conversations. Wiretapping, phone records, and additional data collection by apps, service providers, carriers, device makers, and advertisers have compromised users' privacy. The US Constitution's Fourth Amendment protects US citizens from unreasonable search and seizure. This amendment also applies to telecommunications. Law enforcement needs a court order or a warrant to collect information during a phone conversation.

Figure 9.2 A black rotary phone from the 1960s.

Photograph by the author.

Additionally, several American federal laws prohibit certain types of phone communication surveillance. The Electronic Communications Privacy Act (ECPA) of 1986, and similar associated acts, all work for consumer privacy. The Wiretap Act prohibits the intentional interception of wire, oral, or electronic communications, and the Stored Communications Act prohibits accessing stored communications without authorization (US Department of Justice, 2020a). The Pen Register Act prohibits trap and trace devices, including pen registers, to capture phone numbers dialed or received (US Department of Justice, 2020b). The Foreign Intelligence Surveillance Act (FISA) prohibits electronic surveillance of domestic communications for foreign intelligence purposes (US Department of Justice, n.d.). Telecommunication carriers are mandated by the Communications Assistance for Law Enforcement Act (CALEA) to include surveillance capabilities in their services with restrictions on how law enforcement can use them, including the need for a court order to use the data. The telephone was an essential step in media history. The smartphone brought together telecommunications, computing, and broadcasting. A tiny pocket-sized technology has combined different sound-focused technologies to create a robust digital landscape.

Comm Tech Transformed

The history of the cell phone is global and began in the 1940s when engineers invented cellular frequencies for portable phone use. These ultra-high frequency bands represent a range of frequencies under the radio frequency (RF) spectrum ranging from 300 megahertz (MHz) to 3 gigahertz (GHz). In the US, the FCC and the National Telecommunication and Information Administration (NTIA) assign frequencies for cellphone networks. The NTIA manages the US government's spectrum use, and the FCC manages other uses. Cell phones and other cellular devices use specific frequency areas within the bands to connect and communicate with carrier cells so customers can make calls, text, and access mobile data. The government considers radio frequencies a natural resource because they oscillate waves of electrical and magnetic energy in Earth's and space's natural environment. Technologies like radio, television, and cell phones are designed to harness the waves of the electromagnetic spectrum. In addition to the radio frequencies being a natural resource, like sunlight, water, land, and minerals, they are also a critical communication commodity. Electromagnetic waves can be used for microwaves, cooking, satellite communication, infrared electrical heaters and cameras, cooking, light for fiber optics communication, ultraviolet energy efficient lamps, X-ray technology for medical imaging, and radio and television. Specifically, some waves are long, some are short, and they transmit energy for use. People consider them low, medium, high, and very high frequency.

In contrast, sound is not part of the electromagnetic frequency. Sound is a longitudinal wave that cannot travel without a conducting and vibrating medium like air, water, and solid items. Vibrations create pressure waves that cause particles to form these mediums into vibrational motions. The particle vibrations move to transmit sound. Radio frequencies are auctioned off for all of these uses. License auctions serve as a revenue generation stream for the government. Specific frequencies go to telecommunication companies. The license gives the license holder the right to use that spectrum freely as long as they adhere to the FCC guidelines and standards. The FCC makes money from the competitive bidding at the auction through regulatory and processing fees. Without the magnetic spectrum, the world we know would not exist.

From Sound to Screen

A cell phone is a portable phone that carries many tools in one's hand. The device has become one of the most used and popular multi-use technologies developed. The phone body comprises mainly plastic, metal, lithium, silicon, and ceramic. A mobile phone also includes a camera, editor, sound recorder for content creators, and many other apps for multiple uses. In the 1970s, a person used a 4-pound phone to make the first mobile phone call in New York City. Martin Cooper of Motorola made that first call on a prototype mobile phone. Ten years later, the first Motorola mobile phone was commercially available for nearly four thousand dollars. In the early consumer years, cellular telephones were hard-wired into cars or carried in backpacks and bags. Eventually, they were untethered from wires, but quickly became tethered to people.

Usenet and dialup were among the first internet capabilities. Then, 1G was launched in the late 1970s, before many people owned cell phones. The networks these phones used, and still use today, are described by a "G", indicating their technological generation. Finland's Nokia, Korea's Samsung, and America's Motorola and Ameritech launched cell phones in the 1980s. Texting features were launched just as 2G was integrated in the 1990s. 2G was better than the previous generation because it had encrypted calls, improved sound quality, faster download speeds, and the ability to transfer small media files between phones. Using the internet on mobile devices was crucial for people to access communication and information. Signal dropout, static, and poor sound quality in the early years did not increase consumers' confidence in cell phone use. Numerous geographic locations had no coverage. Services often shared coverage maps so customers knew what to expect from their service when they traveled, as coverage was often regional.

Phone technology shifted from primarily audio to visual technology in the 1990s when screens were added to phones for text messaging by short message service (SMS) and camera integration. IBM and Nokia were among the first to introduce affordable smartphones to the marketplace. IBM's phone had applications for contacts, a calendar, a notes function, text messaging, and internet access. Nokia phones had a branded ring tone and roaming options. In the mid-1990s, Motorola's StarTAC became so popular that it moved the needle on consumer use. Cell phone manufacturers added cameras to their devices in the late 1990s. They were primarily used to take still images, but video cameras were standard in smartphones by the first decade of the 2000s.

The Finnish-built Nokia 3310 was launched in 2000. The phone had exciting options, like interchangeable cases, an excellent battery life, and embedded emoticons, an early precursor to emojis. This popular phone heralded in years of designs with phone screens of all sizes and styles. 3G started in 2001 and brought the age of the Blackberry personal digital assistant (PDA) and the Apple iPhone. Apple introduced the iPhone in mid-2007, with its multi-touch interface and large touchscreen with no physical keyboard. The iPhone was an easy-to-use interface which increased consumer interest and use. Shortly after, the first Android OS, the T-Mobile G1, also called the HTC Dream, was released. This more affordable model also gained popularity, creating a two-operating system landscape for smartphones. In 2009, Samsung introduced the Samsung Galaxy GT-I7500, which used the Android operating system. The Apple App Store and Google Play stores made downloading apps for both operating systems easy. Google, and by extension, Alphabet Inc., has owned the Android operating system since 2005. Just ten years later, telecommunications companies offered 4G as a standard service (Galazzo, 2022). Soon, companies like Nokia, Blackberry, and Palm started producing more affordable and advanced smartphones. Technological advancements made smartphones cheaper for media consumers, leading to a new era of mobile devices. In 2019, 5G became the next generation of wireless cellular technology.

Phones in Cars

Cell phone use has become an ever-present activity. Consumers walk and talk and text on their phones. Consumers also text while driving. Organizations started monitoring cell phone use and car crashes once it became evident that people were texting while driving. "Distracted driving" refers to using cell phones for texting, apps, emails, music, and calls while driving. Young drivers in car accidents were especially charted as being the largest mortality group. Texting while walking also causes accidents. Developers created new technologies and apps to help deter this kind of usage. Car manufacturers now have systems that monitor drivers' head and eye movements, while police can identify mobile phone users in cars. Almost every American state has texting-while-driving laws. Many states don't allow drivers to use handheld devices behind the wheel, and fines come with license points. Some apps are designed to detect motion, which prevents the driver from texting, reading, or typing. Camera-based eye-tracking car technologies can identify driver inattentiveness.

Newer cars allow drivers to operate their phones from the steering wheel for less distraction. Some phones block incoming calls while the vehicle is in motion, and others use voice commands to interact with the driver instead of texting. Some teen and new driver surveillance systems alert parents if their young driver attempts to text. Additionally, forward collision warning systems and other alarm and deterrent systems are becoming standard in new cars. Vehicle safety systems (V2) are working to provide a way for automobiles to communicate to deter crashes and other road hazards. Increased technology use also brings up issues of privacy. Some car companies have outwardly stated that their safety systems do not record, save, or transmit user data. When and how can technologies be used to track user patterns, driving data, and driver video for research and overall government surveillance, aside from its intended and designed initial purpose? As technology advanced, we moved from 3G to 4G, which brought faster data transfer rates and allowed us to access the internet on our mobile phones, make video calls, and send multimedia messages (MMS). Specifically, 4G networks provide faster internet speeds on phones. Smartphone capabilities continued to improve with increasingly more sophisticated processors, sensors, and cameras, and they became thinner and lighter. These increasingly sophisticated data networks allow users to do more with their phones, giving others increased access.

Phones can be tracked, even if location services are turned off. Social media check-ins and posts are often time-stamped. Trackers, alerts, and notifications leave a trail for data analytics to find. Third-party trackers collect and send information about a user's browsing history. Criminals and digital forensic experts have access to the same information. Knowledge of your digital footprint is essential for media literacy. Doxxing, or sharing private and personally identifiable information about someone, is not a crime in the United States. Those who do this may face legal action if they are sued or charged with cyberstalking, harassment, identity theft, or invasion of privacy (Sanger & Lasen, 2005).

New technologies create new cultural experiences. The synergies between music and radio began in slang in the 1950s. Smartphones and text keyboards also fostered a type of slang. Text slang emerged in the 1980s and 1990s with the rise of online chat rooms and early social media. People adapted language and spelling to communicate quickly and informally in SMS text messaging. Initial code-type language included words like "LOL" (laugh out loud), "BRB" (be right back), and "TTYL" (talk to you later). Later, some of these were replaced by emojis. Text slang expanded with instant messaging in the late 1990s and early 2000s. The rise of social media and smartphones in the late 2000s led to increased GIFs, memes, and emoticons like :-). Texters also started to use acronyms and abbreviations. Text slang continues to evolve, and now emojis, GIFs, and memes are ubiquitous in digital communication.

Social media has also added language to dictionaries, including, in the early 2000s, photobombs, selfies, binge-watch, sub-tweeting, dox, YouTubers, cyberbullying, hangry, and influencers. New technologies and platforms continue to introduce unfamiliar words and meanings. Text slang and social media-related lexicons have become deeply embedded in how generations born into digital communication engage in casual written conversation. New designs, such as bendable and foldable screens, unlike earlier flip phone versions, multiple cameras, and more apps than ever, including facial recognition and mobile payments, have facilitated media consumers' communication, work life, entertainment options, and access to information. The smartphone is one of the most transformative and synergistic technologies of the 21st century.

Multimedia Integration

From a media technology perspective, multimedia began integrating with smartphones in the late 1990s and early 2000s, when PDAs like the BlackBerry and Palm Treo integrated basic multimedia capabilities like cameras, audio playback, and simple video playback. These early prototypes heralded an era of more advanced multimedia features seen today, like photos, videos, music, streaming apps, photo touch-ups, and filters, in-app editing with extended battery life, and more in phone storage attached to cloud storage. The screens got more prominent with a higher resolution. Increased video quality with high-definition (HD) video recording and console-quality gaming further helped to solidify multimedia use as an everyday occurrence on a smartphone. Load and stream times and download resolution continue to improve as smartphones reach the quality and flexibility of computers and tablets. Because of convergence and rapid technology improvements, smartphones transitioned from basic multimedia capabilities to comprehensive mobile media devices.

Smartphones continually improve and converge. Besides increased connectivity, for better performance for various needs, such as online mobile gaming, HD video streaming, and other data-intensive tasks, in-display fingerprint sensors allow authentication directly on the screen for security and ease. Multiple and wide-angle camera lenses increase the aesthetic experience of content creation. Phones moved from brick-style phones to folding phones, to flat style, and now back to folding styles. Foldable displays that expand the screen size create a compact phone that can unfold into a small tablet for increased flexibility and usability. Newer chipsets, higher capacity batteries, and more efficient processors make phones that last longer without a charge, using wireless charge ports. Minimized bezels on the screen also create a more immersive experience. Additionally, on-device artificial intelligence (AI) can power many features like objects in cameras, voice assistants, and text messaging AI prompts (Turner et al., 2021).

While the first phones were designed for one-voice communication, the smartphone now has one-to-one and one-to-many communication abilities through social media, including live video capabilities. In addition, written communication has been transformed through texting. The first text message was sent in the early 1990s by Neil Papworth, a software engineer in the UK. SMS texting was created in the 1980s, but phone companies began to support SMS messaging between phone networks in the 1990s. The Nokia 7110's built-in keyboard was designed for manageable texting and set the standard for text-friendly phone designs. "Texting" became popular in the early 2000s as SMS messaging became more popular. In the United States, Apple's iPhone, launched in 2007, helped boost texting rates through its easy texting capabilities. Messaging apps like WhatsApp and iMessage also expanded texting options. The convenience of texting has changed communication habits all over the world.

Texting Communication

Standard fonts have also made the texting experience easier. On both iOS and Android devices, default system fonts like Roboto on Android and San Francisco on iOS are commonly used in texting and messaging apps because they are simple and easy to read on mobile screens. Texting apps use simple sans-serif font families like Arial, Helvetica, or Verdana that provide clarity and legibility at small text sizes on mobiles: options include accessibility features and the ability to change fonts, like OpenDyslexic font for dyslexic users. Apps like iMessage allow users to format their texts with Chalkboard, Comic Sans, Impact, and other free or premium fonts for a more stylized font experience. Standard emoji fonts have become increasingly popular on mobile operating systems. These tiny pictographs include food icons, faces, animals, arrows, and flags. Text windows now have easily accessible locations for emojis, GIFs, memes, and other information.

The ability to format and customize texts with different fonts is part of the appeal and style of contemporary text messaging. Smartphones have a symbiotic experience with media. The website design changed to be more mobile-friendly. Media companies redesigned their websites and apps to optimize for smaller screens and touch interfaces, including optimization through larger buttons and white space and a design that seamlessly adapts to different screen sizes. The content decreased in word length, format, infographics, short videos, and podcasts. This content is called "snackable" because users quickly consume its small bite-sized message. Social media integration grew as media companies leveraged and optimized social content to share. Push notifications allow users to opt-in to alert them of real-time content delivery, like breaking news or "lives". Mobile ads and social gaming also increased. An individualized and personalized design also helped popularize the use of a smartphone. Location services, user preferences, and use and behavior tracking, especially with the help of wearables like smartwatches, enabled media apps, and sites, customize content and ads for each user. Smartphone cameras and sensors in games like Pokémon create augmented reality experiences that continually increase the usage and popularity of specific brands of phones.

Phone accessories have also become a cottage industry. Cases, screen protectors, phone mounts, and a variety of tripods, holders, and other media-related gadgets, such as selfie sticks, can now be hooked up to phones for increased and varied content creation. PopSockets and chains add handles to phones. Materials continually improve and change model sizes as phones increase and decrease in size and flip open, shut, or fold in half. Phone cameras can be rear-facing and front-facing, which means stands and other accessories are required to facilitate ease of use. Clothing, purses, and backpacks have also been altered to provide phone-sized pockets. Mobile adhesive card holders and wallets adhere to phone cases. Cables, chargers, and wired and wireless adapters give consumers choices. Consumers can even purchase a phone case with a stun gun or pepper spray attached (Reyes, 2016).

Participation Matters

Smartphones have also facilitated a more participatory environment. Increased connectivity, access to information, friending and connecting in physical reality, social activism, increased content creation, sharing across platforms, and multiplayer gaming have all fostered engagement. Easily connecting with others and sharing information through messaging, social media, video chat, and more makes it easier for people to communicate for many reasons, whether social or professional. Instant access to large amounts of information makes it easier for people to learn about issues and seek information in groups and online communities. Smartphones allow people to organize quickly, share information about causes, participate in activism through social media campaigns, petitions, and protests, and promote socialization through flash mobs. Mobile apps and websites help media consumers engage civically through their smartphones. Content creation tools in a smartphone, such as cameras, audio capture, and editing capabilities, allow anyone to create content. This environment facilitates participation and sharing. Mobile gaming apps with multiplayer and community features create fun opportunities and experiences that foster human connection and communication. Even calling a group of gamers a "party" helps cross the digital and the physical experience. Smartphones allow people to engage, express themselves, and interact in previously impossible ways, creating a more participatory environment.

In the same way that the FCC created the emergency broadcast system, cell phones can help consumers involved in an emergency. Cell phone users can call or text 911 to access emergency services or search for first aid information and advice. They can collect health information and provide medical history through various apps. They can also track and identify where cell phone users are or might have been through GPS— these location-tracking mechanisms aid search and rescue operations and location-sharing systems. Emergency systems also provide notifications for specific weather and natural disaster emergencies and provide users with information on where they can go for shelter and medical help. An emergency call button can be used if a cell phone has a charge. To receive a wireless emergency alert, a cell phone must be turned on within range of an active cell tower and in a geographic area where the owner's provider participates.

Cell phone use has also been correlated with positive and negative physical issues. Various well-designed and sophisticated studies worldwide have shared no conclusive evidence between cell phone use and cancer. Users have shared stories of eye, neck, and back pain, and some report mental health issues, like sleep disturbance, loneliness, fear of missing out, and body image issues, to name a few. The most dangerous effects of cellphone use are vehicular accidents. However, cell phones can also be worn as fitness gear to track health data to improve one's health. The Food and Drug Administration (FDA) has shared that steps can be taken to reduce exposure to radiofrequency radiation, like using cell phones for shorter conversations, using landlines when available, and using hands-free technology that places a distance between user and technology.

One of the most tech-centric laws involves texting while driving, also called distracted driving. In most states, distracted driving laws focus on any activity involving using an electronic device while driving. Accidents occur when visual, auditory, or cognitive attention is removed from the road, and safety is at risk. The National Highway Traffic Safety Administration (NHTSA) researched and issued a report in 1997 detailing crashes, injuries, and deaths caused by distracted driving (Wellner, 2015; Haque & Washington, 2015; Stavrinos et al., 2013).

The Federal Trade Commission (FTC) is the primary US government commission for cybersecurity. Regulation occurs through state and federal laws. The Department of Homeland Security (DHS) and the National Institute of Standards and Technology (NIST) regulate cybersecurity. Cybersecurity laws are not present in every state. Privacy, security, and data collection are essential considerations for cell phone users and all media consumers. Searches can also be used to track consumers down. If a social media site can identify a consumer's purchase trends, it can also research and identify other personal trends and movements. All companies have these clauses to alert consumers of changes. But new technologies come along every day, and how privacy and data are kept and how secure personal and private information is depends on who owns the company. Data is a sellable commodity. Technologies that hack security and privacy are being created. Many images can be screen-grabbed, even if they fade away after being sent or read. Two-factor authentication (2FA) helps, but criminal teams are working day and night to get through password protection measures. Sophisticated passwords with letters and numbers are helpful. Phishing occurs. Data breaches occur. Media literacy also means recognizing and actively working on digital self-care.

Digital Divides

Almost everyone in the US has access to cell phone service, but not all services are the same. Mobile data is one way to access the web, and broadband is another. A broadband connection provides a faster, more reliable connection and is less expensive than data.

Browsing and streaming speeds differ, and multiple users increase the load. For instance, online learning, work from home, and telemedicine have transitioned from conveniences to critical everyday applications in the contemporary post-pandemic world (Adarsh et al., 2021). The digital divide is real and is focused on access and disparity of information and communications technology (Lythreatis et al., 2022).

While the term digital divide is more than twenty-five years old, the effects of connection or lack of connection are still problematic. It is challenging to be media literate when access is spotty, and information and resources are unclear and often unavailable. Adarsh et al.'s 2021 study confirms network performance is significantly slower in rural and tribal communities. This suggests that users in under-served regions are far more likely to drop out of virtual engagement, such as online lectures and e-learning. Unfortunately, user disengagement will lead to a more significant digital gap. "Broadband deployments that address these access and coverage quality gaps are urgently needed" (Adarsh et al., 2021). People who had access to the internet found jobs and bought/sold products at lower prices.

Regarding social participation, people with network connectivity became overall more social. They found a political party to vote for and new ways to express their political opinions that aren't available in traditional media. In terms of cultural participation, they experienced more educational and entertainment opportunities. In terms of institutional participation, they benefitted more from public and vital health services, such as finding out about their disease and the best hospital (Van Dijk, 2017, p. 8). The quality of broadband services differs based on cost and technological underpinnings. A usage gap is apparent. Digital divides people and their access to many different things.

Tele-Effects

Cell phones include many technologies that came before them, including cameras, both moving and still, audio recorders and players, editors and other digital mixing components, GPS navigators, calculators, answering machines, computers, and writing apparatus (Wellner, 2015). One group of researchers notes that "Cell phones seem to activate a 'keeping up with things' heuristic by triggering the deep-seated need to check in on the ongoing information flows and interactions that happen on that device" (Kang et al., 2019, p. 396). Research on cognitive load was studied, and the researchers found that "an overall pattern appeared whereby those who stopped their tasks to take a break on their cell phones fared worse than any other type of break in terms of their subsequent performance, regardless of the main task medium used" (p. 399). This study concluded that when phone users take a mental break from other tasks to use the cell phone, that cell phone work unintentionally adds to the cognitive load rather than offering a break from it. "The results show that breaks might be better spent without the cell phone if the goal is to have restored cognitive ability for subsequent work tasks" (Taylor & Bazarova, 2021, p. 401). A different mobile phone study used the Media Multiplexity Theory to track an ecosystem of media use. This holistic approach aims to measure the digitally collected life of today's media consumers (Balayar & Langlais, 2021). Both research articles share positive and negative effects on mobile phone use.

Things to Consider

- Consider how cell phone companies, services, or global cell phone network coverage can work together.
- Name the different technologies mentioned in this chapter.
- Ponder some cultural shifts that have occurred from smartphone use.
- Imagine some scenarios of how cell phone use will change in the next ten years.
- List the major cell phone networks and trace their roots back to the early days of telephones.
- Study ways that communication has changed because of the cell phone.
- Should the naming of the smartphone be changed to remove the word phone? Why or why not?

Takeaways

- Cell phones have evolved into all-in-one entertainment devices with functions like gaming, HD video recording, and creative design in ongoing efforts to provide better customer experiences.
- Users can personalize their messaging experience with different fonts and emoticons to illustrate customization when sending communication messages.
- Cell phones have made the world a more participatory place.
- Smartphones have become practical tools for interaction and connectivity, supporting everything from social activism to content development and multiplayer gaming.
- Technology can transform relationships between individuals.
- Name some of your chapter takeaways.

References

Adarsh, V., Nekrasov, M., Paul, U., Mangla, T., Gupta, A., Vigil-Hayes, M., Zegura, E., & Belding, E. (2021, July). Coverage is not binary: Quantifying mobile broadband quality in urban, rural, and tribal contexts. In *2021 International Conference on Computer Communications and Networks (ICCCN)* (pp. 1–9). IEEE.

Agar, J. (2013). *Constant touch: A global history of the mobile phone.* Icon Books Ltd.

Balayar, B., & Langlais, M. (2021). Technology makes the heart grow fonder? A test of media multiplexity theory for family closeness. *Social Sciences*, 10(1), 25.

Bargellini, P.L. (1993). An engineer's review of Antonio Meucci's pioneer work in the invention of the telephone. *Technology in Society*, 15(4), 409–421.Haque, M.M., & Washington, S. (2015). The impact of mobile phone distraction on the braking behaviour of young drivers: A hazard-based duration model. *Transportation Research Part C: Emerging Technologies*, 50, 13–27.

Galazzo, R. (2022, July 28). *Timeline from 1g to 5G: A brief history on cell phones*. CENGN. https://www.cengn.ca/information-centre/innovation/timeline-from-1g-to-5g-a-brief-history-on-cell-phones/

Hounshell, D.A. (1975). Elisha Gray and the telephone: On the disadvantages of being an expert. *Technology and Culture, 16*(2), 133–161.

Kang, S., & Kurtzberg, T.R. (2019). Reach for your cell phone at your own risk: The cognitive costs of media choice for breaks. *Journal of Behavioral Addictions, 8*(3), 395–403.

Lythreatis, S., Singh, S.K., & El-Kassar, A.N. (2022). The digital divide: A review and future research agenda. *Technological Forecasting and Social Change, 175*(6), 121359.

McCormick, A.L. (2004). *The invention of the telegraph and telephone in American history*. Enslow Publishers.

Reyes, I. (2016). Mobile phone: Marketplace icon. *Consumption Markets & Culture, 19*(5), 416–426.

Sanger, C., & Lasen, A. (2005). History repeating? A comparison of the launch and uses of fixed and mobile phones. *Mobile world: Past, present, and future*, 29–60.

Spinelli, M., & Dann, L. (2019). *Podcasting: The audio media revolution*. Bloomsbury Publishing USA.

Stavrinos, D., Jones, J.L., Garner, A.A., Griffin, R., Franklin, C.A., Ball, D., . . . & Fine, P.R. (2013). Impact of distracted driving on safety and traffic flow. *Accident Analysis & Prevention, 61*, 63–70.

Taylor, S.H., & Bazarova, N.N. (2021). Always available, always attached: A relational perspective on the effects of mobile phones and social media on subjective well-being. *Journal of Computer-Mediated Communication, 26*(4), 187–206.

Turner, D., Murphy, D., Pike, C., & Baume, C. (2021). Spatial audio production for immersive media experiences: Perspectives on practice-led approaches to designing immersive audio content. *The Soundtrack, 13*(1), 73–94.

US Department of Justice. (2020a, January 21). *1061. Unlawful access to stored communications—18 U.S.C. § 2701*. Justice Manual | 1061. https://www.justice.gov/archives/jm/criminal-resource-manual-1061-unlawful-access-stored-communications-18-usc-2701

US Department of Justice. (2020b, January 21). *1062. Unauthorized installation or use of pen registers and trap and trace devices-18 U.S.C. § 3121*. Justice Manual | 1062. https://www.justice.gov/archives/jm/criminal-resource-manual-1062-unauthorized-installation-or-use-pen-registers-and-trap-and-trace

US Department of Justice. (n.d.). *The Foreign Intelligence Surveillance Act of 1978 (FISA)*. Bureau of Justice Assistance. https://bja.ojp.gov/program/it/privacy-civil-liberties/authorities/statutes/1286

Van Dijk, J.A. (2017). Digital divide: Impact of access. *The International Encyclopedia of Media Effects*, 1–11.

Wellner, G. (2015). *A postphenomenological inquiry of cell phones: Genealogies, meanings, and becoming*. Lexington Books.

Part Three

Synergies

10 Sports Media

Sports communication and media have embraced technology, following a similar path to the media timeline discussed in this book. Almost from the beginning of sports, there was some kind of fan coverage. Then, newspapers in the early 1800s started covering sports news, and before long, they dedicated a separate section for sports worldwide. Newspaper reporters shared scores, written accounts, and illustrations of sporting events. Sports journalists also shared coverage of sporting events, such as boxing and horseracing in magazines. The coverage often featured more style than specific play-by-play information about the event (Billings, 2011).

As the penny press grew, placing newspapers in the hands of middle-class America, sports reporting became central to printed content. From the late 1800s into contemporary media coverage, sports topics have increased, proliferated, and become an all-encompassing specialized focus across all media, from newspapers to streaming, and everything in between. In the 1920s, baseball became the national pastime in America with newspaper coverage, and college football gained popularity through radio and television. When the Associated Press started the sports wire in 1945, it turned sports coverage into a national business model. The growth of sport as an American cultural phenomenon grew alongside its media coverage. Live baseball coverage over the radio expanded the reach of sports coverage. Fans of specific teams and baseball in general, enjoyed the sounds of the field and the game in real-time (Schultz & Arke, 2015). This chapter works through sports technologies, programming, and new synergistic options for sports coverage.

Live Shots

Television, too, provided visuals for live events in the late 1930s. American television embraced sports with live coverage, talk shows, documentaries, commentary, and shows like *Wide World of Sports*. Local televised coverage of the Olympic Games began during the 1936 Berlin Olympics, but it wasn't until 1964 that the Tokyo Olympics were broadcast worldwide

DOI: 10.4324/9781003397588-13

via the Syncom 3 geostationary satellite. Other innovations include acoustic simulations for the 1984 Summer Games in Los Angeles, advanced modeling of the acoustic properties at all venues at the 1988 Seoul Winter Olympics, and digital audio networking without losses or delays in Sydney 2000. Tokyo 2020 saw immersive video using over 3600 microphones hung throughout venues across the campus (Reiss, 2021). The 2024 Paris Olympics used technologies like Digital Audio Broadcasting (DAB) and digitally enhanced Cordless Telecommunication to prevent wireless radio interference (Despaquis, 2023). Signals from other electronic and digital media in the area can interfere with broadcasts and streams, so precautions must be taken.

In the early 1900s, wagons and trucks were used to move the heavy broadcast equipment needed for a sportscast. Later, people fashioned these vehicles into what is now called the sports live truck or outside broadcast (OB) truck or van. The OB truck took the studio into the world of production, along with reporters engaged in the programming. Electronic Field Production (EFP) is a production technique that uses compact cameras, microphones, tripods, and sound equipment for recording and tape decks. The sportscasting crew had different-sized teams in the studio with all the necessary equipment, like cameras, switchers, recording decks, monitors, audio mixers, and graphics. They also had cables, satellite transmitters, dishes, and specialized equipment for live shots that connected to the studio for a high-quality live broadcast. Mobile control rooms or "trucks" also became a popular way to bring live events to the consumer. The television production truck, used for remotes, field reports, and outside broadcasting, allowed reporters to share "live" news, events, and sports. A satellite dish on the truck made it possible to transmit the programming back to the television studio to be integrated into the daily programming. These trucks and vans (and wagons) have varied in size, but these sophisticated mobile control rooms house an entire production crew with full capabilities. Cameras are connected through the remote-control room with graphics, a switcher, an audio board, and other equipment. Video cameras are shrinking in size, and while most newsrooms capitalized on using better quality recording tape, e.g., ¾ inch and Beta cameras, the camcorder was embraced by consumers in the 1980s. This new camera size created new recording programming methods and different built-in or changeable lenses. In the 1990s, the broadcast and media industries began transitioning from analog to digital recording. This introduced new tapes and files that could record digital images for the first time. In the 1970s, microprocessors were used, and in the 1980s, fiber-optic cables became popular in broadcasting. However, it was in the 1990s that the shift from electronic to digital media happened, because of the internet and the World Wide Web. Flash memory cards and solid-state drives replaced tape and film, pushing consumers to record 4k media at approximately the same technological quality as professional media companies. Mobile and other small surveillance cameras have been improving their recording quality. During recording, drones can also collect metadata, such as time, date, and climate.

Sports Programming

The popularity of televised sports continued to multiply. Before widely broadcasting sports content, cinemas showed short documentary-style newsreels. The ability to watch sports coverage on a big screen has been a viewing pastime ever since. Sports photography also played an important role in sports coverage. Famous images have captured important and memorable moments. Sports magazines also became a popular way to learn more in-depth information about athletes and the sports they played. Since the mid-1950s, magazines have provided in-depth features, analysis, and storytelling. This comprehensive and narrative-driven approach to sports coverage struck a core in media consumers everywhere.

Sports media coverage grew in popularity through cable, satellite, and pay-per-view, and streaming revolutionized the media industry. The way sports programming is produced has changed. It used to be one company bidding for a season license on TV, but now it's different because of digital and streaming platforms. Increased competition for broadcasting rights, the rise of live streaming services, and the interest and innovation of technology companies have presented challenges and opportunities for broadcasters, rights holders, sports streamers, and fans as they seek the best coverage of their favorite teams, hoping not to purchase another of the many streaming services to watch their favorite competition. As more sports content becomes available, the audience both grows and fractures. Several sporting events that use the most contemporary sports media technologies include the Olympic Games, the FIFA World Cup, the Super Bowl, Wimbledon, the Tour de France, the Masters Golf Tournament, marathons and road races, the America's Cup sailing race, and Formula 1 Grand Prix and NASCAR racing.

Up-to-the-minute news, analysis, and live broadcasts of sporting events became central to media coverage. When fans started recording shows on their Video Home System (VHS) recorders and then their digital video recorders (DVR), sports fans could catch the big game outside of the time-confined periods called "appointment viewing". Social media, too, has gained prominence in the media coverage. Sentiment analysis on social

Figure 10.1 Mini iPad, microphone, light, and iOgrapher case.

Photograph by the author.

media can also gauge fan reactions, historically through Twitter, now X, and other social sites. In addition, "broadcasters willing to engage in the tacit or latent constructs that Twitter offers may find that, rather than being displaced by Twitter, their sportscasts can be a supplement" (Hull & Lewis, 2014). Athletes, teams, and sports media outlets created verified accounts on their favorite social media platforms, and fans also started fan accounts. Content creators use many different devices to make sports content. The excellent quality of tablet and cell phone cameras has prompted a new style of field production fashioned with microphone and lighting fixtures specifically designed for tablet use.

Engaging with fans on social media and press conferences became essential for the job. In the 2020s, college athletes can sign media deals, creating NIL (name, image, likeness) agreements. Previously, only professional athletes could engage in these kinds of money-making ventures. Companies also pay athletes to represent their products. Athletes can market their brand by accepting payment for promotional activities, becoming an ambassador for a brand, receiving sponsored products and services in exchange for promotion, and earning money from various media ventures. Before NIL agreements, colleges and non-professional athletes were prohibited from engaging in these money-making activities. Print, radio, television, digital, and social media have all had a part in the contemporary sports media landscape, with increasingly diverse and immersive ways to engage fans with sports on the horizon (Wanta, 2013). Streaming video opened doors to various app-based options for many sporting events. The creation of sports networks like ESPN and the production of sports-themed shows and movies fueled the popularity of sports. High-definition television (HDTV) in the late 1990s allowed fans to see a larger screen when the picture went from 4x3 to 16x9 aspect ratio.

Sports media also pushed the invention of a variety of innovative technologies. Sports media cultivated the invention of various innovative technologies, including the use of Steadicams and other stabilizing camera systems across fields, in the stands, and increasingly through drones, to capture dynamic and fast-paced moments. Specialized small cameras, such as the GoPros, were also essential because they became wearable ways to bring sports fans along for the ride. Providing clear, fluid visuals and capturing different angles of the action-packed visuals in sports like soccer, basketball, or football became essential to fans. Extreme sports and Olympic sports also captured audiences through the use of these newer technologies. Ensuring high-quality and dynamic coverage is just one component of the overall camera setup. Other essential technologies include robotic cameras operated from a distance, strategically placed around stadiums or arenas. Using aerial cameras, SkyCams, and drones can improve production quality.

Drones offer fans unique vantage points and have replaced traditional broadcast helicopters, allowing a close-up view of athletes. Drones capture the action on the field and are featured in elaborate light shows in large sports productions like the Olympics Opening Ceremony. Using drones in sports production reduces costs and enhances safety while delivering high-quality shots suitable for live television. As drone technology improves and more media companies hire skilled pilots, more sports will adopt drone technologies. Wireless cameras also provide flexibility in camera placement, which allows the technology to move freely around the field or court without cable restrictions. High-speed cameras can capture slow-motion replays and give a detailed analysis of critical moments in a sporting event. Fixed cameras can also be strategically positioned to capture specific areas of the field, using pan–tilt–zoom (PTZ) technology to adjust the framing and focus remotely. Wearables like GPS trackers and radio frequency identity (RFID) chips, virtual reality (VR), augmented reality (AR), extended reality (XR), mixed reality (MR), telefitness technologies, data tracking and collection, and performance analytics through artificial intelligence (AI) and big data all play a part in sideline coverage, decision-making, referee tools, video tracking, and content creation to enhance fan engagement.

One significant moment in sports media coverage came in 1979 when news-embedded sports coverage moved to 24-hour cable channel coverage. The 24-hour news cycle offered sports fans a continuous stream of sports content at any time of day. Strategic programming created a platform for sports fans, helping advertisers reach a specific audience. The live-televised Super Bowl professional football championship garners higher commercial rates than any other sporting event. The sports coverage included highlight shows, replays, and commentary shows that gave viewers daily recaps, top plays, and detailed analyses. A constant news cycle also made space for global sports coverage, beyond traditional American sports, incorporating international events into coverage, which broadened the scope of sports fans. ESPN also introduced innovative camera techniques and angles, affecting other media programming, especially live programming like concerts and other live events. ESPN also emphasized sports personalities, such as anchors, analysts, and field reporters, which made sports broadcasting more entertaining (Rowe, 2012). Information on the coaching staff, referees, and umpires also became more available and spotlighted sports infrastructure and organizations at all levels, from streamed middle and high school sporting events to Olympic training camps. ESPN pioneered many dedicated sports channels, a comprehensive website, mobile apps, and streaming services. This cable channel gave fans access to content anywhere, at any time. ESPN's "30 for 30" series and other original documentaries have changed the way we tell sports stories, including profiles of athletes and teams. These feature series have also extended to sports video gaming. ESPN secured broadcasting rights for various live sports events, including major leagues, college sports, and international competitions, which challenge traditional networks' dedication to live coverage. Fantasy sports and esports also became important sports-related pastimes, proliferated by the 24-hour sports news cycle, and actively allowed sports fans to participate in the games they watched.

Televised and streamed sports programming has pushed the envelope on various technologies that enhance coverage. YouTube TV, FuboTV, Hulu, and Direct TV have many sports channels, including international, national, regional, and local leagues. They also offer on-demand and archived content. Advancements in all kinds of cameras, including AI and robotic driven, wireless microphones, video equipment, emphasizing slow-motion replays, multiple camera angles, and close-up shots ensure a better viewer experience. Graphic displays featuring scores, instant replies, highlights, player positions, scores, and other game-related graphics boost the viewers' understanding of the game. Talent can draw on the screen, highlight key plays and movements that break down the game, and provide analysis. Additional statistical analysis tools offer fans in-depth insights for context and commentary during the broadcast. VR and 360-degree cameras also provide immersive experiences for viewers. Communication systems help media teams and editors quickly create highlight packages for social media integration, making broadcasts more interactive. Sports often support live streaming, on-demand content, and interactive features. A 2024 NFL playoff game on Peacock's streaming platform shared that their game was the most streamed program in streaming history.

Sports entrepreneurs and management have worked hard to enhance player engagement through customized and innovative experiences. Real-time marketing and immersive social media technologies can boost revenue, help players develop their brands, and boost ticket sales, generating more income for leagues. Technology also plays a critical role in improving player performance. Athletes use specialized training equipment, including wearable technology, to measure and analyze their performance. Sometimes, athletes share the statistics from these sessions with producers and content creators for on-air sharing. Sports technology has often led to innovation. Sports organizations can now work with broadcasters and new platforms to reach viewers on different devices.

AI has been integrated to track and identify players and other objects during the game, through heat maps and statistics. A social media algorithm can quickly pick up the teams a specific media consumer enjoys. Through social media, AI can further analyze and identify goals, significant plays, or outstanding performances. This process streamlines the highlight creation process for quick post-game analysis. AI also contributes to immersive virtual and augmented reality experiences for viewers. Analyzing biometric data collected from players during a game has also become an essential use of technology. Tracking heart rate, distance, and movements helps create player statistics for coaches' fitness staff and announces real-time performance analysis and post-game commentary. AI models use past and current data to predict game results and player performance. AI can generate personalized content recommendations, interactive features, and targeted viewer advertisements. Language translation services also convert content quickly for a global audience.

A less talked about media connection with sports is betting. Sportsbooks, like the ESPN Bet, owned by Disney, and FanDuel's betting plus content model, merge social media, video games and sports wagering. Sports-focused online casinos are increasingly popular and require a lot of archival footage, sports-themed graphics, and an understanding of sports to create a gamified experience with a gambling twist. Betting can also extend through pre-game, in-game, and post-game to add fan engagement. The convergence of legacy methods, production aesthetics, and converged digital enterprises have taken a separate but known entity, sports gambling, and synergized it. "As advertising and marketing strategies have become integral parts of the business, bookmakers are developing innovative and state-of-the-art tactics to cross-promote and converge separate markets, targeting new gamblers or discouraging the discontinuation of gambling" (Lopez-Gonzalez & Griffiths, 2018, p. 18).

Sports Podcasting

Podcasting was covered in Chapter 8, but it is worth noting the significant impact podcasting has had on the sports industry. This new form of content is changing how fans enjoy and understand sports, and facilitates how athletes can engage with their audience and connect with their fanbase. Diverse sports content has created niche interests, and content on and from specific teams, athletes, and aspects of sports culture is now available on podcasts. The platform helps fans and podcast hosts have in-depth discussions and builds community. The ease of access creates an environment that allows sports fans to enjoy content and entertainment 24/7. Previously, fans had to wait for engagement and new content on the broadcasting schedule. The convenience of listening helps fans stay updated on information about their team. Podcasters' global reach also enables fans worldwide to access content related to their favorite sports, teams, or athletes, globalizing sports fandom. Podcasters can profit from their content through sponsorships, advertising, and premium subscriptions.

Sports media figures have also delved into new technologies. John Madden's video game franchise called Madden and Dick Vitale's College Basketball Sega game are enjoyed by gamers and fans and heralded in the genre of sports video gameplay. Bob Costas has voiced play-by-play for various gaming platforms, and Howard Cosell's distinctive voice has also been used in diverse media content. Al Michaels has also been credited on video games. Electronic Arts featured Erin Andrews on Road to Glory on Xbox360 and PS3.

Things to Consider

- Consider the ways sports media has been at the forefront of media innovation.
- Ponder the use of AI in video gaming. How have these technologies changed the user experience?
- Name some of the most successful sports coverage in video gaming and some areas that can be identified for growth.

- Think about the idea of appointment viewing. Do you still watch live sports?
- Consider ways entertainment lines might become blurred in the growing digital sportsbook ecosystem.
- Name the different technologies mentioned in this chapter.
- Compare live sports coverage to other types of live media coverage, such as concerts.

Takeaways

- Sports media has developed dynamically through different platforms and technology, including streaming and podcasts. It has revolutionized how people consume sports material, making it more individualized and available to a broader audience.
- Sports technology has pushed media technologies as a whole in advanced directions.
- The immediacy of live updates and lively conversations about sports improves fans' interaction.
- Name some of your chapter takeaways.

References

Billings, A. (2011). *Sports media: Transformation, integration, consumption.* Routledge.

Despaquis, L.J. (2023, March 30). *Spectrum management plan for the Olympic and Paralympic Games.* Paris 2024. https://www.paris2024.org/en/spectrum-management-plan-paris-2024/

Hull, K., & Lewis, N.P. (2014). Why Twitter displaces broadcast sports media: A model. *International Journal of Sport Communication, 7*(1), 16–33.

Lopez-Gonzalez, H., & Griffiths, M. D. (2018). Understanding the convergence of markets in online sports betting. *International Review for the Sociology of Sport, 53*(7), 807–823.

Reiss, J. (2021, October 6). *Three thousand six hundred microphones and counting: How the sound of the Olympics is created.* The Conversation. https://theconversation.com/3-600-microphones-and-counting-how-the-sound-of-the-olympics-is-created-164875

Rowe, D. (2012). Sports media: Beyond broadcasting, beyond sports, beyond societies? In *Sports Media: Transformation, Integration, Consumption* (p. 94–113). Routledge.

Schultz, B., & Arke, E. (2015). *Sports media: Reporting, producing, and planning.* Routledge.

Wanta, W. (2013). Reflections on communication and sport: On reporting and journalists. *Communication & Sport, 1*(1–2), 76–87. https://doi.org/10.1177/2167479512471334

11 Marketing, Advertising, and Public Relations

Throughout media history, various professions have emerged that focus on promoting goods and services for media businesses. In legacy media, media marketing focuses on advertising content and generating advertising dollars. Revenue came through advertisements and commercial spots. In many legacy stations, this official departmental office is called Sales. TV stations have a creative services department that handles marketing, design, promotions, and commercials. Professions like public relations have become foundational in contemporary media. These professions, like media content, are focused on audiences. Most media, including social media, make money from ads. Strategies may differ for different media, but advertising dollars keep the lights on and the coffers full. Digital marketing has become more strategic in calculating exact numbers than ever before. Every click, swipe, upload, download, start, stop, click, and heart generates data. Brands and products want to reach audiences. Media programming and content bring that audience. User-generated content means that media does not have to pay for its production. However, creating these platforms and structures is often expensive and technologically complicated. Social media platforms, devices, web interfaces, compression, internet connections, and algorithms, among other entities, must work together to reach audiences with advertising messages. This chapter explores early marketing and advertising technologies, a move to public relations, government oversight, and audience measurement.

The Early Advertising Movement

Advertising in print media, such as newspapers, catalogs, magazines, billboards, and posters, grew due to industrialization. Catalogs were printed as marketing tools for retail businesses, like Tiffany's Blue Book, Montgomery Ward's Wish Book, and Sears & Roebuck's Catalog, to attract attention to store inventory. These tools offer customers a reminder to make a purchase. They provide media consumers with images, photos,

DOI: 10.4324/9781003397588-14

and descriptions of products. Catalogs, like magazines, use pictures and colors to build relationships with potential and existing customers. Catalogs became a good model for influencing purchasing decisions because they brought the products into the home. Some catalogs shared stories and additional articles to increase product interest. Magazine ads focus on specific products, attractive visuals, and sometimes even include scents. The look and style of these printed materials and advertisements have evolved consumers' unique visual experiences. Nowadays, catalogs often combine visual design with interactive features like QR codes and website links.

Diving into Definitions

As media marketing and advertising grew, the professional development of the industry also grew. These industry professionals evolved to have many duties, and advertising and sales are two of them. Marketing also plays a significant role in determining various aspects of a product, including promotion and price point, while advertising specifically focuses on promoting the media product, such as determining the cost of airtime to run commercials. The symbiotic relationship between media and advertising is an important one. Without media content, there is nowhere to sell advertising or market products and services. And without marketing and advertising, media content can't fund itself. In early media, the content was called programming, the process of scheduling media content. Persuasive communication is crucial in marketing, especially in media marketing, to reach media consumers. The word influencer came about based on the idea that someone can influence specific ideas, values, attitudes, emotions, and behaviors. Two professional career positions grew from the need for content creation and revenue. With its concentrated effort in advertising, sales, and public relations, media marketing is a strategic communication model that builds beneficial relationships between a company, its stakeholders, and the public. Advertising makes great ads and marketing campaigns, while public relations (PR) builds relationships between organizations and their audiences. Advertising sales is concerned with making money for a client or company, and public relations has a focus on building awareness and a good reputation for a company through internal and external stakeholders. Both advertising and public relations are essential professions central to media.

Public Relations

The other area of professional growth in media marketing and audiences occurred in the field of PR in the early 1900s. Corporations and governments needed to shape their public image and manage their reputation. Early PR professionals, such as Edward Bernays, Betsy Plank, Belle Moskowitz, and Ida B. Wells created strategies that are still used today in business. PR also has a role in political and government strategy. Modern PR techniques focus on managing media, crafting messages, and influencing public opinion. As journalism has evolved throughout the 1900s and 2000s, PR strategies, like press releases, media kits, and content marketing, have become everyday ways for organizations to get coverage, leading to conversations about native advertising, also called sponsored content, and transparency. PR techniques have also played a role in promoting the entertainment industry. PR agents and consultants work with celebrities and influencers to craft a public image and adjust media narratives. This PR style has contributed to the rise of celebrity culture and entertainment journalism. There are four models of public relations: the public relations agency model, the general information model, and the two-way asymmetric and symmetric models. Each emphasizes different things. The agency model focuses on image creation rather than a specific public-facing effort. Crisis communication firms can also be hired specifically to work on a person's or organization's image. The public information model focuses on providing accurate and transparent information. The asymmetric and symmetric models deal with public perception and messaging that either persuades the audience or listens to audience feedback.

Another critical area of PR is crisis management. Disasters, scandals, and mistakes have led to the need for message management during crises. Information control and the creation of strategic narratives are critical functions of PR in crises. PR studies how organizations, figures, and events are represented in the media. Combining digital media and new data advancements has created various digital tools for PR specialists. The software can track brand mentions, keywords, or topics in the media to provide data and insights. Managers can schedule posts and engage with followers to increase content engagement. Content Management System (CMS) and Search Engine Optimization (SEO) help media professionals create, edit, and publish content for specific audiences. PR specialists use visual content creation tools to make infographics and videos for their client campaigns. Software and tools help analyze data to measure the impact of public-facing content and campaigns to track progress and identify trends. These professionals work with journalists and broadcasters to shorten and simplify press releases, media assets, and company information. They also monitor TV and radio coverage. In addition to other strategies, PR has utilized webinars, virtual press conferences, and events in the digital media landscape. Strategy and branding firms track content and data with media database services. Increasingly, companies are integrating artificial intelligence (AI) chatbots and tools for engagement and auto-replies on websites and social media. Research, too, has become part of this profcs-sional engagement—surveys and polling tools that gather public opinion data (Li et al., 2021).

Ancient merchants in Egypt and Greece used signs, symbols, and word-of-mouth to advertise their products. In ancient Rome, merchants used buildings like billboards to promote public events and games. During the Middle Ages and the Renaissance, merchants and the church used printed materials for advertising. The Gutenberg Press fostered increased adver-tising in those ancient times. The inventions of the Telegraph and the Railroad also transformed advertising by moving information across geog-raphy, so regional and national advertisements and media market buys gained traction. Also, mass media, such as radio and television, brought

Figure 11.1 Magazine advertisement from a 1960s magazine.

Photograph by the author.

mass audiences to advertisers. Post-World War II, America was considered a time for the rise of consumer culture, and advertising made additional technological strides in mass media with the rise of electronic and digital advertising as billboards began displaying video. Social media advertising brought forward monetization on their platforms. Companies use print, broadcast, online, and social media to advertise and reach consumers in various ways. The concept of media markets explains why people in different cities receive different local TV news and radio programming. It's customized based on their designated market area (DMA).

Spot On

Creating an advertisement that works is a work-intensive experience involving a variety of creatives. While the process can be short or long, depending on the type of ad and reach, some parts of the timeline can't be skipped. Market research and strategy start with understanding the identified target audience. In most cases, some type of marketing research is needed. Innovating, catchy, and memorable messaging takes time and effort. Will the advertisement cover digital, web, television, radio, newspapers, streaming, print, or all of these platforms? What is the cost per view versus the cost per click, and how are these sifted out to provide data for the brand? Then, the team needs to identify a platform for the advertisement and a budget. Various content creators, producers, directors, and crew are required. Storyboards, scripts, and rough cuts occur before a final version or versions are released to the public. Once the message is crafted, the budget will help identify the financially viable approach. For more extensive campaigns, focus groups and testing are needed. After the advertisement is shared, the performance needs to be tracked and analyzed. The idea is to move the needle forward on a brand's sales and revenue, so any issues with the messaging mean that the ad needs to be pulled from circulation. In short, is it getting the right buzz?

The Economics of Early Media

Since the birth of legacy media, paying for technology, talent, and programming has been a substantial effort. Media owners want to know who the audience is and how to keep them returning for more. Since early cinema, management and producers have worked to "increase eyeballs". Media companies have a long legacy of creating and producing media content for profit. Monetization models were established once inventors found stable ways for media business models to prosper. Like other businesses, media businesses aim to attract an audience of consumers. "Content is King" became an early media catchphrase because good content brought people to the cinema, radio, and television programs, and digital content. As a commodity, media content is a means to that commercial end. In a capitalist economic model, private media companies, many vertically and horizontally structured in contemporary society because of consolidation, produce and distribute content as a commercial service or product. In this instance, media is purchased, sold, and created for profit. The advertising industry still faces ethical and regulatory challenges, especially regarding truthful advertising and privacy. From simple signs and circular fliers, advertising has come a long way to highly sophisticated and data-driven contemporary campaigns. It remains an integral part of business and culture, constantly evolving to adapt to changing technology and consumer behavior. Innovative tools are transforming traditional geographic media markets and advertising strategies.

Advertising uses a variety of advanced systems for buying and selling advertising. Demand-side platforms (DSPs) help advertisers manage multiple ad exchanges and data sources to bid on ad inventory. Supply-side platforms (SSPs) also help publishers manage and sell their ad inventory. Data management platforms (DMPs) collect and analyze data to create targeted advertising audiences. Native advertising platforms integrate ads into the user experience, and retargeting tools target repeat users. Video advertising and social media platforms are increasingly delivering and managing video ads across various platforms. Fraud prevention solutions stop fake advertising, while ad verification services ensure ads appear on suitable sites. Advertising tools use Geofencing to target user locations, while influencer marketing connects brands with customers to promote products and services.

Market Shares

One key point of advertising comes from the size of media markets. A media market is a geographic area where consumers receive the same media services. Media research companies define media markets based on population size and density and what that media make-up entails, e.g., how many television or radio stations or newspapers, for instance, this same population can consume. This regionalism was part of the vestige of legacy media. Today's media focuses more nationally, meaning advertising dollars are shifting toward a national audience. Online and mobile media have loosened the relevance of geographic boundaries. However, the standard is still used for buying/planning advertising campaigns. The United States has over 200 Designated Market Areas (DMAs). These big city geographic areas like New York City, Los Angeles, Chicago, and Philadelphia combine cities and zip codes to identify a Nielsen corporation marketing measurement area. Larger markets have more media outlets, and smaller markets have fewer. Advertising rates increase in larger markets because of higher audience exposure. Many larger advertisers buy ads regionally and nationally, and local businesses use their advertising dollars for local advertising. Media companies need to know the demographics of their audience to create content and ads that resonate with them.

But media can also be created for the public good. Public affairs offices help with safety information and work alongside government agencies during disasters and emergencies. And local news and information help residents learn about their communities. National and global news helps people choose political candidates who share their values. Knowing media companies' responsibilities aside from the business model is challenging. Still, the American government and governments worldwide have and do put guidelines in place based on their freedoms. Freedom of speech and other legal parameters create different media environments. In the past, during the era of legacy media, the airwaves were a natural resource and governed just like state parks and other resources are protected and managed. Media inventions came about as innovations used by society in different media-minded ventures.

The media landscape is different today. The Federal Communication Commission (FCC) regulates telecommunications and broadband internet, while the Federal Trade Commission (FTC) protects consumers. Other groups like the Internet Corporation for Assigned Names and Numbers (ICANN) and the World Wide Web Consortium (W3C) work to guide web standards. And different countries have different media regulations and models. In the United States, most media organizations rely on advertiser-supported revenue streams. While not profit-driven, public media also receives some government support and depends on commercial or sponsorship revenue streams.

In contrast, while engaging in some commercial efforts in other countries, the BBC is primarily funded through the UK's Royal Charter, which pays for BBC services for all households. In many media newsrooms, the foundational idea of the fourth estate is still relevant and used as a guiding principle for news. Editorial independence has always been suggested as an aim of news agencies in the media business model. However, they still require revenue. The tension between editorial news content and ownership has existed as long as news media has existed. The public interest versus a media company's shareholders has long been debated. By following ethical codes and journalistic standards, a strong division has been established between the two entities.

Media Advertising

The fourth estate is a philosophical idea from the Middle Ages when the press was considered alongside the nobility, the church, and the townspeople or commoners. The output from newspapers influenced the government. In summary, the press became a watchdog over the government, informing the public about its actions and events. In the United States, the traditional aim has been supported by the First Amendment of the American Constitution and a watchdog of the executive, legislative, and judicial branches. In the past, people have considered journalism and media news as a way for the public to hold leaders accountable. Public distrust, bias accusations, and social and digital media competition have affected journalism and news content. Good journalistic content attracts advertisers and benefits the public. Blending media and digital advancements have made it harder to distinguish between media as a business and media for public benefit. Technologies, like online paywalls and subscription models, provide limited public access for everyone. The models that pay for news have changed. The tension between public service and profit will continue to evolve.

Early legacy media advertising models still have relevance today. In the early days of radio, advertisements were inserted into specific television shows or programming hours. Then, the advertising for broadcasting shifted to various short commercials representing different companies. Stations and studios created sales teams that specifically sold local advertising and national cooperative ads, and worked with advertising agencies to find sponsors for programs. National standards for ads, namely the 30- and 60-minute spot times, were created to increase and facilitate ad purchasing. Advertising agencies cooperated and worked together to find sponsors for programs. They made national standards for ads, specifically for 30- and 60-minute spot times, to increase and facilitate advertising purchasing. The cable TV industry's growth created more ways for stations and sales teams to make money. In many cases, sales teams worked on a draw and were only paid a percentage of the advertising they directly sold.

The invention of cable television put pressure on broadcast media because, initially, media consumers paid a monthly subscription fee for commercial-free viewing. However, after a time, even cable channels moved to a commercial model along with the monthly payment. Streaming services also use this model. Cable channels advertise to specific audiences by creating commercials tailored to their interests and locations. In the 1980s and 1990s, the model shifted to product placements and product and toy tie-ins in movies and television shows, infomercials, and television show-length advertisements couched in an often talk show-style format. Recording media programming content also affected commercial advertising. Consumers purchased technology that blacked out and forwarded through commercials, and digital video recorders skipped ads. As technology shifted entirely to digital transmission, interactive ads, more flexible targeting, pop-ups, banners, and personalized ad targeting have proliferated as sales strategies across content. Media advertising is increasingly data-driven, analytically informed, targeted, and interactive. OTT, called over-the-top content delivers streamed content.

In cinema, previews, and movie trailers have moved out of the theater and onto streaming platforms to create product buzz. Transmedia has shown increased use of movie characters and advertising-specific products that air for top advertising dollars on TV channels and during major live events. Print ads and movie posts still provide opportunities to showcase movies, actors, and movie release dates. Social media marketing, podcasts, premiers, and live web clips have also become integral ways to release behind-the-scenes (BTS) content and teasers to get fans to share content and increase anticipation. Advertisers also embrace virtual reality (VR) and augmented reality (AR) to create interactive, immersive theme parks, website experiences, and games that allow fans into the world and experiences shared in the movie. New technologies enable broadcasters to automate better ad sales, target audiences, and deliver specialized content across broadcast and digitally branded platforms. Due to consolidation, sales teams now sell advertising for local stations, cable/satellite options, and digital platforms. As viewer habits change, data, analytics, and media changes continue, as do sales strategies that evolve advertising.

Measuring Audiences

Media consumers, the audience, are at the crux of all media decisions. The viewers, the players, the gamers, and the listeners provide the attention advertisers strive to reach. Getting products and services in front of target audiences to gain revenues is the primary commodity model for contemporary media. Media audiences are studied more than ever, through demographics, interests, audience behaviors, and appetites. Technology can pinpoint and connect advertisers and publishers with the audiences they want to reach, facilitated by automated ads across many sites and platforms. Integration of on-demand shopping experiences through social media enables product purchase. This results in individualized social media and search engine advertising. Advertisers can now leverage influencers' branding opportunities across various social media platforms. Interactive near-immediate audience response and engagement have opened digital doors for increased revenue.

But what kinds of technologies are used to measure audiences accurately? Broadcasters use various methods to measure TV viewership, including the American Research Bureau, which later became Arbitron and Nielsen ratings. Both companies surfaced in the 1950s to try to accurately measure how many media consumers were using radio and television. Arbitron created ScanAmerica to monitor how people use media, while

Neilson developed the PeopleMeter. In the 1990s, Arbitron moved to internet radio measurement, and Neilson Research Group Inc., now called AC Nielsen Corporation, measures radio, television, and additional platforms. Contemporary digital media has many ways to measure the usage created through streaming. In the beginning of media measurement, companies relied on the consumer for usage information. Arbitron sent books out to consumers through the mail and asked them to complete the diaries of content use and who was viewing or listening and return them. The company included a small amount of money in the envelope as a perk for their time. Arbitron developed measurement by testing the area of dominant influence (ADI), and Neilson developed its Designated Market Area (DMI). Research points, such as audience trends and composition, diversity of the listening audience, demographics, hour-by-hour, and quarter-hour listening estimates, overnight listening, listening locations, and loyalty to specific talent were measured, among other things.

When the quarterly rating "book" comes out, stations react and recalculate their programming to gain more ground or get viewers back. This reshuffling results in talent, programming, and management shake-ups. Sweeps Week, or the Sweep period, occurs during four weeks in the year, usually around November, April, June, and October, as well as a monthly expanded rating period in over two hundred media markets. During Sweeps Week, programming increases, and media groups "up their game" for higher Neilson ratings. Shows may have special guests, a new plot twist might occur in a dramatic series, or special programming might be aired. While it may not seem like television and cable garner a large share of viewers, a chunk of advertising dollars goes to this kind of media programming viewed live and on demand. Increased ratings mean increased advertising revenues. The onset of streaming has altered the way measurement occurs. Traditional broadcasting is converging with streaming opportunities, which has increased different kinds of monetization.

The ratings generated during Sweeps Week determine advertising rates for the year. November sweeps have been historically very important because the ratings share if programming put in place in the fall is getting audience attention. Advertisers want to buy video commercials during these times because viewers are more engaged. In the 1950s, Neilson invented ratings to track TV viewership and set advertising rates based on the audience and target audience. While ratings and rates are part of the same process, they differ. Ratings show a viewership measurement, and rates are the number or cost to run advertising during a specific period of media programming. For instance, a show that is highly popular by measurement will cost more to advertise on. Significant costs are associated with purchasing commercial time during televised or streamed high-level sporting events, playoffs, and final games. The Neilson company uses its patented portable PeopleMeter to measure TV and cable viewer habits. At one time, the company also sent paper diaries to media viewers in the mail and asked them to fill them out and return them. Contemporary rating systems through the PeopleMeter show when media is being viewed and who is viewing it. Each station has a unique ID that allows the technology to recognize which station the consumer is watching or listening to. Neilson has changed their business model through the years and now measures broadcast radio, audio streaming, podcasting, and television, cable, and video streaming across all platforms on a global level.

Nielsen's rating process tracks TV viewership in the US by asking people to install meters on their TVs that record the programs they watch. Throughout the history of legacy media, advertisers estimated viewership and used these metrics to determine advertising rates for programs. Cable and satellite companies can track viewership using the programming boxes they provide to their subscribers. Set-top boxes store precise data on overall channel use and time of use, but it is difficult to know who is in the room watching. Streaming platforms track viewer numbers based on streams or views, but these numbers don't show the actual demographics of the audience, only information on the subscriber. Social media analytics is another way media companies can gauge engagement. When individuals share their profile information, compiling demographics and ideas about specific target audiences is easier. Posts and hashtags can measure buzz about a topic but not necessarily viewership. Media companies and networks use surveys to learn about viewers' preferences and habits. Self-reported data is often helpful, but is only completed by a subset willing to take the survey. Ratings have historically been used to set advertising rates, but newer ways to datify usage mean more accurate analytics, which translates into more targeted audiences for advertisers. Correct viewer and participant metrics are essential for advertising revenues. Identifying a sure thing for determining who is watching or using specific media is difficult, but digital tools are increasingly more sophisticated ways to measure an audience. Advertisers want to be sure, as much as possible, that the shows they run their commercials in will be shows that viewers will watch. TV programming predictions can be made using historical ratings data, pilot testing, pre-release metrics, and the talent involved. Additionally, social media chatter around a show, and its stars and creators and the size of the marketing and promotional partnerships, can give a sense of the building buzz. Stations and companies pay for rating services.

Television networks have been making money from a big event called the annual TV Upfronts, where they secure advertising dollars for their shows and programs. The idea came from the network management pitching programming to potential advertisers. They wanted to showcase their fall line-up by including actors, snippets, or trailers of shows to create buzz and increase sales before the season started. The idea is for advertisers to commit to buying ad time and pay a rate based on projections of the buzz or popularity around a show. This marketplace is significant to the business side of the television industry. Advertisers want to put their dollars into the commercials on a hit show, one that will connect with the viewer. TV Upfronts guarantee networks a chunk of ad revenue upfront, and some streaming services are also participating in the Upfronts each May. OTT offerings and data analytics increasingly back up these presentations. The revenue from commercial airtime pays for the production of programming and management of the network. In the past few decades, the television industry has changed with the rise of cable, streaming, and short-run series. This shift has made the opening of the traditional fall TV season less significant. However, Upfronts remain important for networks, especially when generating revenue from sports programming.

Social Demographics

Social media has been digital from the beginning, so audience and user measurement has been more manageable, but still not exact. Tracking demographic, usage, engagement, advertising, and loyalty metrics measures a social media platform's user base's value, retention, size, and activity, which informs advertiser offerings. Social media sites can quantify the number of users with accounts, how active or inactive each user is, and user interaction, called engagement. An engaged user base is a good measurement for solid advertising. Clicks, ad recall, purchases, searches for external websites, and shares for other accounts can qualify advertising engagement. Social media platforms gather user information, such as interests, age, and location, to identify targeted ads for different groups of people. Analytics can further predict usability through user patterns, like time spent on the app, other platforms, habit formation, and something measurement professionals call stickiness. This means getting consumers to a specific digital place and holding their attention through interactivity and content engagement to keep them there. The stickier the location it is, the more users are engaged. Another way audiences can be measured through social media includes net promoter scores that are identified through surveys that ask users how likely they are to recommend the platform. The aim is to increase the habit, loyalty, and user experience satisfaction. Even deactivation and deletion are measured. This churn rate identifies a lack of interest or low user retention.

Networks and advertisers rely on each other for financial gain. The network needs ad revenue to create programming that brings an audience, and advertisers need that audience to see their commercials and other advertising content to generate income. Advertising and sales started with simple text ads in newspapers and magazines describing products and services. As advertising grew as a profession, so did the mass circulation of newspapers and magazines. Advertising agencies gained popularity by helping companies create and place ads in certain publications. Sales teams were established to sell print ad space and commercial airtime later. The rise of radio and television advertising brought audio and visual elements into ads for the first time. Advertising agencies made national ads, while TV and radio stations made local commercials too. Media sales teams now had to sell airtime slots and print space. As advertising grew, media sales expanded, and product placement became an additional way to promote revenue.

Media sales adapted to cable's niche audiences when cable became a popular way for media consumers to get new programming, because advertisers could now target specific demographics on specialty music, news, or sports channels. Sales continue to grow as the world converges through digital media, online ads, and data-driven digital ads. The contemporary media environment means advertisers buy audiences across an integrated multimedia landscape.

Influencer Brand Work

Social media marketing and influencer use have become an increasingly popular strategy in marketing. "The increase in the number of users has resulted in social networks becoming a very important element in the advertising for various companies. Companies strategically consider branding and communication on social networks, constantly adapting to new trends by carefully planning their strategies. Billions of dollars are spent on social network advertising in the United States every year" (Milas & Lesinger, 2022, p. 28). Sometimes, influencers work with a brand to expand both the audience and the experience of the specific product. According to a study by Liu and Zheng, marketers can benefit from partnering with sales representatives who have a strong reputation with their followers. Brand credibility and purchase intentions are an essential part of this strategy. How followers view an influencer's values and authenticity greatly impact their influence. Their study notes that when building brand trust, an influencer's followers' persuasion can negatively affect brand credibility (Liu & Zheng, 2024). Consistent influencer ads on social media and timed social media spots can fatigue followers. While recent mobile phone filters can remove an ad's ability to track the user's data and prevent advertisers from tracking the success of their ads on social networks, users cannot blank out the ads. Because most social media sites are advertising-driven, technological ways to deter ads have been thwarted. Brand loyalty is the goal, but alienating followers and consumers can be problematic.

Audience Research

Audience measurement is an integral component of a strategic marketing plan, with social media interaction being a key element. Audience measurement research can be divided into two categories: theoretical research, which focuses on general explanations and identifying effects, and methodological research, which involves product testing and research and development (Webster et al., 2013). One media effect-focused research project using consumer engagement theory noted that engagement by drivers, inputs, throughputs, and outputs reports passive and active engagement. The key findings of this study show that companies choose their social media marketing strategies based on their goals, resources, and organizational capabilities. They note the need for more research on appropriate measurement metrics because social media is unique as a marketing tool that marries social media and marketing.

Things to Consider

- Take into consideration current streaming models with commercials and a subscription fee. How does that revenue model work?
- Ponder the kinds of advertising you see each day. What platforms are they on? Now, ask someone ten years younger or older, where do they see commercials?
- Deliberate the differences between advertising and public relations. Research some case studies for each.
- Contemplate the position of the influencer. Is it a sustainable freelance career?
- Brainstorm the idea of demographics. How do these measurements relate to an audience?

Takeaways

- Public relations are vital to media advertising and have four general operation models.
- Media marketing dates back to ancient times, with word-of-mouth and symbols used in Ancient Egypt and Greece, and advertisements written by merchants on buildings in Ancient Rome.
- Media marketing has grown in multiple fields, from print, television, social media, and broadcast.

- Marketing, advertising, and sales share a strong link. Without marketing, you won't have advertising; without advertising, you won't have marketing; without either, you won't have sales.
- Name some of your chapter takeaways.

References

Li, F., Larimo, J., & Leonidou, L.C. (2021). Social media marketing strategy: Definition, conceptualization, taxonomy, validation, and future agenda. *Journal of the Academy of Marketing Science*, *49*, 51–70.

Liu, X., & Zheng, X. (2024). The persuasive power of social media influencers in brand credibility and purchase intention. *Humanities and Social Sciences Communications,* 11, 15 https://doi.org/10.1057/s41599-023-02512-1

Milas, J., & Lesinger, G. (2022). The relationship between the perception of advertising, FOMO, social network fatigue, and privacy concerns among social network users. *Communication Management Review*, 7(01), 26–47.

Webster, J., Phalen, P., & Lichty, L. (2013). *Ratings analysis: Audience measurement and analytics*. Routledge.

12 Social Media

In the survey of media, social media, as a construct, is very new. However, many synergies connect legacy media to contemporary social media. At the start, this kind of social interaction was called social networking. The earliest social sites include SixDegrees, in the mid-1990s, and Friendster, in the early 2000s. Not long after that, social networking-focused apps, some installed on phones at purchase, started popping up and, in some cases, buying each other. Companies combined and separated, making it hard to distinguish between tech and media companies. This chapter explores the relationship between social media and participatory culture, including ideas about social expression through GIFs (Graphics Interchange Format) and memes, social monetization and effects (Jenkins, 1992, 2006; Jenkins et al., 2013).

In contemporary studies, the term social media is more popular than early social networking language. Social media extend from early forms of digital communication, like the Talkomatic chatbox style of digital communication, Bulletin Board Systems (BBS), and online forums. All digital citizens leave a path, and social media has pushed those boundaries in new and different ways (Thorburn et al., 2003).

Historically, media consumers might think of MySpace, Facebook, Instagram, YouTube, Twitter, X, Snapchat, TikTok, Pinterest, LinkedIn, Twitch, Discord, Redditt, WhatsApp, BeReal, and WeChat as well-known social-facing media. Others, like Google Hangouts, Periscope, and Vine, went by the wayside as their parts were used for other apps. Periscope and Vine were purchased and incorporated by Twitter, now X. Social media apps usually require users to be at least 13 years old, due to a law from 1988 that prohibits collecting children's data without parental consent. The overwhelming majority of guardians favor these guidelines, but less than half of those under 13 are in favor. Child-focused social media, like Togetherville, was short-lived, and longer-running PopJam closed its doors in early 2023. The Grom Social App is still available. According to the Grom Social Enterprises website, Zach Marks started Grom Social at age

DOI: 10.4324/9781003397588-15

11 after getting in trouble with his parents for lying on social media (Grom Social Enterprises Inc., 2024).

While it is unclear who said it or thought of it first, adding the participatory (social) side to the media experience happened on the cusp of the 21st century. The lack of clarity is expected when using the phrase for the first time, as media, inventions, and ideas were all emerging simultaneously. At some point in the 1990s, the term social media was coined. In some ways, it mirrors the era of early tech exploration and Web 1.0. In the history of media, we've gone from one-on-one communication to mass media and now to interactive media. Some researchers have considered Samuel Morse's first Morse code transmission as an early history link to social media. Others have considered the military an early contributor to the social media experiment in the 1960s. Each of these moments had a lot to do with, and continue to have a lot to do with technology. Still, other researchers note the creation of SixDegrees platform as the moment social media began.

In the early 2000s, websites that allowed users to create and connect with media content became popular. This trend continued with the rise of Web 2.0. The "social" at this stage is in parentheses because, at that time in history, philosophers, educators, and media pundits were all discussing whether or not online connection could indeed be called "social". Many years later, in our post-pandemic world, we've learned a few things about what accounts for being social, but the debate raged on at the beginning of the 21st century. While monetizing social media as a business model took some time, joining and participating through social media was a solid and significant upward trajectory for quite some years. Early social networks include SixDegrees, MySpace, LinkedIn, Facebook, and Friendster, also advertised as dating apps, followed later by Twitter and Instagram.

Early Social Developments

The beginning of social media aimed to create content that would bring consumers back to a website hub. The introduction of hashtags, mentions, real-time participation, photo editing and sharing, digital video clips, and a variety of iterations, like Pinterest, and e-commerce sites, like Etsy and eBay, started in the late 1990s as an early frontrunner of the e-commerce push. Messaging apps like AOL Instant Messenger, WhatsApp, Slack, and other proprietary message apps worked alongside texting as alternative ways to gather groups for conversations. The idea that messages, videos, and photos could disappear, slid social media from a repository of digital diaries, notations, and personal pithy and not-so-pithy insights, to a disappearing communication experience similar to the telephone, invented over 150 years ago. Because their content vanished after viewing, Snapchat "seemed" like a safe space for communication. The quotes here note the idea that there are digital traces on all digital media. The idea of untraceable movement is a misnomer. Ephemeral content disappeared quickly and changed the focus from curated posts to casual, in-the-moment messages. Stories were introduced to share additional online content in a channel-like structure, but these could also be saved as well in disappear mode. These early social media platforms integrated emojis and later GIFs and memes into the cultural lexicon used daily in mobile phone texting communication. Memes are similar to music sampling because they use already produced snippets or clips of media content, and remix or re-use them as a new form of communication. American meme creators are protected by the Fair Use Doctrine for using someone else's copyrighted work, but they cannot copyright that work. Copyright protection goes to the original copyright holder who created the work. Additionally, technology companies merged with, traded and purchased other less popular or less financially solvent social media companies and integrated their products to untap more potential social capabilities. Websites like WebMoney and PayPal made it easy to transfer money online, which helped social networking advertising grow. Sites with sharing and content capabilities, like YouTube and Tumbler, added another layer to distribute content through phones and small digital devices.

Figure 12.1 HD video Flip camera used to record social video.

Photograph by the author.

One of the kinds of content facilitated by digital means that has been popular for many years is the meme. The word meme is short for the Greek word *"mimeta"* which means imitation. The content of a meme comes from an often, but not always, culturally relatable image, photo, or clip, often already generated. "Meme culture" refers to the prevalent use of memes in texting and social media. Personal profiles, timelines, feeds of all kinds, content sharing, and mobile apps were all in use by 2010. In the first ten years of social media, sites competed fiercely to gain users and make money. Almost all social networking sites continue to have an age limit of 13 to open a social media account. Early social app legal teams picked that age because it was a historical marker used in a US law called the Children's Online Privacy Protection Act (COPPA), which barred websites from collecting data and information from children under 13 without parent or guardian permission. The Surgeon General continues to uphold this age and encourages later use for some young people. The World Health Organization and the American Association of Pediatrics (AAP) suggest that we pay attention to the kind of screen activities children and teens participate in rather than just the total screen time. The areas of passive and active communication, and content creation have been identified as ways to weigh the quality, time, balance, and positive nature of the time on a device. The AAP notes that children under 18 months should avoid all screen time, except video chatting. Parents of children aged 18–24 months are encouraged to find high-quality programming, if possible, and encourage co-viewing, watching, or playing together. The AAP urges parents with children ages 2–5 to limit screen time to no more than an hour a day of high-quality programming, create a family media plan, and enforce it.

Some early online social spaces focused on children and young teens included Club Penguin and Webkinz. Club Penguin was a paid online site launched in 2005 by Disney that did not have an age requirement for registration and play. Players could sign up for monthly, 6-month, or yearly memberships to participate in this massively multiplayer online (MMO) game with a vibrant online community. They could create avatars, chat with fellow players, and engage in various games. Another 2005 game was Webkinz World, launched by Ganz. This online community targeting youngsters had stuffed animal merchandise tightly connected to an online community. When purchased, the stuffed animal had a tagged code that could be used to register the animal on Webkinz World, connecting the consumer's physical world of play with online play in the digital community. A player could also purchase a pet in a game to feed and play with. The game had its economy, where players could accrue KinzCash by adopting pets and playing games. With the more significant number of Webkinz stuffed animals a player possessed, their bonus points and Kinz-Cash increased. If players did not play regularly, the game would lock them out of their accounts, and when their current pet died after a year, they had to buy a new one. An adult could turn off the game's interactive feature with other players. The game moved from a free online community with the pet purchase, to a membership fee model, gaining a large and dedicated player following. The game also has in-game ads (Gehl, 2014).

Second Gen Social

As social media entered its second decade of use, it solidified itself as a technological movement, similar to the media that came before, and it changed the way prior media, now referred to as legacy media, moved into a less participatory category of media existence. New Applications developed, like the Chinese company ByteDance developed TikTok, a short form video platform, and the Brain, a French social media app that asks users to heighten the experience of authenticity of their social media experience by opening randomly picked short windows for a user to post what they're up at that moment. These different takes on the participatory experience bring new users into the social media habit. User platforms became an embedded part of daily use and influenced politics, business, education, and culture. Concerns over fake news and data privacy, as discussed in Chapter 7, started to come to the forefront.

Social media creates data from likes, clicks, post content, comments, hashtag indexing, shares, and check-ins, and media consumers wondered, who owns my data and who owns this site? Consumers also started to pay more attention to polls and games that took them out of the app. Each social media app has its privacy policies. Companies can buy and sell a data commodity provided by algorithms and data collection. This data is culled from users' activities, political views, spending habits, interests, demographics, and online behaviors. Companies gather data from multiple platforms they own to gain more specific insights. The Federal Trade Commission's (FTC) consumer protection authority stretches to social media users and the data that user creates. The increased scrutiny of the collection, purchase, and sale of social media data, and the ways social media collects data, has led to increased concern over international ownership of social media sites. Certain restrictions are placed on international ownership of legacy media, but fewer boundaries are required for internationally owned social media companies. The US Government has stepped in to strengthen consumer protections regarding sale of social media data, which the government says presents a national security risk.

Celebrities have always been part of the media story, and influencers add to their popularity by amassing a quantifiable digital following on social media that increases with activity. Another term, viral, has also been used to explain how media content quickly becomes popular through social media. Viral YouTubers gain popularity by creating timely and exciting videos that have a large following and are monetized through ads or sponsorships. Influencers are social media marketers, earning a large following because of their expertise and skills. Social media use for kids that started with Webkinz stuffed animals and Club Penguin, and then moved on to Live Streaming. Twitch, Facebook, Instagram, and YouTube Live allow users to broadcast real-time videos to their audiences. Snapchat and Instagram filters enable users to add interactive elements to the user's photos and videos. Social media platforms use artificial intelligence (AI) algorithms to suggest content, posts, and ads for users' interests and behaviors. Social media platforms utilize chatbots and digital assistants for automated customer support and addressing frequently asked questions.

Social media platforms are adopting virtual tools to foster immersive social interactions. Social listening tools are evolving into advanced analytics tools that assist brands in monitoring conversations about their products or services on social media. Integrating social media and podcasting through applications like Discord creates another platform for engagement. Geotagging and location-based services continue to allow users to tag their posts with locations, creating a need for enhanced privacy settings to give users greater control over their data and who can see their content. In the contemporary converged world, data is a commodity to buy, sell, and store. Community building and connecting is the key reason this kind of media is called "social". Soon, personalized advertising crept onto the walls and into the accounts and emails of social media users, as platforms provide highly targeted and customized advertisements by culling and scraping data. Users can now manage multiple social media accounts more easily with real-time emoticon reactions, influencer marketing, and advanced social media management tools. Scheduling and timing information is one strategy to entice users into habitual use. The idea of FOMO, the fear of missing out, earned its place in the dictionary in 2013. This idea was fostered on social media platforms. The social ramifications of constant social media apps, platforms, and usage increase research on eye strain, and dark mode options were offered, reducing eye strain and conserving device battery life. Voice-activated features made it easier for users to interact with platforms. As some social media platforms grew, others fizzled out, or were purchased by other social media companies to pollinate cross-platform sharing or additional components and features for their central platform. For example, Google, Meta, Twitter, Microsoft, and Yahoo purchased other companies to build on their social offerings and experiences.

Building Expression

GIFs and memes were two types of converged media content that moved through social media sites, texting apps, and messaging platforms. Both user-generated and website-generated GIFs and memes were designed to compress and display images in color in early internet use, when information travel through the web was slow. Increased service speeds and compression have increased creation and use. Animated GIFs have also become popular, allowing multiple images to be displayed sequentially in a single file, creating simple animations. One early animated GIF that proliferated through the Web, social media, general pop culture, and television was the "Dancing Baby" or "Baby Cha-Cha-Cha". It featured a 3D-rendered baby dancing to a looped animation and became a cultural phenomenon. In the late 1990s, website domain names and HTML shortcuts became more standardized. Popular website creation platforms included Geocities, Angelfire, Wix, Weebly, and WordPress. These too, proliferated GIFs and memes and contributed to the early visual aesthetics of internet culture. Close to ten years later, GIF design services and websites such as Giphy and Tenor have made it easier for users to search for, sometimes create, and share GIFs across technologies and websites, and eventually support and embed them into device messaging interfaces. One of the issues for GIFs and memes centered around, you guessed it, copyright issues. What were the legal ramifications for shared copyrighted material in GIF or meme form?

GIFs are improving with advanced animations, compression techniques, and use in augmented reality (AR) and virtual reality (VR). Throughout its history, the GIF has played a significant role in online culture, from its early days as a simple image format to its current status as a dynamic and versatile medium for online expression and communication. These emotional digital objects continued to develop and were the seed that created non-fungible tokens (NFTs), unique digital assets stored on a blockchain. Retail investors also use memes and social media to influence the stock market. Social media, throughout its history, has influenced fashion trends, music tastes, and the food industry. It has helped connectivity thrive through increased device use and content creation. As consumers become more dependent on online information, more individuals and organizations use these platforms to raise awareness and advocate for many different things.

Sociocultural Trends

Social media connects people globally, making the world smaller digitally. This environment can provide people with easily facilitated ways to both connect and alienate people. Social media platforms are now also a significant hub for explicit content and sexual exploitation. The variety of platforms has made it easier to connect media consumers to pornographic material and, also, to increase a variety of illegal sex trade-related activities that facilitate an environment to create media content. Another consideration comes from "cancel culture", the practice of a large group of media consumers who remove various types of support for a public figure who has done things that a specific demographic of media consumers deemed socially unacceptable. This shunning, avoiding, or rejecting as a form of hurting someone often extends to social or professional circles and can act as a tool for holding public figures accountable. Cancel culture cuts communication and fosters censorship of public discourse.

Monetization

Social media content creators can profit from their content generation and strategic branding. User-generated content makes the social media world go around, and most of the content is unpaid labor for fun and shared as a hobby or interest. A high number of followers does not explicitly show income-earning potential. Building and growing a following is an important step. Content creators make digital content, while influencers advertise products to followers. In short, they persuasively influence others through their personal cache and charisma. Social media content creators make more money when they develop a cross-platform following for cross-promotion. Repurposing content can also be a helpful strategy. Collaborations with other content creators can also be possible. Selling merchandise has also been profitable for some content creators on the way to developing their identifying brand. Some content creators sell other art, music, products, or services. A newsletter can also be a helpful way to provide more concentrated information about a brand or idea. Followers can enjoy exclusive content, like podcasts and videos, through platforms, like Patreon and other social media programs. Building brand partnerships can boost income while promoting other brands or products through affiliate links can increase earnings. Other sites might also pay for high-performing content, so there are ever-changing opportunities to reach a larger audience. Teaching what you know, sharing tips and tricks, freelancing, coaching, voice talent, and consulting are all ways to earn additional funds as a social content creator. Content creators are entrepreneurs in the freelance or gig economy. Each opportunity for collaboration and all funding opportunities comes with an obligation to read the fine print and contracts, so it is clear how funds are generated and received, and how to save a portion of earnings for taxes.

Social Media Effects

Social media is like previous mass media studied in this text because it involves the same message and many receivers. While streaming altered the time of media consumption, and media consumers can now pay to enjoy their niche content at their own pace, as media programming options have increased, social media has added another layer of complexity to the landscape. It is not only the participatory nature of social media and a user's ability to comment on many platforms, but how the content can be instantly available (Quan-Haase & Sloan, 2022). This means instantly made, shared, and immediately commented on, liked, and shared again. This kind of mass personal communication blends mass communication elements (O'Sullivan & Carr, 2018). Effects like antisocial behaviors and interpersonal changes are also studied (Turkle, 1995, 2008). Researchers also study the content of social media messages and link them to brain reception responses, as well as study the additional avoidances of social media (such as sharing, liking, and commenting) from a neuroscientific perspective (Meshi et al., 2015; Scholz et al., 2019, p. 13). The variety of research on social media effects and experiences is still growing.

My Digital Profile

The total of a person's movements in the digital world is a digital profile. Another name for a person's social media engagement is their digital footprint. When someone searches for you through various methods, you can often decide what they find. A media-literate individual knows what photos, accounts, and information to share and which to leave as personal. A social media presence helps people see a side of you that you have crafted. Only share personal information that shows you in a positive light. Stalking someone is easy, and people spend excessive time looking up information on an individual. Manage your profile, or it will manage you.

Things to Consider

- Should you update your social profile?
- Think about some crisis communications situations involving social media and research the outcome.
- Deliberate on ways you can use social media skills to your advantage.
- Study some social media monetization trends.
- Map out the different owners of social media companies, and consider the potential ramifications of international ownership.

Takeaways

- Social media can work toward changing people's lives, allowing people to go viral for their content and be seen on the internet. These platforms immediately facilitate users' access to media content, replacing cable TV subscriptions and fixed TV schedules.

- Social media allows the usage of its platforms for pornography, sexual trafficking, and more.
- "Cancel culture" tends to go to the point of bullying others and ruining the lives of some people. While the platforms work in different ways to benefit their users, the users are the ones who tend to shift the proper usage to something negative at times.
- GIFs and memes have allowed for creative expression and profit all across the internet. People have integrated these media types into texting, social media applications, and more. These GIFs and memes can be anything from movie or TV show frames to random relatable images. Creators started profiting a few years later, but GIF services were developed to simplify usage. As these different types of content constantly evolve, creators have integrated GIFs into AR and VR.

References

Gehl, R. (2014). *Reverse engineering social media [electronic resource]: Software, culture, and political economy in new media capitalism.* Temple University Press.

Grom Social Enterprises Inc. (2024, January 16). *Grom Social.* https://gromsocial.com/about/

Jenkins, H. (1992). *Textual poachers: Television fans & participatory culture. (Studies in culture* and communication). Routledge.

Jenkins, H. (2006). *Convergence culture: Where old and new media collide.* New York University Press.

Jenkins, H., Ford, S., & Green, J. (2013). *Spreadable media [electronic resource]: Creating value and meaning in a networked culture.* (Postmillennial pop). New York University Press.

Meshi, D., Tamir, D.I., & Heekeren, H.R. (2015). The emerging neuroscience of social media. *Trends in cognitive sciences, 19*(12), 771–782.

O'Sullivan, P.B., & Carr, C.T. (2018). Masspersonal communication: A model bridging the mass-interpersonal divide. *New media & society, 20*(3), 1161–1180.

Quan-Haase, A., & Sloan, L. (Eds.). (2022). *The SAGE handbook of social media research methods.* (Second ed.). SAGE.

Scholz, J., & Smith, A.N. (2019). Branding in the age of social media firestorms: How to create brand value by fighting back online. *Journal of Marketing Management, 35*(11–12), 1100–1134.

Thorburn, D., Jenkins, H., & Seawell, B. (Eds.). (2003). *Rethinking media change: The aesthetics of transition.* (Media in transition). MIT Press.

Turkle, S. (1995). *Life on the screen: Identity in the age of the internet.* Simon & Schuster.

Turkle, S. (2008) (Ed.). *The inner history of devices.* MIT Press.

13 Video Gaming and
   the Metaverse

Gaming is a significant form of screen entertainment in today's world. This chapter focuses on games and their link to transmedia, the interconnection across media from connecting games with film and TV genres, characters, and worlds, and their periods in media history. The chapter covers various topics, including the origins of gaming, gaming technologies, essential factors in game history, and the development of the metaverse. Video games, also called computer games and general gaming, combine a device with storytelling content through video, audio, and digital interactivity. Video games provide a storytelling narrative that includes entertainment and information through hardware devices, such as mobile phones, computers, consoles, screens, and software within the device or in the cloud.

People recognize video games as a protected form of media, like radio, television, and film, regarding free speech. Video games have more generic genres, including action, action-adventure, adventure, puzzle, role-playing, simulations, strategy, and sports, and subgenres within each. Massively multiplayer online (MMO) games are online games that allow many players to play together, including role-playing, shooting, and strategy games. The sandbox video game is unique because it doesn't fit a specific genre. It's all about building, being creative, and making your content. Video gameplay has evolved into educational versions that use gamification to enhance learning and strategic thinking. This chapter starts with gaming history and moves on to ideas about video game technology, economics, virtual worlds, and the metaverse. The chapter ends with research on gaming effects.

Gaming History

Gameplay has been explored for centuries, starting with children's games, pretend play, and more serious games, such as chess. It all begins with the idea of play, for both serious and fun pursuits, as part of culture. One of the

DOI: 10.4324/9781003397588-16

earliest historical accounts of gameplay is the book called *Homo ludens: A study of the play element in culture* (1949), written by Johan Huizinga. His work took a deep dive into the culture of play, noting the nature and significance of play as a cultural phenomenon and naming different types of play, like war, poetry, philosophy, and art. Huizinga shares that "Play cannot be denied. You can deny, if you like, nearly all abstractions: justice, beauty, truth, goodness, mind, God. You can deny seriousness but not play" (p. 3). His text considers the difference between seriousness and play and the game's role. At the end of the book, Huizinga notes that the player can abandon themselves body and soul to the game, pushing the consciousness of it being "merely" a game into the background. The joy inextricably bound up with playing can turn into tension. "Frivolity and ecstasy are the twin poles between which play moves" (Huizingas, 1949, p. 20–21). The idea of abandoning body and soul to the game has often been linked to video games. Still, all gameplay is associated with experience in another world separate from our embodied one. Huizinga explains this as "ordinary life". "The play's mood is labile in its very nature. At any moment, 'ordinary life' may reassert its rights, either by an impact from without, which interrupts the game, or by an offense against the rules, or else from within, by a collapse of the play spirit, a sobering, a disenchantment" (p. 21). Such is the experience for gamers, and especially those who play media infused games. Early video games often had interactive fiction, where players could use text commands to change the game world. These literary narratives moved into integrating either role-playing games or adventure games. Text-based adventure games started including graphics as technology advanced and online gaming communities expanded. Choose Your Adventure books and other interactive fiction fostered the contemporary video game landscape.

Gaming Technologies

Video games and digital video innovation started percolating at several different universities around the globe in the 1950s and '60s. At the time, cinema, television, and radio were popular media, taking up solid shares of the media pie, and consumers were increasingly developing media habits. In the early days of these media, inventors, and engineers pushed the boundaries of computer technology and how computers and video could combine for game development. In the late 1950s, physicist William Higinbotham created the game called *Tennis for Two*. Multiple person interactivity design improved and interactivity popularity grew through the 1960s and 1970s when arcade games like *Pong* and *Space Invader* became very popular. At the time, most consumers left home to play games. When Atari released its 2600 home console in the late 1970s, video games could be played at home, increasing the gaming audience. A console is a specific branded computer used to play video games. Other game companies had to upgrade console parts and features, which led to increased competition. An informal and well discussed sales competition between gaming companies, known as the "Console Wars in" the 1980s, 1990s, and early 2000s, occurred between many different companies. Atari vs. Intellivision (released by Mattel), Nintendo vs. Sega, and Sony vs. Sego vs. Nintendo were all calculated and marketed among companies and in-game player culture. The technological issues between game companies included improving sound and graphics, increasing game libraries, and developing better advertising strategies. The alternative to console play is personal computer (PC) gameplay. PCs are popular because they are multipurpose machines. They can run games with a higher frame rate, creating faster response times, render times, smoother graphics, and shorter game load times.

Soon video games adapted to education with gamified versions. The 1960s and '70s saw tremendous growth in educational video games, such as *Lemonade Stand* and *The Oregon Trail*. "In 2003, a movement for video games in education and training began. Minecraft education edition and other serious games have transformed education for the network generation" (Utoyo, 2018, p. 57). Games, such as *Lego Digital Designer, Roblox,* and *LittleBigPlanet, Civilization,* and the *Kerbal Space Program,* provide a transparent educational experience, based on learning various information.

Arcade Game Era

In the 1980s, popular arcade games like *Pac-Man* and *Donkey Kong* were turned into home games. Each decade brought improvements in visuals, speed, music, and interactivity. In the early decades of gaming, the components were part of a computer or a console entertainment system, like a proprietary computer. Increased in-game voice communication via voice chat started with Sega Dreamcast and is now standard in most gameplay. The 2000s saw a shift to online play, introducing linked systems and multiplayer experiences through the gaming console. Microsoft's Xbox and Xbox 360 entered the fray, and Sony's PlayStation 2 and PlayStation 3 became dominant games consoles.

The top gaming companies making the most money are Sony, Tencent, Microsoft, Apple, and NetEase. The United States holds the largest market share for gaming, and China, Japan, South Korea, the United Kingdom, Germany, France, Canada, Italy, and Brazil also show strong gaming revenues. However, most game players come from China. In the United States, games like the *Nintendo Wii* and *Dance Dance Revolution* introduced a

Figure 13.1 Gaming controllers.
Photograph by the author.

new aspect to game development by incorporating full-body movement (Katatikarn, 2024). Nintendo Wii games used a specialized Wii remote, a Nunchuk, a balance board, and a regular controller to manage the games based on movement. Shortly after, the video game platform was again pushed by games like *Guitar Hero* and *Rock Band*, which increased the popularity and idea of a video game. These games used controllers modeled like musical instruments to track movements and sync them to music.

Once the mobile phone moved into the smartphone era, mobile gaming acquired popularity. Video game development opened a media-related career path for artists—companies needed game developers, publishers, marketers, researchers, testers, and retail and manufacturing partners. Video game developers at Microsoft started the first game-specific union in 2023. As technology became more accessible to personally own and access, the indie game industry soon cropped up. Another growth area occurred in live play through streaming channels, e.g., the Twitch livestream platform, YouTube, and Facebook Gaming. Streamers fund esports teams, play games live or on-demand, and bring spectators to esports. A way to grow a celebrity profile is by engaging through categories not related to gameplay. Gamers increase their influence by sitting and conversing with fans on the chat using text and emojis. "Just Chatting" category streamer have special guests or host events to boost their popularity. Other streamers simply stream their day online, shopping or using social media. This kind of reaction-based entertainment sometimes entails a "you-laugh-you-lose" challenge. Most Just Chatting streamers have energetic personalities, quick wit, and humorous antics. If Just Chatting and gameplay are not your thing, Twitch has Art and Travel & Outdoor categories. The Twitch UserVoice forum works through engagement and upvotes. Online influencers also attend conventions, including TwitchCon, PAX East, and DreamHack.

Virtual reality (VR), augmented reality (AR), and metaverse play have not yet been integrated into consumer reality, but VR headsets are becoming increasingly popular. Each new gaming technology has faster processing power, load times, and increasingly immersive experiences. Advanced features, like real-time ray tracing, make graphics look more realistic, and cloud gaming allows people to play without needing game consoles. Facial recognition, eye tracking, gesture controls, and haptic feedback during gameplay work to use facial expressions and body language to personalize the game experience, and artificial intelligence (AI) programs integrate all levels of gameplay, from advanced procedural content generation to anti-cheating systems (Bender, 2019). Blockchain in gaming allows for ownership of in-game assets, microtransactions, and decentralized gaming. Matching open-world streaming technology and algorithm game generation will be ahead for gamers.

Graphic Capacities

Realistic video game visuals require vast teams of specialized artists and engineers. Advanced 3D (three-dimensional) modeling software allows artists to model detailed 3D environments, characters, and objects. Motion capture is when models or actors wear special suits that track their movements, creating a realistic player experience. The natural human motion data is captured and mapped to animated characters. Additionally, photogrammetry, ray tracing, performance capture, and procedural animation, pushed by AI and algorithms, continually push the envelope for world-creating environments and life-like visuals.

Video games overlap with cinema, television, and video in obvious and less obvious ways. Cinematic sequences, virtual camera movements, high-resolution files, interchangeable lenses, and different visual styles have influenced video game aesthetics.

Gaming Economics

Vertical integration of media companies and media conglomerates provides an economic model that creates business across various digital media more easily, creating a transmedia environment. In this way, characters and worlds can increase across multiple platforms and formats. This movement can be seen across books, zines, comics, TV, cinema, online video, video games and apps, blog writing, radio, and advertisements. Much-loved characters and worlds can be adapted to video games, movies, television, or streaming shows. In some cases, the book, comic, film, TV, or streamed programming comes first; in others, the game comes first. Gaming techniques are increasingly becoming part of visual effects in cinema and television. All forms need many creative writers and artists in the process, but the platform of gaming interactivity is essential in video game creation. In cinema and television, the director controls the action of the story. In video games, the player drives the story, bringing different probabilities and expectations.

Early on, comics or books transitioned to radio dramas or television series. Linking multiple platforms while retaining characters and stories is an intriguing way to build a franchise. Transmedia storytelling is founded on the transition between legacy and digital media platforms, facilitated through content creation and distribution models. The process includes creating and sharing a story experience across different platforms. This newer participatory content experience invites the audience to become active collaborators in the story experience, facilitated through online video, audio, mobile, game, social, and immersive media multi-platforms. When each medium serves the story and the media consumer well, a story can be introduced in one medium and expanded through others. Different forms of media like film, TV, books, comics, and games come together to boost creativity and keep consumers interested. Nowhere is transmedia storytelling more evident than in the contemporary video gaming world.

In video game history, the economic or business side comes from forming franchises by establishing a series of related video games that create a brand. The franchise improves the series and any spin-offs or cross-over products. The franchiser started the trademark, and franchisees pay to use the trademarked products, characters, and other items associated with the franchise. Transformative works, like fan art or fan fiction, are not liable to pay the franchiser because this work does not break copyright laws. It does, however, engage and leverage the existing fanbase. Activities like theme-based conventions and cosplay costumes pique the interest and involvement of fans. Tie-ins continue to engage fans as a digital extension of the series or, by extension, the franchise. Other video games include scripted games and live video gaming with commentary. Esports competitions and tournaments have become more popular, attracting younger audiences. Platforms like Twitch and YouTube made watching live and recorded video game play possible as entertainment. How the game is played, not the in-game components and built world, has shifted ideas about video games.

Screen Changes

Mobile phone screens have also increased in sophistication, partly due to increased viewing and gaming. TV screens are much larger, so everything down to the action on the screen is considered differently on a small screen. While cinema and television programming may be viewed on a mobile phone screen, content like webisodes, are specifically designed for mobile phone viewing and philosophically and technology are directed differently. Cinematic pans are traded in for lots of close-ups. Mobile phone screens range 5–7 inches, so the information on the screen is much smaller. Mobile phones also lack the higher resolution of television monitors. Most televisions today also have a wider 16:9 aspect ratio. Mobile phones are taller with aspect ratios like 19.5:9 or 21:9, so sometimes, work created for television looks different when viewed on a mobile phone. Horizontal video standards have made way for vertical video recording for consumer-generated content. Mobile phone screens are also designed for better contrast, increased brightness, and deeper blacks for a better small-screen viewing experience. Sound-wise, televisions' high-quality built-in speakers provide a better listening experience, but mobile phones have made successful strides in listening using wireless speakers or headphones.

Technologically, the actual screens of video games have also pushed sophistication. Video game screens have a higher refresh rate, which means images are displayed faster and with less delay in action response to give players a smoother and more immersive viewing experience, with improved picture quality and color settings, tailored for gaming. Games also became popular on social media, and the small screens provide gamers with hand entertainment at will. Games like *Angry Birds*, developed by a Finnish company and now owned by Sega, are situated in the history of social media gaming. *Pokémon Go* improved mobile app integration by using augmented reality and location tracking to make catching Pokémon more exciting in real life. Gaming apps have now solidly integrated mobile phone play.

Virtual Worlding

At the opposite end of mobile phone screens lies virtual world screens, often powered by larger screened monitors or computer monitors. The

1960s game *Spacewar!* is often shared as one of the earliest digital multiplayer games. While early media innovators are called inventors, in gaming, most inventors are described as developers within the computer software industry. Developer Steve Russell created the space combat game that showcased two battling spaceships. It was popular in hacker culture and then loaded into games for some players. Roy Trubshaw and Richard Bartle created text-based multiplayer adventure games in a virtual world. Their MUD1 (Multi-User Dungeon) became a base for many different game designs. Lucasfilm developed a virtual world called Habitat for the Commodore computer. It had a persistent world and allowed people to interact socially. This is one example of filmmakers and game builders merging to develop games. In the early 1990s, there was a game called *The Palace*. It had a chat platform where users could create virtual rooms and use avatars. This was one of the first instances of users creating and performing in virtual worlds. Ultima Online also pushed the envelope, creating a massively multiplayer online role-playing game (MMORPG) that launched a gameplay genre. The game gathered a large player base and illustrated players' interest in these games. Cross-pollination from different games continues to move the needle on how players play and enjoy games.

The serious study of the cultural experience of games and play took a different turn when, over 20 years ago, an experience called *Second Life* captured the attention of gamers and those interested in immersive experiences. *Second Life* was similar to a MMORPG but emerged as a world for exploration. Is *Second Life* the metaverse? While both are virtual worlds, *Second Life* is less immersive, scalable, and advanced than the metaverse. The experience is primarily based on 3D user-generated content. The official Second Life.com website shares that residents can make friends in virtual hangout spaces and remote meetings, shop virtual fashions, find a like-minded community, and explore the *Second Life* world. Users in this experience could create an avatar, join communities, and interact in a three-dimensional world. Linden Lab started Tilia, a virtual world economy where real-life content creators can profit from their creations. At first, Linden Lab made Tilia to manage the economy of *Second Life*. It lets users purchase different things for their virtual world, like furniture, clothing, houses, and vehicles. These items can be found in the *Second Life* marketplace. Linden Lab, who sold the virtual world to Meta in 2023, created *Second Life*. Blizzard Entertainment's *World of Warcraft*, a highly successful MMORPG, set new standards for immersive worlds, ushering a resurgence of interest in virtual worlds driven by advancements in virtual reality.

The birth of Second World and other virtual platforms like OpenSimultor and MozillaHubs provides users with a virtual, interconnected digital universe where they can interact, socialize, and engage in various activities. This idea has evolved into the metaverse, which takes virtual reality to a new level with more immersive experiences. Once languages like avatars, shared online commerce, and virtual economies took hold, MMOs like *World of Warcraft* increased in popularity. These large-scale online environments demonstrated the popularity and potential for shared digital spaces. VR technologies, like Oculus Rift, pushed innovators to make virtual headsets more affordable and realistic. Virtual economies continued to increase, allowing users to buy, sell, and trade digital assets through blockchain technologies and cryptocurrencies, like Bitcoin, altcoins, or Ethereum, run through apps with decentralized computing. Using blockchain-decentralized virtual worlds and empowers users to create and shape their user-driven economy. Large technology companies invest significantly in research and development to advance metaverse technologies and fuel their growth. The aim is an extended virtual space, or metaverse, with applications in remote work, social interaction, and education. Digital assistants have also become part of the gaming world. Players can use these assistants to access the game, talk to a game agent, or use the digital assistant for a variety of other needs while gaming. AI-powered chatboxes, or AI agents, are now essential in gaming for things like in-game purchases and managing digital currency. Immersive retail offers new ways to augment spending through 3D images and virtual experiences. Popular brands create 3D images and holographic displays so customers can see all sides of a product and place it in their virtual room, create worlds with games and products intertwined, and create a completely personalized virtual experience with a brand and product.

The Federal Trade Commission (FTC) is an independent agency of the US government. It is often linked to conversations about the internet and metaverse because this government entity enforces competition and marketing laws online. The agency is focused on consumer protection. This is different from the Federal Communication Commission (FCC), which is charged with protecting American natural resources. The FTC Act empowers the agency to prevent unfair competition, unfair or deceptive acts or practices involving commerce, seeks compensation for injury of consumers, establishes requirements for products, gathers information and conducts investigations on products, and makes legislative recommendations to Congress and the public, based on their agency research.

Future technologies, such as fifth- and sixth-generation cellular networks, increased connection through wearable technologies and the Internet of Things (IoT), AI, AR, and extended reality (XR), network function virtualization (NFV), software-defined networking (SDN) will all become integrated with games and video game experiences in the metaverse. Cloud computing and storytelling improve service delivery by creating efficient virtual networks and combining communication channels as big data analytics and fiber optics improve. With the increasing need to protect high-tech infrastructure, fast data transmission, cyber threats, and robust security solutions are more critical than ever. Beamforming that focuses signals on specific devices will also improve network efficiency for gamers.

As games develop, dynamic difficulty adjustments will become more central to the experience. When in-game AI adjusts to player strategy, it makes games more exciting and challenging and keeps players engaged for longer. Procedural content generation, dynamic resource allocation, and personalized non-player character (NPC) interactions keep the game interesting for players. Additionally, gaming AI systems continuously analyze player data across the entire player base to find and fix exploitable flaws, optimize challenge balance, and improve over time with accumulated experience.

Wide Demo Reach

Video games have a broad and far-reaching effect. Media users say they play games to make friends, learn new things, improve their skills, stay healthy, and have fun. In many cases, games fall into action games, adventure games, and overall play experience games. Over 60 percent of video gamers say that video gameplay builds skills in communication and leadership, and over 80 percent share it raises cognitive, creative, and collaboration skills and introduces them to new friendships. Interestingly, players aged over 65 say they play to use their brains, and over 70 percent play video games to pass the time, unwind, and relax. Over 90 percent of players note that video games can create accessible experiences for players with different abilities. The gameplay is challenging and involves problem-solving, and the chemical rush from the win becomes an intoxicating effect. Disadvantages include isolation from the physical world, increased risk of obesity because of a lack of physical activity, an increase in poor educational performance because time is spent gaming, the expense of gaming technology, and exposure to improper language and themes, which can increase aggression within players (Elad, 2023). Two-thirds of surveyed individuals say they play a video game; most players are over 18. While the average gamer is in their early thirties, the demographic ranges from children through age 65. In addition, 71 percent of kids under 18 share that they play digital games. There is about a 52–48 percentage split for male versus female play. From a tech perspective, over 60 percent play games on a smartphone, and close to 60 percent play games on a computer.

More than 70 percent play more than three hours a week. Video game revenue topped over 60 billion dollars with growth projections in the 2020s. On the PC/console side, the top game sales for PC and console include *Call of Duty*, *Madden*, *Pokémon*, *Battlefield 2042*, Marvel's *Spiderman*, and *Mario Kart 8*. Top-grossing mobile games include *Candy Crush*, *Roblox*, *Coin Master*, *Garena Free Fire*, and *Pokemon Go*. Buyers rely on videos and streams of gameplay, user and professional reviews and trailers, and ads to make their purchasing decisions, and more than 65 percent make in-game purchases a few times a year (Urbanemujoe, 2022). Teens access their smartphones, desktops, laptops, tablets, and gaming consoles during screen time, with more than 80 percent accessing gaming consoles for screened activities. Not surprisingly, more than ninety-five percent have access to a mobile phone (Pew Research Center, 2024).

In the mid-1990s, based on pressure from various stakeholders, the Entertainment Software Rating Board (ESRB) created rating information on all publicly available video games. Contemporary labels are placed on the packaging of publically available games for everyone (E), those aged 10+ (E+10), teen (T), mature aged 17+ (M+17), adults only 18+ (A), rating pending (RP), and RP but likely 17+. Ratings are required to be physically listed on boxed games and in advertising. Other countries also have game ratings based on the International Age Rating Coalition, so rating ages remain similar worldwide.

AI, AR, VR, XR & the Metaverse

There is much on the horizon for video gaming and its link to AI, AR, VR, Mixed Reality (MR), and XR. The metaverse, first described in 1992, has become a concept used to describe 3D VWs (virtual worlds) in which people interact with each other and their environment without the physical limitations of the natural world (Narin, 2021, p. 1). The main crux of the idea is the understanding that these experiences, while not part of physical reality, are still actual experiences. Along with growing digital games in these environments, the idea of the metaverse shares a central role. Some experts note media consumers are already in a quasi-metaverse, noting that mentally virtualizing comes from imagining, creating, camouflaging, deception, fake news, curiosity, and planning for the future as examples of quasi-experiences to current realities. A synonym for metaverse is the often-used word cyberspace, and AI, AR, VR MR, and XR are all mixes and extensions of that digital medium. The metaverse is becoming more like the real world with increased intelligent data, machine intelligence, and immersive media. Distraction, cybersecurity, personal privacy, and fake media will continue to be struggles, and media, digital, and internet literacies will continue to be essential skills. This 360° version of the digital world will come from synergies in immersive multiplayer games, video-based social media connections, virtual travel, remote work, and training and education.

Gaming Effects

Media effects study on computer games, usually now called video games, has been relatively pervasive since the beginning of video gameplay. Across the board, research shows both positive and negative effects from gameplay. Studies have shown improved hand–eye coordination and improved problem-solving skills through video game play, but also lack of physical activity, game addiction, and the impact on mental health. Media consumers are increasingly using the persistent virtual space called the metaverse. While still in the early phase, this digital ecosystem is already being studied by researchers. One study examines whether young Koreans socially benefit from logging onto the virtual world, a sub-category of the metaverse that allows massive numbers of users to interact in a virtual space (Oh et al., 2023). The two digital spaces used in this research study were Roblox and Zepeto. The study's hypothesis was supported; a positive relationship between the number of friends in the metaverse and the sense of social presence users perceive in the metaverse occurred. It is crucial to explore digital realities and metaverse experiences to grasp the future of online experiences. Contemporary research also examines gambling, violent games, addiction, harassment, racial/homophobic slurs, sexually explicit content and portrayal of sex, and hate speech but also in educational games and gamification, recreation therapy, and the cognitive psychology of play. Voice chats have opened communication for gamers but also provide openings for crime, sex slave trade connections, and other criminal activities. Almost all games have ratings, but open games played on the internet and new areas opened in-game bring forward issues for the video game industry and players.

End Game

Video and digital game technologies, newer digital processes and components, and digital twin technologies all play a part in the future of extended digital gaming and metaverse experience. Moving to the metaverse is the ultimate video endgame, where players return for more play beyond the main game as an extension of reality. Contemporary economic links, like blockchain and the sale of non-fungible tokens (NFT) are fostering a digital economy, and more powerful generations of mobile networks, increasingly sophisticated hardware technologies, and media content and connection need to occur before the next gaming frontier, the metaverse is fully developed.

Things to Consider

- Name the different technologies mentioned in this chapter.
- Ponder the use of AI in live game reporting. How have these technologies changed the viewer experience?

- Ponder the difference in experience between in-person and online games.
- Deliberate over reasons some games become more popular than others.

Takeaways

- Gaming is a significant style of screened content in the contemporary world.
- Games are part of transmedia, the interconnection across media that connects games with film and TV genres, characters, and worlds in their periods in media history.
- Video gaming has increased due to technologies in other media industries.
- Creating a video game involves a large crew of developers from different media and different animation software to create realistic or specifically stylized visual graphics.
- There is a connection between arcade games and video games.
- Name some of your chapter takeaways.

References

Bender, S. (2019). Headset attentional synchrony: Tracking the gaze of viewers watching narrative virtual reality. *Media practice and education, 20*(3), 277–296.

Elad, B. (2023, September 11). *Video gaming statistics – by countries, market growth, region, company, demographics, addiction, type, and subscriptions.* Enterprise Apps Today. https://www.enterpriseappstoday.com/stats/video-gaming-statistics.html

Huizinga, J. (1949). *Homo ludens: A study of the play element in culture.* Routledge and Kegan Paul.

Katatikarn, J. (2024, January 16). *Online gaming statistics and facts: The definitive guide (2024).* Academy of Animated Art. https://academyofanimatedart.com/gaming-statistics/

Narin, N.G. (2021). A content analysis of the metaverse articles. *Journal of Metaverse, 1*(1), 17–24.

Oh, H.J., Kim, J., Chang, J.J., Park, N., & Lee, S. (2023). Social benefits of living in the metaverse: The relationships among social presence, supportive interaction, social self-efficacy, and feelings of loneliness. *Computers in Human Behavior, 139*, 107498.

Pew Research Center. (2024, January 5). *Teens and internet device access fact sheet.* https://www.pewresearch.org/internet/fact-sheet/teens-and-internet-device-access-fact-sheet/

Urbanemujoe. (2022, June 10). *2022 essential facts about the video game industry.* Entertainment Software Association. https://www.theesa.com/resource/2022-essential-facts-about-the-video-game-industry/

Utoyo, A. W. (2018). Video games as tools for education. *Journal of Games, Game Art, and Gamification, 3*(2), 56–60.

14 Digital Synergies

This book has highlighted the development and use of media technologies that have made positive and negative differences in the world. Just by each medium's invention, the world is a different place. At both ends of the spectrum, from startups to multinational, vertically and horizontally integrated companies, media leadership and media-literate individuals who understand and negotiate this landscape are essential to the job market. It is a negotiation between convenience and economics, habit, and preference. Digital synergies follow us, as we follow them. This chapter shares ways new media technologies are synergistic. The chapter ends with thoughts about media literacy.

The printed newspaper brought a ripple effect into the world. Printed media shared information, but mass production brought pollution. Cinema brought entertainment, but also propaganda. Senses overload with the advent of visual media. Television brought audiences together to share cultural references and laugh and cry together, all at the same time, but produced caricatures and stereotypes in its wake. The media habit also formed with the invention of this medium. Cable companies dug up neighborhoods to deliver new programming choices, as round-the-clock music and news became a stability and cable, become a "utility." People organized their lives based on the days and nights of the programming grid. This became known as appointment television. Journalists met quick deadlines for morning and evening newspaper distribution. People turn the "boob tube" on and watch the war at the dinner table. Video became the streamed content that traveled to devices for everyone to access and view. And everyone did. Media was on demand. And with the content came embedded metadata that shared a lot more than the content of the stream.

Sounds abound as radio and music become "portable" in big and small devices. Listeners carried them in pockets and on shoulders. Speakers were connected or paired. As the music went digital, file sharing, ownership and creative rights became nebulous. Who owns what, and who gets paid for it? Radio can find the listener almost anywhere

DOI: 10.4324/9781003397588-17

they can catch a signal. But the listener pool has become fragmented. Music, sports, information, and talk have splintered into many genres and ideologies. People find the message that speaks their ideology or taste in music and stop there. As the medium evolves, diverse ideas and thoughts lead to targeted and narrowcasted messaging. Podcasting took the signal from radio and continues to increase many individually packaged bites of programs that listeners download for play. Consumers cultivate their day with a personally designed media landscape, free from the intrusion of alternative ideas, thoughts, information, or sounds. The earbuds and noise-canceling headphones make sure of that. Phones invented for talk have turned to text as media doubles back onto itself in communicative wonder. The telephone set the tone for being home to catch a call. Now, the call greets the listener with the caller's name, so "hello" isn't even necessary. But spam also greets the caller, who ignores the message. Senses overload with the advent of visual media as the message goes to voice mail because the user is doing something else or has the ringer off or slept through the alarm because they binged on a streaming show all night. The phone ring no longer indicates a pickup. Text is the preferred mode of message delivery. Additionally, generative obsolesce means consistent upgrades are a standard business model and a constant need.

Synergies abound. Sports media has created a sports-centric environment with a programming grid of choices available on digital. The question becomes who gets coverage and who makes the profit from the programming content athletes of all ages generate from the content. Sometimes, consumers connect to "Just Chat". Video games and social media have become central for entertainment and communication. While surfing and gaming were once considered antisocial behaviors, consumers turn to digital content to consume, integrate with other people's content, duet the content, and throw on a headset to talk about the content being made. Others comment on audio content and then integrate it into their music. All the consumption comes with messaging to do, or do more, to make, or make more, to listen, or tune out.

Marketing algorithms design loops that bring consumers back to visit sites time after time, day and night, 365 days a year. Engineers created search engines, indexed web pages, web servers, data centers, application programming interfaces (APIs), web hosting services, CDNs (content delivery networks), algorithms, browsers, advertising networks, social networks, aggregators, and cloud storage to organize and index digital communication on a global scale. These technologies connect to the internet and the media consumers who use them. Are you being nudged toward a preferred choice, behavior, or feeling? Possibly. Probably. Manipulation or personal curation or preference? You decide. Who are the ring leaders, the kingmakers, the naysayers, and the pundits, the advice givers and cyber bullies, the influencers, the streamers, and the cancelers, the educators, and the violators in this synergistic environment, and can we tell the difference? Where is the hive mind and the canceled culture? However, with the identification of the media messenger, the consumer becomes more media literate. Technologies are not neutral. They have positive and negative effect.

While synergies increase education, research information, and opportunities, misinformation and disinformation multiply. If one's media is specifically curated, then the effects are also personally and specifically curated. Everyone's media experience is different. Those effects need to be evaluated and considered on a daily basis. Media-literate individuals are capable of considering the positive and negative aspects of this digital connection (Bryant & Oliver, 2009).

Deep Collaboration

These increasingly new and often changing synergies have created variations in work, as more businesses use online and digital tools and allow some level of online work. While artificial intelligence (AI) and automation, and in the early days of media, electronic and mechanical modes of operation, have replaced some media jobs, other career paths involving digital tools have been created. Businesses and global commerce have embraced the digital domain through online shopping and digital retail, digital payments, cryptocurrencies, and blockchain to facilitate financial transactions more synergistically.

The deep web references a subsection of the internet that is unavailable through standard search engines and browsers. Private enterprises that general browsing cannot access, take up this subsection of unindexed websites. Users secure personal communications in the deep web with unique or pay-walled content and databases. A subset of the deep web is called the dark web. As the name suggests, this is a hidden small subsection that requires inscription programs to facilitate anonymous browsing and access to deep websites. Illegal and criminal activities and illegal content, viruses, and scams are more likely to occur on the dark web. In contrast, the dark web facilitates communication in countries where digital communication is monitored, and free speech is limited. Law enforcement monitors the dark web for illegal activities.

The convenience of the digital economy has been embraced by most companies worldwide. Entertainment has become more digitally created and enhanced, individually tailored and on demand. Streaming services for almost any kind of media, including video and audio content, allow instant access for a price. Media economics and business models have shifted, converged, and become more synergistic. Consumer usage and purchase

Figure 14.1 Music concert with a digital light show.
Photograph by the author.

patterns have become more researched and identified than ever. The personalization and customization of media use, called by some narrowcasting as a juxtaposition to broadcasting, is tailored to individual interests and needs based on data collection and algorithms. Privacy and surveillance concerns have also become central to this environment of synergies and convergence. Consumers have changed their media use and behavior based on digital tools.

Information Loading

The Freedom of Information Act (FOIA) ensures that the public can access records from any federal agency. The process requires federal agencies to disclose requested information unless it falls under nine exemptions, including harm to the government or private interest. Some areas of exemption include those classified under executive order, specific and private personal issues, confidential trade or commercial interest, some maps and geographical regions, and some law enforcement records, among other exemptions. Anyone can submit a request on the FOIA.gov website. An organization like WikiLeaks, sometimes called a whistleblower organization, was a group of political activists that provided or leaked documents to journalists, the press, and the public. Just like with any other information, journalists need to verify website information. WikiLeaks was an online publisher that "specializes in the analysis and publication of large datasets of censored or otherwise restricted official materials involving war, spying, and corruption. It published more than 10 million documents and associated analyses" (Freedom of the press Foundation, n.d.). Cryotome is another similar library of documents, which closed down in 2023. Watchdog and investigative journalists use various digital tools for research and investigation, including sophisticated social media searches, finding, and accessing archived chats, people tracking through digital footprints, and getting unique story leads through themed podcast transcriptions.

Compression Goals

One of the significant ways these media synergies have been facilitated is through the technological invention called compression. While it is not

Figure 14.2 32 GB SD card for a digital camera.
Photograph by the author.

always studied within a survey of media, this vital idea and invention has encouraged synergy in the contemporary media environment. Without compressed files, media does not go places. Compressing complex ideas into efficient visual streams of information has existed for centuries. An earlier chapter mentioned the invention of Morse code in the 1930s, which is one place to start a compression timeline. Transmitting textual communication across long distances using dots and dashes, using telegraph wires, was one early way to compress written language effectively. Twenty years later, the Huffman coding algorithm became widely used for lossless data compression, creating efficient data storage. Another twenty-year jump brings run-length encoding (RLE) into existence for early computer systems to compress text and images, creating an earlier platform that facilitates later files like the GIF. The Lempel-Ziv-Welch (LZW) algorithm capitalized on the RLE idea, which allowed the integration of popular compression formats like GIF and TIFF. The 1980s saw lossy image compression, which effectively brought image compression techniques like JPEG (Joint Photographic Experts Group) into existence, and allowed the storage and transmission of digital images with reduced file sizes. The MPEG (Moving Picture Experts Group) compression allows for efficient video content storage on SD cards and upload using MPEG-2, MPEG-4, and H.264 codecs.

Modern data compression is a technology in constant flux, as digital files and streaming become a significant component of media products. And so on. Who owns these patents, and who uses them? Who gets around patents for their end-game use? Words themselves have become compressed. Text language, white space between letters, and 120-character limits in text boxes have compressed communication. The compression is not only technological but personal. Time on task is shortened as people try to use technology for time-saving enterprises. Life is genuinely squeezed, compacted, condensed, constricted, packed down, and crowded together because of the experience of media compression. But the synergies, working together toward collaboration, cooperation, and combined effort, bring people together.

What's Next

In the mediated environment, the "what's next" soon becomes "retro". What is different, is that this media-linked environment is not going away unless electricity goes away. And that is a whole other story. Many media platforms share similar invention timelines because inventors, engineers, and experts worked simultaneously across various linked technologies that would become part of the media. The telegraph and telephone technologies converged in the late 1800s when telephone networks started carrying telegraph traffic, creating the first integrated telecommunications systems. In the mid-1900s, broadcasting and computing joined to develop personal computers and the internet, and heralded the age of multimedia convergence, integrating mobile phones with web access, cameras, and global positioning systems (GPS) to create the smartphone. The convergence of the internet and television in the early 2000s has resulted in many technologies that use extensive data analysis, machine learning, and AI to give inanimate objects "smart" technologies; "smart" devices such as phones, speakers, cars, homes, and TVs, to name a few, along with streaming services and on-demand content. Traditional cable and satellite television have had to adapt to this new digital landscape.

Wearable technology involving the collection of quantified data, sensors, computing, and connectivity has created smartwatches and fitness trackers, which offer a range of functions in their original and historical usage. Smart devices have heralded in the age of the Internet of Things (IoT), the convergence of internet connectivity, sensors, and everyday objects. The economic and industrial structure of agriculture, healthcare, and manufacturing have all been altered by IoT innovative technologies and cloud computing, and increased algorithmic connections continue to proliferate changes and improvements for access and management of data and applications.

As 5G technology rolls out, the convergence of telecommunications and data services enables faster and more reliable connectivity for various applications, including IoT and autonomous vehicles. Blockchain technology will be an essential aspect of future media technologies, as a meaningful way to continually reduce storage and transmission costs associated with data storage. Blockchain also adds more information to data compression. Compression is one of the founding innovations and principles of convergence, which gives us contemporary media synergies. Convergence means the integration of various technologies, experiences, or roles into a single device or platform. AI continues to converge in multiple industries and markets. Cryptocurrencies and decentralized finance (DeFi) platforms continue to grow. Our lives have been impacted by the convergence of media and digital technologies that have driven innovation, altered entire sectors, and shaped work and play. Virtual reality (VR) and augmented reality (AR), combined into extended reality (XR), have revolutionized gaming and various immersive experiences. XR technologies immerse users in digital environments and overlay digital content onto the real world. While the first VR headset was invented in the 1960s, VR didn't gain mainstream attention until the 1990s. Oculus Rift Inventor, Palmer Luckey created the VR headset in 2012. Google Glass and *Pokémon GO* demonstrated AR's potential for gaming and entertainment early in the 2000s.

Mobile AR experiences are making inroads in the education, healthcare, and manufacturing industries. Physical and virtual content in real-world environments create new-level experiences. Combined with advanced optics and AI, immersive experiences will continue to drive XR hardware. Expect significant improvements in resolutions, field of view, form factors, and user input. As technology companies work to decrease motion sickness, develop compelling content, increase security and accessibility, and reduce manufacturing costs, the global XR market is forecast to grow. XR will undoubtedly bring media into new immersive digital experiences, transforming how citizens interact with the world around them. In time, media consumers will become consumers, as almost all technologies integrate media to inform, design, train, enjoy, connect, and experience the world.

Union Fallout

Changes in technologies and platforms have been at the forefront of union work stoppages within media and entertainment industries in many converged and synergistic areas of media. The Screen Writers Guild notes that "changes in the entertainment industry, often driven by technological change, have presented each generation of union members with new challenges and opportunities to pursue that goal" (Writers Guild of America West, n.d.).

Many media and entertainment trade unions worldwide help their members have a voice in their workplace environment and business. Employees in media employment will often see these acronyms.

African Union of Broadcasting (AUB)
American Federation of Musicians (AFM)
American Society of Cinematographers (ASC)
Arab States Broadcasting Union (ASBU)
Art Directors Guild (ADG)
Asia-Pacific Broadcasting Union (ABU)
Caribbean Broadcasting Union (CBU)
Casting Society of America (CSA)
Communication Workers of America (CWA)
Costume Designers Guild (CDG)
Directors Guild of America (DGA)
European Broadcasting Union (EBU)
International Alliance of Writers Guild of America (IAWG)
International Association of Broadcasting (IAB/AIR)
International Brotherhood of Electrical Workers (IBEW)
International Brotherhood of Teamsters (IBT)
Location Managers Guild (LMG)

Make-Up Artists and Hair Stylists Guild (MUAHS)
National Association of Broadcast Employees and Technicians (NABET)
National Association of Broadcast Employees and Technicians-
  Communication Workers of America (NABET-CWA)
North American Broadcasters Association (NABA)
Producers Guild of America (PGA)
Screen Actors Guild-American Federation of Television and Radio Artists
  (SAG-AFTRA)
International Alliance of Theatrical Stage Employees, (IATSE)

These groups represent all the different parts of the creation of entertainment media. Some groups are called unions, and others are called guilds (See https://www.freelancevideocollective.com/filmmaker-resources/film-unions/). Both set standards for their industries and craft.

The 1980s also saw several work stoppages from media-related unions. The 1981 WGA strike resulted in writers winning a share of the revenues from the emerging home video market. After many years of ABC, CBS, and NBS networks, Fox was launched in 1986, offering additional network programs to viewers nationwide. Shortly after, NABET strikes at NBC, involving TV technicians and engineers, focused on the network's use of non-union freelance workers and job security. Additional NABET work stoppages occurred against ABC, CBS, and NBC. Technical workers continued to strike over issues with new technologies, outsourcing of jobs, new platforms and compensation for them, syndication, and other rerun compensation in domestic and foreign markets, as well as benefits. More recent concerns grew from streaming platforms and AI use within the media and entertainment industries. These union issues continue today and often focus on new and changing technologies used in the industry and their benefits (Kisselhoff, 1996). Other work stoppages came with the WGA strike in 2007–2008. Their aim was residuals for DVDs and New Media. In 2012, SAG and AFTRA merged into one union to meet the more holistic needs of the industries they champion.

The complete fallout and shift from the nearly 4-month SAG-AFTRA strike in 2023 is not yet available, but so many hours of work stoppage means that many projects will need the same type of people power, expertise and technology all at the same time, to start and catch up or shift. Postponements and canceled projects happened, and new rules will change entertainment workflows and economic contracts moving forward. Some of the most significant American strikes have come from media-related unions like SAG-AFTRA and the IBEW in less than forty years. Arts, entertainment, and recreation work stoppages are pretty low relative to other industry union groups in manufacturing, education, healthcare, construction, and transportation (Writers Guild of America West, n.d.).

Overarching Effects

One of the main emphases of media studies moving forward will be to better understand media effects of digital technologies. This effort requires cross-disciplinary work that brings together many strategies and perspectives. One cross disciplinary research area that may be helpful is psychology. This discipline is developing formal models to measure and explain complex media processes involving algorithms, wearable and ambient communication technologies, and augmented, virtual, and extended realities. Certainly, other disciplines will also join in this kind of research. Media history can also build upon and forecast the future of media-related effects, by helping us learn from our mistakes and create new innovations. Realizing the path of the past can also open the doors to consider and improve the present and future ethical and technological considerations. Chapters 2 through Chapter 5 of this text shared ways in which print and text-based media, cinema, television and video, and journalism developed and shaped the current media landscape. Chapters 6 through Chapter 8 capitalized on music recording and Foley, radio, audio, podcasting, and sports media and their recent proliferation in the digital landscape. Chapters 9–13 explored the synergistic convergence of all media, creating media messages in the form of content and a proliferation of devices, platforms, and technologies to push that content to the media consumer. These chapters all explore the value of the interconnected technology to create a whole, more powerful than the parts, through mobile phones, media marketing and audiences, social media, gaming and metaverse, and the digital synergies of all media considered in this survey.

Recent technological developments change how consumers select media devices and content, and how media plays a role in human–technology–world relations. For instance, in an algorithmically personalized media environment, specific actions using media technology, clicking a link, or listening to music can be tracked, and the user can be technologically nudged in a particular direction of use or experience. If a human's action, like task switching in multitasking, can be identified, and inferred through AI, those actions can be reasonably confidently predicted. This decision science is becoming increasingly valued and necessary for the media industry as technologies integrate more seamlessly with media. "To understand modern—and future—media behaviors, media psychology scholars must push forward in developing theories that can account for the complex interplay between cognitive, social, and algorithmic processes that characterize the modern media landscape" (Fisher & Hamilton, 2021, p. 222). While FlowGPT organizes ChatGPT, data tracking, algorithms, and data mining churn away, social media, dating apps, and security services integrate, and Vimeo and Cash App swap stories with the wearable technology, speculative realists consider all of it, and synergies abound.

Media Literacy

Media literacy is about finding the most fruitful ways of living in a world founded on centuries of media invention, innovation, and development. Critical thinking involves becoming more media, technologically, digitally, and internet savvy and literate. Understanding media history helps us become active participants instead of passive observers. Awareness of how media impacts us allows us to make responsible decisions on a personal and societal level. We are being analyzed and judged for online activity and dollars. We must explore media content and infrastructure. In short, media industries research us, so we should study them. Media content is telling our cultural story. Are we in it? Understanding how something is made helps us to understand it better. Media criticism helps us deconstruct and analyze media texts. Resources about media technology and philosophical approaches to media can be helpful when digging into a media literacy study (Potter, 2018; Potter, 2015; Christ & De Abreu, 2020; Van Den Eede et al., 2017; Irwin, 2016; Massey, 2002). At the end of each chapter, the Things to Consider and Takeaway sections were designed to get you thinking in a media-literate direction. Observe your experience and think about how daily media use makes you feel. Evaluate the time you are on technology. Think about the reasons you are using media. What do you and others observe about your media habits? Understand your relationship to the media you use. Here are fourteen short suggestions to start your journey as a media-literate consumer.

1 Keeping a log of your media usage is a tremendous, low-stakes way to start. This small week-long exercise helps you focus on your media consumption habits.
2 Spend a day without using any media. See what that is like.
3 Read some headlines. Do they match the story?
4 All media are constructions. How many decisions go into what you watch? Take it way back to the original makers—list who is involved.
5 What do you watch on television that you consider "real"?
6 Who owns the media you watch? Find the company's name that holds your favorite streaming show, film, or social media. Do a little research on that company. What do they own?
7 What values do your media uphold? How can you tell?
8 Look at three news stories written about the same topic. Are the facts the same? Add two more media portrayals of the story. Still the same? Pick a news outlet you never use. Is that story different?

9 Do you read? How often and by what means do you read: books, online, eBook, magazine?

10 Who owns the music you listen to? Do you know how the musician or actor is paid for their work?

11 What can't be shown on broadcast television? What are the Federal Communication Commission (FCC) decency rules?

12 Check out the branding of your favorite celebrity. What messages is their PR team creating about them?

13 How do influencers influence you?

14 Where are you seeing negative stereotypes in the media you view? Others view? Compare.

Things to Consider

- Deliberate cross-disciplinary work on media effects. What disciplines and research areas could be involved?
- Study ways that algorithms might be nudging your media choices and habits.
- Contemplate what you'd like to request from the government under the FOIA. What information is the government protecting from journalists?
- Name the different technologies mentioned in this chapter.

Takeaways

- Media are synergies when the different aspects of legacy media intertwine and converge with digital technologies to shape our contemporary media landscape.
- Media synergies have significantly impacted how we use and view media and this affects our everyday lives.
- Compression technology is crucial to media synergies because it helps different digital technologies converge into new pipelines to improve media technologies and products.
- Multidisciplinary work deepens our comprehension of the intricate workings of contemporary media and their consequences.
- Examining the development of various media forms provides crucial insight and a more complete picture of the media environment.
- Technology advancements motivated by algorithmic personalization and its effects on user experiences shape a user's decisions about media devices and content.
- Name some of your chapter takeaways.

References

Bryant, J., & Oliver, M.B. (Eds.). (2009). *Media effects: Advances in theory and research*. Routledge.

Christ, W.G., & De Abreu, B.S. (Eds.). (2020). *Media literacy in a disruptive media environment*. Routledge.

Fisher, J.T., & Hamilton, K.A. (2021). Integrating media selection and media effects using decision theory. *Journal of Media Psychology: Theories, Methods, and Applications, 33*(4), 215–225. https://doi.org/10.1027/1864-1105/a000315

Freedom of the Press. (n.d.). *WikiLeaks.* https://freedom.press/organizations/wikileaks/

Irwin, S.O. (2016). *Digital media: Human–technology connection*. Rowman & Littlefield.

Kisseloff, J. (1996). The box: An oral history of television, 1920–1961 (Book Review). *Journalism and Mass Communication Quarterly, 73*(3), 754.

Massey, K. (2002). *Media literacy workbook*. Wadsworth Publishing Company.

Potter, W.J. (2015). *Introduction to media literacy*. Sage Publications.

Potter, W.J. (2018). *Media literacy*. Sage publications.

Van Den Eede, Y., Irwin, S.O., & Wellner, G. (2017). *Postphenomenology and media: Essays on human–media–world relations*. Lexington Books.

Writers Guild of America West. (n.d.). *A history of WGA contract negotiations and gains.* https://www.wga.org/the-guild/about-us/history/a-history-of-wga-contract-negotiations-and-gains

Index

1996 Telecommunications Act 117, 120, 202
24-hour news cycle 5, 58, 77, 82, 86, 152

above the fold 80
above-the-line 38
advertisers/advertising 7–8, 86, 100, 115, 120–123, 130–131, 152, 154, 156, 160–169
aerial cameras 151
agenda setting 5, 90
aggregate/ aggregators 195
Aldus Manutius 26
algorithm(s) 5, 8, 75, 84, 99, 101, 107, 109, 121, 153, 157, 175–176, 185, 195, 197, 199, 203
AM radio/ Amplitude Modulation 106, 112–114, 119–121
AM for Every Vehicle Act 121
American Association of Pediatrics (AAP) 174
American Booksellers Association (ABA) 20
amplifiers 120
analog-to-digital 101, 124
animation 43–44, 177, 185
announcer 60, 81, 104–105, 115–116, 121–122
APIs 195
arcade 102, 182–183
Area of Dominant Influence (ADI) 165
ARPANET 54
American Society of Composers, Authors and Publishers (ASCAP) 121

artificial intelligence (AI) 27, 41, 72, 82, 85, 99, 121, 124, 137, 151, 158, 176, 185, 196
aspect ratio(s) 44–46, 57, 69, 151, 187
attentional synchrony 47
audience measurement 156–157, 161, 165–169
audio mixing 96, 99, 101–102, 141
augmented reality (AR) 27, 45, 71–72, 83–85, 125, 138, 151, 153, 164, 177, 185, 187, 200, 203
automation 86, 106, 114, 124

Baby Bells 130
backpack journalists (BPJs) 82
bandwidth 71, 73
beamforming 190
behind-the-scenes (BTS) 70, 164
below-the-line 39
Betamax 6, 55, 67–68
big data 151, 190
billboards 27, 157–160
binge-watch/binge 67, 75–76, 136, 195
blockchain 28, 85, 102, 177, 185, 189, 192, 196, 200
Blu-ray 40
Book Expo 20
bookstore 20, 21, 24
bookstore culture 24
bootlegged 106
box sets 75
branding 46, 108, 119, 158, 164, 168, 178
broadcast journalism 78, 81
broadcast quality 71–72

broadcasting 50–53, 57–58, 63,
   66, 70–71, 97, 104, 112, 114,
   119, 120–124, 129, 132, 148,
   149, 152, 154, 163, 165, 197,
   200, 201
broadcast Music Inc. (BMI) 12r
Bronze Age 22–23

cable 8, 51, 54–60, 63, 70–71, 75,
   82–83, 87, 117, 124, 129, 138,
   148–152, 163–168, 179, 195, 200
camera obscura 32–33
camera stabilizers 45, 52
carbon footprint 26–27
CDNs (content delivery networks) 195
cell phone 7, 70, 72, 86, 132–135,
   139–142, 150
chatbot 158, 172
Chat GPT 203
Children's Internet Protection Act
   (CIPA) 59
children's literature 21–22
Children's Online Privacy Protection
   Act (COPPA) 174
cinema 9, 22, 32–47, 51, 57–58, 68,
   69, 78, 96, 97–99, 121, 125, 149,
   160–161, 164, 182, 185–187, 194,
   201, 203
cinema as media 33
cinéma vérité 42
cinematographers 38, 201
citizen journalist 5, 83, 85
clickbait 84
codes of ethics 87–88
college radio 104
color tube 6
color TV 63
Comics Code Authority (C.C.A.) 23
Comics Magazine Association of
   America (CMAA) 132
comics 22–24, 29, 186
commercial spots 157
commercials 56, 71, 114–122, 157,
   163, 165, 166, 167, 168
communications Assistance for Law
   Enforcement Act (CALEA)-9
compression 71–74, 101, 157, 177,
   198, 199, 200
computer-generated imagery (CGI) 43,
   45, 53

conglomerate 60, 61, 83, 186
connectivity 7, 54, 58, 85, 124, 137,
   138, 141, 177, 200
console 58, 68, 71, 113, 136, 182–183,
   185, 190–191,
consumers 5, 6, 8, 27–33, 46–50, 53,
   56–59, 63, 68–71, 78, 82–89, 100,
   101–102, 107–108, 113, 116, 118,
   119, 120, 123, 134, 136, 138, 139,
   140, 141, 148, 149, 157, 160–169,
   172, 175, 177, 178, 182, 186, 189,
   191–192, 195, 197, 201, 203
content 116, 120–124, 125, 129,
   133, 137, 138–139, 149–154, 156,
   160–168, 172,
content creator 2, 7, 8, 33, 44, 53, 69,
   72, 74, 82, 85, 86, 108, 133, 150,
   153, 160, 178, 188
content delivery networks CDNs 195
content is king 160
Corporation for Public Broadcasting
   (CPB) 54, 123
counterculture 24
crisis management 158
critical thinking 8, 41, 204
cryptocurrencies 189, 196, 200
cybersecurity 84, 140, 189, 191
cyberspace 191

Dark Age 23
dark web 196
data Tracking/collection 151, 203
decentralized finance (DeFi) 200
deep web 196
Demand-side platforms (DSPs) 161
demographics 5, 19, 27, 166, 167, 168,
   175, 178, 190
democratization 85
Department of Homeland Security
   (DHS) 140
Designated Market Area (DMA) 7, 21,
   160–161, 165
digital assets 177, 189
Digital Audio broadcast (DAB) 114,
   120, 148
Digital audio recording (DAT) 101
Digital Cinema Package (DCP) 45
digital footprint 135, 179, 198
digital Intermediate (DI) 45
Digital Light Processing (DLP) 69

digital profile 179
digital rights management (DRM) 27
digital Synergies 195, 203
Director of Photography (DOP) 38
Disc Jockey (DJ) 105, 107, 115–116,
    119, 123
Dogma 95 43
Domain name system (DNS) 83
Don Ihde 3
drive time 116
drones 45, 82, 84, 86, 149, 151,
    75, 202
DVD 39, 40, 56, 68
dyslexia 18

eBooks 24, 26
electromagnetic waves 112–113,
    132–133, 112–113
Electronic Communications Privacy
    Act 132
electronic communication 129
electronic media 6, 63
Electronic News Gathering (ENG) 67
electronic surveillance132
embedded journalists 78, 86
Emergency Alert System (EAS) 117
emergency broadcast system (EBS) 117
Etruscan script 25
Extended Elaboration Likelihood
    Model 47
Equal Time Rule 82
Extended Reality (XR) 27, 41, 96, 125,
    151, 189, 200

facial motion capture (MO-CAP) 45,
    84, 136, 185
fake news 16, 84–85
facial recognition 45, 84, 136, 185
Federal Radio Commission (FRC) 81,
    112, 117
FEMA 117–118
film editing 37, 40, 41
film preservation 44
film stock 33, 36
Flow GPT 203
Foley 9, 95–100, 203
FOMO 70, 176
fonts 25–26, 137
Food and Drug Administration
    (FDA) 139

Foreign Intelligence Surveillance Act
    (FISA) 132
Fourth Estate 162
frames per second fps 36
Freedom of Information Act 87, 197
Freedom of the press 87–88
frequency modulation/FM Radio 106,
    111–112, 114

gambling 153–154, 192
gameplay 99, 154, 182–192
gaming companies 183–184
gaming platforms 154
gatekeeping/gatekeeper 5–6
generations 21, 61, 136, 192
George Gerbner 62
Global Music Rights (GMR) 121
golden age of animation 43
GPS 54, 72, 139, 141, 151, 200
graphics interchange format .gifs
    177, 199,
Gutenberg Press 159

handheld games 42–43, 135
haptics 46
High-definition (HD) 57, 70–72,
    136–137
high-frame-rate (HFR) 45
horizontal integration 44, 61, 187

Ihde, Don 3, 32
Industrial Revolutions 10
influencer(s) 107, 136, 157–159, 164,
    168–169, 175–178, 185, 196
Instructional Materials Motivation
    Survey (IMMS) 125
intellectual property 59–60, 79, 108
Internet Corporation for Assigned
    Names and Numbers (ICANN) 162
Internet of Things (IoT) 72, 102,
    189, 200

journalism 5, 9, 19, 71, 77–88, 158,
    163, 203 as a practice 75–78,
jukebox 102–103
just chatting 185

leadership 38, 60, 118, 133, 190, 194
legacy 67, 29, 71, 122, 154, 158–163,
    166, 186 as media 1, 5, 59, 77–78,

83, 86, 97, 120, 122, 160, 171, 175, as platforms 61, 120 as television 5, as news organizations 5, 83, as radio 8, of print 21, of cinema 43–44
Lempel-Ziv-Welch (LZW) 199
letterpress 18
liquid crystal display (LCD) 57, 69
literacy 17–21
lithograph 18
live news 148
live shots 5, 85, 147–148
long term evolution (LTE) 72

magazines 16, 19–27, 79, 147, 149, 156–157, 168
market share 161, 183
marketing 39, 71, 107, 153, 154–169
mass communication 4, 15, 117, 179
Massively multiplayer online (MMO) games 181
Massively multiplayer online role-playing game (MMORPG) 188
Media System Dependency 75
media effects 1, 5, 8–9, 15, 28–29, 46–47, 62–63, 89, 107, 178–179, 192, 203
media influence 9, 28, 61–62
media literacy 4, 8–9, 41, 84, 135, 140, 194, 204
Media Multiplexity Theory 141
media oversight 59, 117
Media Priming 12
media research 9, 161
meme culture 174
Metaverse 10, 46, 181, 185–192, 203
MIDI Controllers 98, 102
military media 118
Mixed Reality (MR) 191
mobile apps 27, 139, 152, 174
mobile control rooms 148
mobile games 191
mobile phone 2, 5, 44, 53, 57, 69, 71–72, 82, 85, 108, 114, 118, 120, 128, 131, 133, 135, 141, 168, 173, 182, 184, 187, 191, 200, 203
mobile-friendly 24, 44, 138
Model of Narrative Comprehension and Engagement 47
Monastic scribes 18

monetization 39, 70, 108, 122, 160, 165, 171, 178
Mood Management Theory 75
MozillaHubs 188
multi-track recording 99, 101
multimedia journalists (MMJs) 72, 82
multimedia messages (MMS) 135
Mumblecore 43

National Anthem 56
Narrative Comprehensive and Engagement 47
National Association of Broadcasters (NAB) 81, 120
National Book Week 21
National Institute of Standards and Technology (NIST) 140
Near Field Communication (NFC) 27
Network Function Virtualization (NFV) 189
networks 49, 53, 54–60, 71
new media 6. 70
newspapers 15–19, 43, 60, 78–83, 86–89, 148, 156, 160–164, 168, 194,
Non player character (NPC) 190
noncommercial radio 111, 123
nonfungible tokens (NFTs) 85, 177, 192
National Telecommunication and Information Administration (NTIA) 132

On Demand 46, 58, 70, 120, 122, 152–153, 164, 185, 194, 200
one-party consent 87, 131
online distribution 95, 108
online video platform (OVP) 74
OpenSimultor 188
OTT 70–71
Outside Broadcast (OB) 148
Owned & Operated (O&O) 60

Payola Scandal 107
Print On Demand (P.O.D) 27
pamphlets 15
papyrus 17
parchment 17–18
participatory 62, 83–87, 128, 138–139, 171–172, 175, 179, 186

pay-walled content 196
Peer to Peer (P2P) 107
Peoplemeter 165–166
performance analytics 151
performance capture 185
photography 19, 38, 43, 52, 54, 79, 149
photogrammetry 185
photogravure 19
pirate radio 118, 119
platforms 136, 138, 149, 150, 153, 154, 156, 160, 161, 164, 165, 166, 167, 173, 175, 176, 177, 178, 179, 186, 187, 188
podcasting 9, 84, 106, 112, 122–124, 154, 166, 176, 195, 203
point of view perspective (POV) 47
pop culture 3, 177
portable 19, 27, 51, 53, 68–69, 79, 132–133, 166, 194
press pass 5, 80
Print-on-demand (POD) -2
Printing press 2, 14, 15, 18, 78–80
Privacy 27, 59, 70
Privacy Protection Act 82
procedural animation 82
programming 6, 49–63, 66, 70, 74–75, 100, 111, 148, 149, 152, 157, 160–168, 174, 186–187, 194–195; for cable 57, 75; for radio 104, 105, 106, 113–125; for television 53–56, 5982
propaganda films 41
public affairs 122, 162
public relations 7, 156–158
publishing 7, 15–29, 78–79

Quick response (QR) codes 27, 157
Quilting 17
QWERTY 72

Radio Data System (RDS) 114
radio formats 105–106
radio operations 116
Radio Television Digital News Association (RTDNA) 88
radio 8–9, 49, 51–55, 58–68, 80–87, 95–97, 100, 103–108, 111–125, 132, 136, 139, 147, 151, 158–159, 161–168, 181, 186, 194–195, 202

ratings 164–166
ray tracing 185
Really Simple Syndication (RSS) 122
recording formats 67
Renaissance 18, 25, 159
Reporter's Privilege 82
RFID chips 151
ring tone 134
Run-Length Encoding (RLE) 199

sandbox video game 181
satellite 54–59, 80–82, 106, 111, 117–124, 132, 148–149, 164, 166, 200
saturation 7–8
screens 2, 15, 32, 40, 45, 49, 57–58, 66, 68–73, 95, 134, 136–138, 181, 187,
search engine optimization (SEO) 27, 158
sexually explicit content 192
Shield Laws 82
Short Message Service (SMS) 74, 134, 136, 137
SkyCams 151
slang 136
Slow Cinema 43
smartphone 27, 72, 86, 128, 132, 134–139, 184, 190, 200
smart devices 102, 200
SMART TV 58, 63, 70
social demographics 167
social media effects 178–179
social media 5, 8, 27, 29, 39, 44, 46, 59, 62, 66, 69–74, 82–86, 106–109, 118, 135–140, 149–153, 156–169, 171–179, 186–191, 195, 198, 203,
Society of Professional Journalists (SPJ) 88
Society of European Stage Authors and Composers (SESAC) 121
sociocultural trends 177
Software-Defined Networking (SDN) 190
sound/sounds 95–109
Soundscape 46, 95–98, 102, 111–114, 119–121, 123–125, 128, 132–133, 147, 148, 183, 187, 194–195
Sports media 54, 147, 149–154
sportsbooks 153

Stored Communications Act 132
streamers 75, 149, 184, 185, 196
streaming platforms 33, 39–40, 57, 58,
    61, 70, 75, 84, 102, 107, 149, 164,
    166, 202
Sunshine Laws 82
supply-side platforms (SSPs) 161
sustainable inks and facilities 27
synergies 77, 95, 99, 136, 171, 191–203

Technicolor 36, 43
telefitness technologies 151
telegraph 117
telephone 2, 73, 80, 117,
television furniture 51, 57, 68, 113
television 5, 7, 9, 22, 33, 38, 39, 44,
    49, 63, 66, 68–75
terrestrial 61, 120
texting 2, 72, 128, 133–137, 139,
    172–176
The American Film Institute (AFI) 44
The Associated Press (AP) 80
The Book of Kells 18
The Entertainment Software Rating
    Board (ESRB) 191
The Federal Communications
    Commission (FCC) 59, 60, 82, 112,
    114, 116–120, 123, 130–133, 139,
    162, 189
The Freedom of Information Act
    (FOIA) 87
The Latin American Cinema Novo 42
The National Highway Traffic Safety
    Administration (NHTSA) 140
The Pen Register Act 132
The Penny Press 79, 88, 147
the press box 80
The United Nations International
    Covenant on Civil and Political
    Rights (ICCPR) 89
The World Health Organization
    (WHO) 174
Transmedia/transmedia storytelling
    21–24, 99, 164 182, 186
Two-factor authentication (2FA) 140

US Department of Defense Advanced
    Research Projects Agency
    (DARPA) 54

Unauthorized use 107–108
underground comix 24
unions 201
Upfronts 166–167
Uses and Gratification Theory 75

Vehicle safety systems (V2) 135
vertical integration 61, 99, 186
vertical video 44, 187
video calling 73–74
video chats 66, 72, 74, 82, 96,
    138, 174
video conferencing 73–74
video formats 73
video games 10, 22, 24, 103, 153, 154,
    181–187, 190–192, 195
video games rating 191
Video Jockey (VJ) 122
Video Journalists (VJs) 82
Video On-Demand (VOD) 70
video stores 40, 68, 5–9, 22, 27, 39
video 5–10, 22, 27, 44, 45–46,
    49–63, 67–76
virtual economies 189
virtual reality (VR) 27, 41, 71, 83, 102,
    151, 164, 177, 185, 188
virtual worlding 187
viruses 196
visual style 24, 185
Voice chats 18, 192

watchdog approaches 77, 84
wearables 138, 151
Web 2.0 172
web hosting services 195
Web Open Font Format (WOFF) 26
Wikileaks 97–98
Wireless Emergency Alerts (WEA) 118
World Television Day 63
World Wide Web Consortium
    (W3C) 162
WW I 19
WW II 19, 41, 50, 160
WYSIWYG 83

Y2K 10
young adult fiction (YA) 22

zines 22, 186

For Product Safety Concerns and Information please contact our EU
representative GPSR@taylorandfrancis.com
Taylor & Francis Verlag GmbH, Kaufingerstraße 24, 80331 München, Germany

www.ingramcontent.com/pod-product-compliance
Ingram Content Group UK Ltd.
Pitfield, Milton Keynes, MK11 3LW, UK
UKHW021027180425
457613UK00021B/1086